**BRITISH ASSOCIATION OF
ADVISERS & LECTURERS
IN PHYSICAL EDUCATION**

Safe Practice
in
Physical Education

D1493059

SAFE PRACTICE IN PHYSICAL EDUCATION

Safe Practice in Physical Education
Copyright ©

The British Association of Advisers and Lecturers
in Physical Education 1985, 1990, 1995, 1999.

ISBN: 1 871228 11 5

Original edition published 1979; this revised edition written and compiled 1999 by:

The British Association of Advisers and Lecturers
in Physical Education

Design: Jean Longville, Dudley LEA

Published and distributed on behalf of BAALPE by:

Dudley LEA
Saltwells Education Development Centre
Bowling Green Road
Netherton
Dudley
West Midlands
DY2 9LY

Telephone: 01384 813706/7

ACKNOWLEDGEMENTS

The help of many individuals and organisations is gratefully acknowledged by BAALPE for their valued contributions to the contents of this book, through offers of advice, the provision of material and the revision of drafts.

They include BAALPE Council and members, national governing bodies of sport and schools' sports associations, together with many others.

The co-operation and advice from the Adventure Activities Licensing Authority and the Outdoor Education Advisers Panel have been invaluable.

The Association is deeply indebted to all concerned.

Abbreviations

Abbreviations used include the following:

AALA	-	Adventure Activities Licensing Authority
AOTTs	-	Adults Other Than Teachers
BAALPE	-	British Association of Advisers and Lecturers in Physical Education
BS	-	British Standard
BSI	-	British Standards Institute
BS EN	-	British Standards European Norm
CEN	-	Committee for European Normalisation
DENI	-	Department of Education for Northern Ireland
DfEE	-	Department for Education and Employment
EA	-	Education Authority (Scotland)
EN	-	European Norm
HSE	-	Health and Safety Executive
IAS	-	Impact Absorbing Surface
LEA	-	Local Education Authority (England and Wales)
LMS	-	Local Management of Schools
RoSPA	-	Royal Society for the Prevention of Accidents
SED	-	Scottish Education Department
SEN	-	Special Educational Needs
SENCO	-	Special Educational Needs Co-ordinator

♦ The term 'headteacher' is consistently used throughout the book. This includes principals.

♦ Similarly, the term 'teacher' includes lecturers.

♦ 'Subject leader' is the term used to include curriculum co-ordinators, heads of department and other subject managers.

INTRODUCTION

This book will be of special interest to all those involved with the teaching and managing of physical education.

Safe practice in physical education should be an integral feature of all aspects and in all phases of education, from the very early years of playgroup and reception through to adult, further and higher education. Every tragedy or accident that occurs serves to highlight the importance of safe practice and the need to learn lessons and to adopt procedures that will minimise the likelihood of a recurrence of such incidents. More importantly, careful forethought and preparation will help to prevent such occurrences. Teachers, and others in positions of responsibility, have a duty of care for those in their charge to ensure that planning and implementation take full account of safety requirements.

Humans encounter risk in many aspects of their lives and to attempt to remove risk entirely would be neither possible or desirable. Absolute safety is rarely achievable. The challenge for education is to ensure that young people are properly prepared to manage reasonable risks with which they are faced and to help them develop the generic skills and awareness which may be usefully applied in any situation to enable their own and others' safety.

Physical education has a significant role to play in this learning process. Dance, gymnastics, games, athletics, swimming and outdoor and adventurous activities combine to provide a broad and balanced range of experiences which incorporate safety education. Each of these areas will enable the growing child or young pupil to face challenges and goals which will equip them with the skills and understanding to meet reasonable risks with competence and sound judgement. The child who learns to lift, carry, assemble and check apparatus correctly in the gymnasium or hall is acquiring fundamental knowledge about safe practice which will translate in a general way to safe and competent movement in the wider environment.

There are two complementary strands in meeting safety requirements. The first embraces the responsibilities of the teacher in charge of a group of young people engaging in an activity. The law requires that a duty of care should be exercised in these circumstances, with those responsible under school regulations being in loco parentis. Local education authorities, education authorities, governing bodies and headteachers in varying capacities, depending on the type of school or institution, must ensure that employees appointed are suitably qualified and experienced to undertake the duties required of them in a safe and proper manner. Where a duty of care is breached, an action of negligence may be brought resulting in possible litigation and proceedings through a court of law.

The second strand is concerned with the process of education. Young people should learn about the principles of safety as applied to themselves and to the care and well-being of others. This should be a planned and intentional aspect of the curriculum. Physical education clearly has a major contribution to make to safety education in heightening awareness in the broader context whilst providing knowledge and understanding about safety procedures relating to specific activities.

The purpose of this book, now in its fifth edition, is to advise on safe practice across the range of activities which may be included in physical education programmes. It aims to inform teachers on aspects of good and accepted safe practice brought about by experience in the field. Safe practice is dynamic and developmental. Technology, the law, parental expectations as well as significant incidents contribute to a changing scene which invariably puts an ever higher premium on the safety of participants. Teachers of physical education need to ensure that they keep abreast of developments which may affect or change accepted good practice.

This edition has two parts. The first covers general matters of safe practice and is recommended text for all. It includes advice on risk assessment, management issues and guidance in meeting the requirements of pupils with special educational needs. Attention is drawn to the requirements for the inspection, maintenance and repair/replacement of equipment which have clearly become less consistent as schools have taken greater responsibility for their own budgets. The use of mats in physical education continues to be featured, being an issue of concern often raised by teachers and a frequent focus for litigation. The chapter on question and answer gives practical examples. Teachers will find it beneficial to refer to this section and to the appropriate chapter for specific guidance. The second part is particular to physical activities in which young people may be involved through physical education. Advice on outdoor and adventurous activities will be of particular relevance following unfortunate incidents, some tragic, which have occurred.

It is hoped that the advice will provide a sound framework against which teachers may analyse and adjust their own practices. It is important to recognise that however specific and fine-tuned the content may be there will always be a need for professional judgement to be exercised in the context of a particular situation. The duty of care is an inherent responsibility carried by all who are employed to teach pupils. Those who work in the field of youth, community and adult recreation are likewise responsible for the exercise of a duty of care for those in their charge.

Finally, to avoid unnecessary anxiety, it should be noted that the criteria to be applied in circumstances where safety is a factor for consideration is that of 'reasonableness'. It is not expected of anyone that s/he should be perfect; only that they should act in a manner which is reasonable in the light of commonly accepted and approved good practice in the context of the activity with which they are concerned. Safe practice is good practice.

It is hoped that all educational establishments will own and use at least one copy of this edition. Although based on the advice given in previous publications under the same title, extensive revisions and amendments have been made to ensure that the advice proffered is the best available at the time of going to press. It is intended to be prominent and to be available for reference by all who may benefit from the advice contained. Any further request for help should be addressed to the General Secretary of the British Association of Advisers and Lecturers in Physical Education.

CHAPTER DETAIL

PART 1: GENERAL ADVICE

1 Physical Education and the Law

2   Qualifications and Supervision

3   The Curriculum and Extra-Curricular Activities

7 Clothing, Personal Effects and Protection

8 Pupils with Special Educational Needs

9   Accidents, First Aid and HIV/AIDS

10   Insurance

PART 2:   ACTIVITIES

16   Gymnastics and Trampolining

Gymnastics

Trampolining

17 Outdoor and Adventurous Activities

18 Swimming, Diving and Life-saving

Swimming

20   Other Activities

Appendices

PART 1:

GENERAL ADVICE

1: PHYSICAL EDUCATION AND THE LAW

1.1 Introduction

1.1.1 "He who would be his own lawyer has a fool for a client". This book does not attempt to interpret the law. That said, experience gained from accidents that have led to court cases has often helped to shape good practice.

1.1.2 Common law and statute law impose general duties on individuals and bodies. Any breach of these duties which causes injury or loss may give rise to a claim for damages (compensation), or sometimes even to criminal penalties. Although accidents will occur because they cannot always be foreseen, teachers have a legal duty to work within a system which demonstrates a realistic use of methods which successfully anticipate and eliminate foreseeable risks.

1.1.3 The law now expects that all physical education teachers will work within a 'modus operandi' which identifies all the foreseeable safety problems associated with the activities undertaken. The school must declare its own policies and practices which will eliminate foreseeable risks. The headteacher must ensure that such a system is operable, even by recently appointed staff. At least one teacher should be identified whose responsibility it is to see that safe practice is realistic and working day to day.

1.1.4 Part of this preventative system will include the educating of all the pupils. They must receive, appropriate to their needs, age and intelligence, clear guidance and experience in order to develop their own safe practice and knowledge. Young people should not be caught out by their own ignorance. Teachers should teach safely and teach safety.

1.1.5 The law will reasonably expect that an individual school's 'code of safe practice in physical education' will reflect its own particular needs according to its programmes and premises in addition to factors which it may have in common with other, similar establishments.

1.2 Duty of Care

1.2.1 Everyone is required to take reasonable care in any situation to try to foresee that others are not harmed by their actions or omissions.

1.2.2   All teachers must operate this duty when they have children in their care. This applies to all activities within the school curriculum, to extra-curricular activities during or outside normal school hours, whether on or away from school premises.

1.2.3   Teachers should note that when they are in charge of pupils involved in school-organised activities on school trips, including residential visits and ventures abroad, the duty of care obligation is for twenty-four hours a day, seven days a week. The duty of care cannot be diluted by any association of the words 'holiday', 'abroad', or 'weekend'.

1.3   In Loco Parentis

1.3.1   In loco parentis forms the basis of duty of care for teachers when responsible for children. It is a standard of care set by the courts and is judged as the level of competence associated with the proper discharge of one's professional duties.

1.3.2   There are long established and important common law requirements for those acting in loco parentis.

What teachers should do was clearly expressed as far back as 1898 when Justice Cain said:

"The Schoolmaster is bound to take such care of his boys as a careful father would take of his boys".

No doubt the language would be a little different if spoken today but the essence has become and remains a fundamental consideration by the courts in the assessment of negligence when claims are brought against teachers.

1.3.3   Teachers with this legal responsibility must exercise the same duty of care as would a reasonable parent in the school situation. In the case of pupils on outdoor and adventurous activities, or at recreational and sports centres, this overarching legal responsibility remains with the accompanying teachers and cannot be delegated to instructors or coaches acting on behalf of the teacher.

1.3.4   It is the responsibility of the headteacher and teacher to judge the competence of other helpers and decide the limits of their duties.

1.4   Higher Duty of Care

1.4.1   It is expected that duty of care will be exercised on a basis of reasonableness rather than idealism. Teachers will have need to make themselves aware of what, in the present day, is reasonable practice. In the past, this was associated with what might be expected of a reasonably prudent parent.

1.4.2　Over the years it has been established through the courts that a school teacher should be expected to know a good deal more about the propensities of children than might a prudent parent. Add to this that some aspects of physical education have a high level of risk and required awareness and a higher duty of care is now expected of physical education teachers.

1.4.3　A higher duty of care is the standard of care expected with increased experience and specialist expertise. Through training or experience, one may be expected to be more clearly aware of the results of one's actions in one's area or areas of specialism.

1.5　Negligence

1.5.1　The standard of care required of a teacher has been expressed as that of a 'reasonably prudent parent, judged not in the context of the home but in that of a school', (Lyes v Middlesex County Council, 1962).

1.5.2　Negligence may be alleged where someone has fallen below the standard of care required in the circumstances by some act or omission which fails to protect others from the unreasonable risk of harm.

1.5.3　A claim for damages on grounds of negligence will only succeed if it can be shown that there was negligence on the part of a teacher (or any other employee) which has directly resulted in injury to a pupil. The claim would normally be made by the parent or carer against the local education authority or governing body on the grounds that they, as employers, were vicariously liable for the negligent acts of their employee.

1.5.4　It is most unusual for a teacher to be sued personally. If, however, damages are awarded against a local education authority or governing body on account of the grossly negligent act(s) of a teacher, then that teacher can be asked for a contribution towards the damages. This has happened occasionally in instances of gross negligence.

1.6　Defence Against Charges of Negligence

1.6.1　Teachers have some protection against charges of negligence. These may be formal defences recognised in law or more informally be the basis of what is considered to be good practice.

1.7   Vicarious Liability

1.7.1   The law will expect that a teacher's employer will be responsible for any acts of omission or commission made by that employed teacher during the course of that teacher's normal work (Scope of Contract), during lessons or outside normal curriculum time.   This is vicarious liability.

In the past, vicarious liability has placed the responsibility on local education authorities but local management of schools has changed matters, with greater responsibility now directed at schools and their governing bodies. Whatever the situation, the law will require that in the event of proven negligence, the responsible agent will be able to meet any costs awarded. It therefore behoves every teacher to know precisely who is the responsible agent in order to ensure that liability will not be directed personally at the teacher.

1.7.2   Teachers should be aware that vicarious liability will not cover acts which happen outside their scope of employment. For example, if a teacher should take a group away for a weekend without the knowledge and agreement of the headteacher and someone was injured then this would be outside the teacher's contract and the employer may not be liable. Teachers will need to have their own insurance cover to provide financial support in such circumstances.

1.8   Contributory Negligence

1.8.1   Where the person injured can be shown to have contributed to the cause or aggravation of the injury by some irresponsible act or omission they may be held partially responsible for the injury. In such circumstances this may be taken into account when responsibility is being determined.

1.9   Voluntary Assumption of Risk

1.9.1   It may be claimed that a willingness to participate assumes an acceptance of the risk of injury. This would be difficult to apply in a school situation as most activities are compulsory. It may also be difficult to show that the child was fully aware of the risks involved and was legally able to accept them.

1.10 Good Practice

1.10.1 Charges of negligence will be very much easier to refute if it can be shown that:

a The teacher (or the coach or parent) was qualified to teach or instruct the activity involved and appropriate supervision was provided.

b All reasonable steps had been taken to ensure the safety of the working environment and equipment.

c The class had been taught about the need for safety and had been warned against foolhardiness in a manner appropriate to the age, intelligence and experience of the pupils.

d The class had been systematically prepared for the activities being undertaken and attention had been paid to appropriate footwear and clothing.

e The work and the manner in which it was accomplished was compatible with regular and approved practice in other similar schools across the country. Over the years, teachers have established and regularly used teaching practices and procedures which have reliably avoided foreseeable accidents without reducing challenge.

f Any local visits, overseas visits or outdoor and adventurous activities, had proceeded with the prior agreement of informed parents by means of signed participation agreements. A senior manager in a school will normally be responsible for compiling a suitable form for this purpose.

g The use of effective record keeping such as attendance registers, lesson preparation and assessment records, shows what pupils have experienced and of what they are capable.

h Helpers (adults other than teachers) were fully briefed and had been given a clear role in the lesson.

i Teachers and governors kept themselves up-dated on safety development and the managers in schools were sufficiently professional to provide in-service training opportunities as necessary to enable staff to influence and improve safe practice. This is particularly important at an early stage in helping newly qualified or inexperienced physical education teachers to make the right decisions and arrangements on safety.

j Appropriate risk assessments have been undertaken.

k Governors are aware of and have approved the activity.

1.11 The Health and Safety at Work Act 1974 (HSW Act)

1.11.1 Under this legislation employers, which in the context of education includes local authorities, school governing bodies, managers of other premises including outdoor centres and the self employed, are legally required to do all that is reasonably practicable to ensure the health and safety of employees (teachers, instructors, coaches and all other staff) and non-employees (which includes pupils and others who enter the premises, such as parents) who are affected by their undertaking.

1.11.2 In a community school, this duty will rest with the local authority. In voluntary aided or foundation schools, the governing body will be responsible. In independent schools (including city technology colleges) the proprietor will normally carry this responsibility.

1.11.3 Section 2(3) of the HSW Act 1974 places a duty of care on every employer to prepare and, as often as appropriate, to revise a written statement on general policy with respect to the health and safety at work of employees and the organisation and arrangements for carrying out that policy. The employer must also bring the statement and any revision of it to the notice of employees.

1.11.4 The system must also provide for safe premises and a safe environment in which employees and pupils will work. This is an important consideration when working on or in any facility external to the school, or when involved with outdoor and adventurous activities where the vagaries of climatic change can produce a rapid change in circumstances.

1.11.5 The Health and Safety Executive (HSE) and local authority health and safety inspectors have powers to ensure that schools comply with the requirements of the HSW Act. Prosecution may be invoked in cases of non-compliance.

1.12 The Management of Health and Safety at Work Regulations 1992

1.12.1 These regulations, which include risk assessment, came into force on 1 January 1993. They require employers to introduce measures for planning, organising, controlling, monitoring and reviewing their arrangements for the management of health and safety. Assessments must be made of the risks to which employees, pupils and others who visit the premises are exposed in order that appropriate action might be taken to protect their health and safety.

1.12.2   The governing bodies or management teams and the staff of the relevant premises need to work together to establish and implement effective health and safety policies. Employees should be provided with information on these measures and be given adequate health and safety training.

1.13   The Reporting of Injuries, Diseases and Dangerous Occurrences Regulations 1995 (RIDDOR)

1.13.1   The requirements and implications of this legislation are considered in some detail in chapter 9 on Accidents, First Aid and HIV/Aids.

It should be noted that accidents or occurrences which fall within the stated categories and which take place away from the school premises, for example during outdoor and adventurous education at an outdoor activities centre or at a recreation or sports centre, are subject to precisely the same procedures of recording and reporting as those which take place on the school site. Failure to comply may result in prosecution.

1.14   The Fire Precautions (Workplace) Regulations, 1997

1.14.1   These Regulations require fire precaution checks to be carried out and risk assessments to be recorded. This includes checking emergency exits, the presence of fire extinguishers, fire evacuation drills and communication systems, such as alarms or telephone. This is a whole school responsibility but subject areas may include relevant aspects in their subject risk assessments.

1.14.2   It is good practice to include those aspects which impinge on physical education within a risk assessment.

1.14.3   In the event of a fire, having a completed register and plan of the buildings would be helpful to the fire brigade.

1.15   The Occupiers Liability Acts, 1957 and 1984

1.15.1   These Acts of Parliament are used only in association with civil claims such as negligence. The Acts impose a duty of care on those who manage premises to ensure that visitors, such as pupils and parents, are reasonably safe in the premises for the purposes they are allowed to be there. This places a responsibility on school managers to ensure that the premises are safe to use.

1.16   The Children Act 1989

1.16.1   This legislation requires that all persons who have substantial access to children must provide information which is laid down on the matter of their suitability. This information should be subject to vetting by the authority concerned. This has implications for any new appointments and for voluntary input by non-employed personnel working with pupils (reference chapter 2 on Qualifications and Supervision).

1.16.2   Many local education authorities and independent agencies now provide codes of conduct on purposeful physical contact with children. Those working with children where physical contact is sometimes deemed to be necessary, such as when teaching certain specific gymnastic skills, should ensure that they are aware of and follow such guidance. Any physical contact should be such that it is for the safety of the child and the child is aware that support will be given. Contact should be of such a nature that its use cannot be misconstrued. (See Section 3.11.3)

1.17   The Activity Centres (Young Persons Safety) Act, 1995

1.17.1   This is a very important piece of legislation which requires commercial providers of climbing, watersports, trekking and caving activities in remote or isolated areas for young people under eighteen years of age to undergo inspection of their safety management systems and become registered as being licensed. From 1 October 1997, it became a legal requirement that only licensed activity providers offer such activities on a commercial basis.

1.17.2   There are exemptions from licensing, such as where schools operate their own centres or where profit is not involved. However, schools should check carefully that any commercial centre being used is currently licensed.

1.18   Transportation

1.18.1   The use of cars, mini-buses and coaches for carrying pupils is also important. The law and regular and approved practice in the transporting of pupils is currently in a state of change. Schools will be expected to exercise whatever legal requirements are brought in regarding transport, however recent. There should be no reduction in provision on grounds of cost.

1.19 Teachers and Unions/Professional Associations

1.19.1 All teachers should consider joining a teachers' union or professional association that offers legal advice and financial support to members. Any teacher involved in litigation should contact the union or professional association at an early stage.

1.20 Guidance on Legal Requirements and Some Further Reading

There are numerous relevant publications and a very small sample is given below:

From HSE Books, PO Box 1999, Sudbury, Suffolk CO10 6FS:

♦ The Health and Safety Commission approved codes of practice and guidance aimed at schools, e.g. 'The Responsibilities of School Governors for Health and Safety'.

♦ 'Reporting under RIDDOR' (Health and Safety Executive).

♦ 'Five Steps to Risk Assessment' (Health and Safety Executive).

From Croner Publications Limited, Croner House, London Road, Kingston upon Thames, Surrey KT2 6SR:

♦ 'Health and Safety in Schools' by Barry Stock, 1994.

♦ 'Head's Legal Guide'.

♦ 'The Teacher's Legal Guide'.

♦ 'The Management of Health and Safety in Schools' (a loose leaf file allowing for regular updating).

From Menthuen Publishers:

♦ 'Teachers and the Law' by G R Barrell and L A Partington.

From the DfEE:

♦ 'Health and Safety of Pupils on Educational Visits', 1998.

♦ 'School Governors: A Guide to the Law' 1999. Appropriate variations of this are distributed to the different categories of schools. It contains a section on managing health, safety and the site.

2: QUALIFICATIONS & SUPERVISION

2.1 Qualifications for Teaching Physical Education

2.1.1   A qualification may be defined as having the skills, knowledge, understanding and competence necessary to plan, deliver and evaluate a programme of activities to a class or group of young people in safe and effective methods approved through regular and accepted good practice. Qualified individuals should be experienced, trained, assessed and accredited to a level at which those with responsibility may reasonably express confidence of a successful outcome in the planning and delivery of the activities being undertaken.

2.1.2   There is no requirement in law that a teacher must hold a specific award before teaching an activity in physical education. However, it behoves all such personnel and it is prudent to be able to show that they are appropriately qualified to undertake the tasks in which they engage with young people. Specialist teachers of the subject in secondary schools will normally have undergone a period of initial teacher training where they will have focused on the areas to be taught. Primary school teachers should likewise have experienced physical education appropriate to that age-range during their initial training. In-service training courses provide supplementary additional opportunities for teachers to further and extend their expertise in areas of physical education. Headteachers should check on the level of initial training of staff involved in teaching physical education. Qualification is enhanced by regular professional development.

2.1.3   Local education authorities and governing bodies of schools may establish their own policies and insist on certain minimum qualifications before a teacher is allowed to teach some aspects of physical education. For example those activities where there are potentially hazardous elements, such as swimming, trampolining, gymnastics and many outdoor and adventurous pursuits. It is vital that anyone teaching such activities is qualified by training and experience to handle the known inherent dangers. Appropriate professional development may be organised by local authorities, higher education institutes and national governing bodies of sport. Certificates may be awarded which indicate the level at which the recipients are regarded as competent to teach the activities concerned. Such evidence can be of assistance to headteachers when considering a request for the introduction of a potentially hazardous activity into the physical education programme. Teachers should keep a record of their continuing professional development.

2.1.4   It should be noted that some national governing bodies require that their qualifications be revalidated periodically in order to be of current value, not simply to endorse previous requirements but to inform on changes and developments which may have occurred in the interim period. This information is available from the issuing body or through the local education authority advisory service.

Primary schools

2.1.5   Teachers in primary schools may be required to teach gymnastics, dance, games and athletics, swimming and water safety, and some aspects of outdoor and adventurous activities. Teachers with little or no initial training in physical education run risks if they undertake to teach more than simple skills. Such teachers should be given appropriate in-service training before being allowed to present a full range of activities. Headteachers must be satisfied that all teachers who are required to teach physical education are able to do so in a safe environment, with an understanding of the needs and stages of development of all the children in their classes.

2.1.6   Teachers should obtain the permission of the headteacher before introducing any new activity and this is particularly important if the activity is potentially hazardous. Some local authorities do not permit the use of certain items of equipment in primary schools (for example, rebound equipment such as trampettes or trampolines) and headteachers should ensure that they are aware of any such policies.

Secondary schools

2.1.7   Teachers who have responsibility for the planning and delivery of physical education programmes in secondary schools should have satisfactorily completed appropriate initial and/or in-service training which embraces all those aspects of activity required to be taught, as recognised by the Department for Education and Employment in England and the equivalent authorities in Northern Ireland, Scotland and Wales.

2.1.8   As the curriculum develops some schools may include so-called emergent activities for which codes of safe practice may still be in the process of formulation. Headteachers are advised to proceed with caution in these circumstances and to contact their own local advisory service, their insurers or the national governing body of the sport, for the best advice available.

2.1.9   Headteachers may ask teachers to take designated lessons or activities. They should recognise that it is unwise for teachers to teach in areas where they lack the appropriate experience and expertise, particularly when there are implications for safe practice.

2.2.1   All teachers are in loco parentis so far as pupils are concerned. School governing bodies must set up a system that can be seen to apply a reasonable degree of safe management of the pupils whilst working within their educational system. All teachers act in loco parentis regardless of time or date or place, so long as the pupils have been properly involved and invited to take part in an activity in pursuit of education arranged by a school. Parents should be kept fully informed on the activities in which their children are involved, including extra-curricular involvement and the arrangements for safe dismissal outside of normal school hours.

2.2.2   Governors have a strategic responsibility for the management and curriculum of schools. Headteachers particularly should be aware of the need to adopt and implement a system of pupil management, especially where higher risk physical education is involved. Governing bodies should ensure that their establishment's physical education programme meets the legal safety requirements. They should be aware that anyone engaged by them must have appropriate training and expertise that meets standards which would be approved by the Department for Education and Employment and the equivalent authorities in Northern Ireland, Scotland and Wales.

2.2.3   Teachers in loco parentis must be able to demonstrate that they are exercising a duty of care which would be acceptable to a reasonable parent or guardian of a participating pupil. In physical education, because of the increased risk levels which occur, a higher duty of care is expected of teachers and it would be necessary to demonstrate that this higher level of care could be met by appropriately trained and qualified personnel.

2.2.4   A qualified teacher in charge of any class of pupils cannot transfer or delegate in loco parentis to an assistant. The services of an assistant may be utilised where this person can exercise a proper duty of care by virtue of known experience and skills. It is the responsibility of the teacher to check that the duty of care system is operating reliably while an assistant is working with the pupils.

2.2.5   The implications for the education establishment using off-site facilities or other partnership arrangements are significant. The institution must have a system which can assess and monitor the quality of the teaching and the management which is to operate with their pupils in such circumstances.

2.2.6   BAALPE recommends that where BAALPE members are available to educational establishments, s/he should be asked for advice on setting up safe partnerships between those establishments and external agencies. The subject leader for physical education should be asked to set up and monitor partnership arrangements on behalf of the headteacher and governors. Whoever sets up the system for the school, the following should be addressed:

a   Headteachers should be mindful that all aspects of the establishment's curriculum and its management fall under their umbrella as the foundation stone of the system of care.

b   A safety policy for the working of the physical education department should be laid down as part of the total safety policy for the establishment and be approved by the governing body.

c   All teachers working within physical education should be suitably qualified by training and experience to discharge the level of duty of care which applies in the activities they are teaching.

d   The class teacher is the one holding in loco parentis which must be seen to be reasonably exercised and operational. This responsibility cannot be transferred to a non-teacher.

e   Vigilance is necessary where pupils receive help from personnel who are not trained as teachers. Those providing such help should be properly trained and qualified to give assistance. The levels of expertise conferred by any national governing body award or national vocational qualification held by non-teachers should be known and be acceptable to the school.

(Note: Teachers should note that many local education authorities have their own requirements with regard to the teaching of certain activities.)

f   The management system of a school should require and enable all external assistance to be checked, tutored and monitored. This is a legal duty as explained in chapter one. The BAALPE document "Adults Other Than Teachers" (AOTTS) contains more detailed guidance. Where such arrangements are undertaken, parents should be informed of the level of involvement of the external personnel.

2.3 Help from Non-Specialist Teachers

2.3.1 Secondary teachers of another subject who have no specialist training in physical education are sometimes timetabled to assist with the delivery of the physical education curriculum. This arrangement should be exceptional and be implemented with the greatest care. Under no circumstances should non-specialist teaching staff take full responsibility for any aspect of physical activity where there are elements of hazard and attendant risk. Whenever possible, a teacher assisting in this way should work with a qualified specialist colleague and so benefit from that protection and expertise in the delivery of the programme.

2.4 Students on Teaching Practice

2.4.1 Students on teaching practice should always be supervised by qualified teachers, even though they may reasonably assume greater responsibility for classes as their initial training progresses. It is important to realise they cannot be in loco parentis until they are finally qualified on satisfactory completion of their courses. This responsibility is retained by the class teachers and cannot be transferred to the pupils.

2.5 Assistance from Adults Other Than Teachers

2.5.1 The help of an adult in school may be considered provided they have the appropriate experience to assist with the activity in which they offer their support and meet the requirements of the Children Act 1989. They should always work under the supervision of a teacher, for it is the teacher who remains in loco parentis at all times. No AOTT should be left to work totally on their own with young people. This will apply equally to either a curricular or an extra-curricular activity. Care should be taken to ensure that the insurance arrangements are adequate to cover the adult in this role.

2.6 Teaching Group Sizes for Physical Education

2.6.1 In determining the size of teaching groups in physical education, headteachers and teachers need to take account of the nature of the activity; the age, experience and developmental stage of the pupils; the requirements of the National Curriculum and the working space available.

2.6.2   The ratio of pupils to teachers should typically reflect normal classroom organisation but, because of the risk element in physical education, more favourable staffing may be necessary in some circumstances.

2.6.3   Advice contained in this book includes reference to teaching group size where the activity requires numbers that may vary from that of normal classroom organisation and learning. Pupil teacher ratios should be determined by a risk assessment of the circumstances specific to the event.

2.7   Non-Participation by Pupils

2.7.1   The same duty of care by the teacher applies to all the pupils in classes. Those pupils excused physical participation should be as involved as reasonably possible in the work of the lesson; as officials, observers, recorders, critics, so that they may learn and understand the work alongside their more active peers and be better prepared to rejoin the class as active participants in due course. Where this arrangement is not practicable, then alternative supervision by another teacher should be arranged. The use of attendance registers at the beginning of lessons following the movement of pupils is essential in schools in case of fire. Registers also further enable the accounting of all pupils and thereby contributes to the duty of care required of the teacher.

Further guidance:

BAALPE 'Adults Other Than Teachers'.

3: THE CURRICULUM & EXTRA-CURRICULAR ACTIVITIES

3.1 Safety Education

3.1.1 In addition to the requirements of the National Curriculum in physical education, most schools provide a voluntary and varied programme of extra-curricular activities in which pupils may engage on a basis of choice, often beyond normal school hours. Both curricular and extra-curricular aspects require the same duty of care from teachers and provide many continuing opportunities to involve young people in safety matters.

3.1.2 Awareness of safety is an integral part of the education process and its development will enable greater responsibility to be accepted and exercised by pupils as they mature. The knowledge derived has wide application outside and beyond school, where the principles of safe practice are significant in underpinning the tasks and challenges of daily living. Safety is a cross-curricular theme but it will be most effectively demonstrated and applied in the practical areas of learning and nowhere more so than in physical education.

3.1.3 The principles for learning about safety are contained within well recognised procedures in schools, and include:

a The need to develop and promote respect and care for self and others as fundamental to all activities. In effect 'everyone owes a duty of care to everyone else at all times and in all situations'.

b Careful planning, with attention given to the inherent risks in any activity and how these will be managed.

c Knowing and applying the accepted techniques for learning an activity and the progressive stages leading up to that activity.

d Involving all the pupils with the assessment and management of risk as an integral part of their education.

e The use of tasks which allow for differentiated inputs and outcomes.

f Ensuring that pupils as individuals are sufficiently mature and physically able to understand and to cope with tasks which involve a degree of risk before these are presented to them.

g Establishing procedures which are contained in a written safety policy, adopted across the department and by the wider establishment.

h   The taking of a register to account for all those present in a lesson or extra-curricular activity.

i   Deciding not to embark on or to proceed with an activity where an inherent hazard cannot reasonably be managed and therefore where safety may be compromised.

j   Ensuring that appropriate progressive steps in learning an activity are included and that each step is thoroughly consolidated before moving on to the next. This is particularly important where 'higher risk' or 'more challenging' activities are concerned.

k   The need for the teacher to adopt a position whereby s/he may safely and effectively supervise all the pupils while they are working.

3.2   Continuity

3.2.1   Continuity in learning is an important element in safe practice. Where pupils experience more than an intermittent break in their learning, particularly when illness is a factor, teachers will need to give careful consideration to the reintroduction of these pupils to the programmes of work being followed. In such circumstances, it may be necessary to revisit and to consolidate activities previously undertaken by the pupils before they progress further. A young person who moves between schools and joins a class as a new pupil will need special consideration in this regard.

3.3   Progression

3.3.1   Activities, particularly those which are more challenging or which contain hazardous elements, should be broken down into progressive stages and each stage should be learned and consolidated by the pupils. The rate of progress of pupils in passing from one stage to the next will vary according to their respective abilities but it is important that all pupils should follow the appropriate sequence and consolidation of stages in their learning.

3.3.2   Progression in an activity from one stage to the next by a pupil will be dependent on consolidation and readiness. Both the teacher and the pupil should be confident that the previous stage has been satisfactorily practised and accomplished before moving on to the stage which follows.

3.4 Differentiation

3.4.1 Teachers must recognise that individual pupils in a class will vary in their stages of development and in their capacities to meet and respond to the challenges with which they are presented. It is essential that pupils are not challenged beyond their individual capabilities and the use of tasks, equipment and time by the teacher which allow for differentiated inputs and outcomes is helpful on both educational and safety grounds. If a specific skill is taught, the teacher must be satisfied that it is appropriate for those pupils concerned, whether as a whole class, a group or individually. No pupil should be placed at risk by attempting a movement for which s/he is not ready or capable.

3.5 Physical Preparation

3.5.1 Pupils should be physically capable of undertaking the tasks with which they are presented. Factors such as size, weight, strength, mobility and endurance should be taken into account in assessing whether or not individual pupils may reasonably be expected to engage in an activity.

3.5.2 The physical education programme will include elements which are centrally concerned with the development of the body in respect of fitness. Warming up should be an integral part of all lessons which involve vigorous physical activities, with attention given to the stretching of major muscle groups and to cardiovascular preparation. Where a lesson has been particularly vigorous it may be useful to help the pupils to return to a calm state.

3.6 Pupils' Growth and Development

3.6.1 The stages of growth and development experienced by all young people, particularly during adolescence, and the individual differences which occur at such times must be taken into account when pupils engage in physical activities. Periods of relatively rapid body change, when 'growth spurts' take place, will significantly influence performance and may in some instances cause temporary regression of physical skill, strength, endurance and co-ordination. Empathy, understanding, and explanation by the teacher will help to ensure that physical activities are appropriately modified to meet these changing individual circumstances.

3.7 Fatigue

3.7.1 Teachers should be vigilant in watching for signs of pupil fatigue. This is generally associated with prolonged activity and is demonstrated by a reduced level of concentration, by slower reaction time and by a deterioration in the quality of performance.

3.7.2 Where fatigue is apparent, activity should stop and the pupil should rest. This is particularly important where a pupil is engaged in activities such as gymnastics, trampolining and swimming.

3.8 Schemes of Work

3.8.1 Schemes of work which are carefully constructed to provide appropriate content for the ages and stages of educational development and which incorporate safety education provide the essential foundation for safe practice in physical education. It is necessary for all schools to have such schemes on which lessons may be planned, consistent with the framework of the national curriculum in physical education but also geared to local circumstances and needs.

3.8.2 Operable schemes of work provide the cohesion, continuity and progression which ensure that the experiences of pupils are at all times appropriate, with risks assessed and managed so that safe practice is addressed and implemented. A safe system will identify pupils with any special educational or health needs and ensure that young people are not exposed to unreasonable challenge. Record keeping is therefore vital.

3.9 Supervision of Pupils

3.9.1 Pupils should always be supervised when they are engaged in physical education and teachers should ensure that the following requirements are met:

a All pupils should know what is expected of them.

b The teacher to pupil ratio should be modified according to the maturity, competence, intelligence, experience and behavioural/emotional characteristics of the pupils and the nature of the activities in which they are involved.

c Teachers should be aware of any recorded individual needs of young people, including special educational needs, disabilities or medical conditions. Lack of awareness by teachers in this regard has sometimes been significant in cases of alleged negligence.

d   Teachers should be aware of any medical treatment, particularly drugs, which a pupil may be receiving and take account of its known effects on the sensory perception, motor control and co-ordination of the pupil.

e   Special safety precautions in determining the appropriate nature and level of an activity will be necessary when a pupil is inexperienced, immature, has a disability or experiences behavioural disorder.

f   Class numbers should be checked through registration at the start of a lesson. In swimming and cross country running, counting checks should be made at the beginning and the end of activity.

g   Whenever possible, pupils should be accompanied by a responsible adult on journeys to and from inter-school events which take place at venues other than their own school. They should be organised to travel as a group or in several groups when numbers are large. Parental consent should be obtained when direct supervision on such occasions cannot be provided.

Parental Notes

3.9.2   A note from a parent requesting that a pupil be excused active participation in physical education on given grounds should always be treated seriously and accepted where a specific illness is stated. Subsequent tactful enquiries of parents may be appropriate in cases of reasonable doubt.

3.9.3   Prolonged periods of inactivity through ill-health or injury on the part of a pupil should result in a letter from the school to the parent(s) expressing concern for the child's well being and requesting a medical report. If there is no response, the school welfare service should be asked to investigate.

Pupils with Special Educational and Medical Needs

3.9.4   It is most important that the headteacher should request parents to provide information on any significant physical or mental medical conditions and associated requirements of pupils. Teaching staff, particularly physical education teachers, should be informed accordingly. The implications are covered in greater detail in chapter 8.

3.10.1   Handling apparatus, as in gymnastics, involves the lifting, carrying and lowering of equipment which will be vary in weight, size and shape and which will involve the application of sound techniques for safe management. Every lesson in gymnastics will provide opportunities for learning in this area and children should be taught how to assemble, lift, rearrange, dismantle and store apparatus as required by the teacher.

3.10.2   Lessons where apparatus is left out for use by successive classes are not recommended, since this practice will deprive some children of learning opportunities which they need for handling apparatus. Moreover, the working space filled by apparatus will be hazardous during the warm up and developmental stages of the lesson. The apparatus arrangements will not necessarily be suited to the specific needs of each class using it.

3.10.3   Every child should be taught the skills of apparatus handling, beginning in the early years of reception and nursery.   Once taught and consistently practised these skills will remain with the child throughout life. Time and practice will be needed initially but acquisition of the skills will provide success and enjoyment for young people and the investment will prove highly beneficial.

3.10.4   The following suggestions are offered:

a   Ensure that apparatus is stored in accessible positions.

b   Allocate sufficient children to any one piece of equipment to enable it to be lifted with relative 'lightness' for each individual.

c   Demonstrate and direct operations in the first instance, using some pupils with the remainder of the class observing to see each unit safely assembled in the working position.

d   Point out safe hand positions which will guard against toppling or premature release.

e   Select lighter pieces and simple arrangements at first and build up to larger and more complex combinations of apparatus over time.

f   Teach 'tandem lifting' and walking with planks or benches so that the foremost lifter sets the pace and looks in the direction of travel. The rear lifter supports, does not push and finally assists to lower the apparatus on arrival at the working position.

g   Benches should be set down quietly and gently and carefully rolled if required to be inverted, with the balance rib up.

h   The lifting of boxes, stools or similar apparatus should involve sufficient children to make the apparatus 'light'. Pupils should be taught where to place their hands and to lift together on the leader's signal, by bending and straightening the legs and keeping their backs straight. Lowering the equipment should be done together, again on the leader's signal, using the stronger muscles of the legs. Four pupils will normally be required but this may be reduced to two when the pupils are older, bigger and more able.

i   Folding trestles should be opened out and the bars locked before being carried to the working position.

j   When fixing connecting bars between stools, one end of the bar or beam should be secured first and the second stool then positioned appropriately for the fixing of the other end.

k   Only one child is required to operate ropes on a pulley mechanism. The pull on the drag rope should be even and steady and the ropes secured in position by the drag rope being firmly wound on the wall cleat.

l   Initially mats will be required to be lifted by four children, one to each corner. Two children will be appropriate when competency is established.

m   Children should be taught never to begin working on the apparatus until permission to do so is given by the teacher after checking that:

- the whole class is involved in lifting, carrying and positioning the apparatus until it is all assembled and ready;

- everything is where it should be;

- space around the apparatus units is safe;

- mats are correctly positioned;

- all fixings are secure;

- apparatus units will not be used by too many pupils at one time. The children should know this limit and should respond accordingly;

- children should not stay too long on any one unit or combination of apparatus if free choice and circulation is encouraged.

n   Leave sufficient time at the end of the lesson for all apparatus to be stored away tidily and with care by the children.

o   The teacher should be involved in helping to move the largest or most awkward pieces of apparatus in the initial stages of learning.

p   The order for placing apparatus should generally be that which is fixed first; followed by larger mobile pieces, then benches and finally mats. This should be reversed when the apparatus is put away.

3.11   Supporting

3.11.1   Supporting is an inherent part of some aspects of physical education, particularly with regard to elements of dance and formal gymnastics where the path of an action is predictable. It may take the form of one pupil physically supporting another as an integral part of an activity (for example, balance work in pairs) or it may be the support of one individual for another in the learning of a movement which might not otherwise be successfully experienced or accomplished.

3.11.2   When any pupil is working on an activity where, because of the child's lack of skill or knowledge, there is foreseeable risk of an accident then the teacher has a duty of care to protect that child. This is enabled through an appropriate method of 'support', 'standing by' or 'catching' to see the pupil safely through the activity.

3.11.3   The law in respect of child protection has implications for supporting and 'standing by'. Teachers will need to be certain of how to set up support systems which, in application, give no grounds for doubt or objection. Educational establishments should have a written policy which covers 'contact', especially that between a teacher and pupil, which clearly distinguishes between what is and is not acceptable.

3.11.4   Where supporting is a part of a physical task, care should be taken by the teacher to ensure that pupils:

a   Understand clearly the principles of stability and handling which underpin successful and acceptable supporting.

b   Understand fully their respective roles in performing the activity.

c   Are able to exercise the essential responsibility of care.

d   Have practised, under guidance, the techniques for holding appropriately and safely.

e   Are physically able to manage the activity without undue physical stress or exertion.

f   Are fully aware of any risks inherent in the activity and how these will be managed, including any physical action necessary, in the event of the activity not being successfully accomplished.

3.11.5   Where physical support is given to a pupil who is learning a new prescribed movement, and has been assessed by the teacher to be capable and ready, this may be provided by the teacher or by a pupil who is well practised in the skills necessary and is able to undertake this responsibility in a mature and safe manner. In either instance, the following points should be implemented:

a   There should be a clear understanding and acceptance between the performer and the supporter on the action itself and the support to be provided.

b   Contact should not be such that it might be construed as over-zealous, unusual or inappropriate.

c   The risks should be fully assessed and their management clearly understood.

d   There should be a readiness by both parties to undertake their respective roles of performing and supporting.

e   Supporting is generally better arranged between pupils, one with another, rather than the teacher being the only person who undertakes this function.

f   Pupils who support each other should, whenever possible, be of the same gender to avoid overtones of personal intimacy.

g   If a pupil's level of skill is variable, it is better that the work of the performer should be redirected to an earlier and more consistent stage where the need for support is foreseeably minimal. Support might then reasonably be provided by pupils so long as they have been trained in the required techniques.

h   Where only the teacher is sufficiently reliable to effect safe support for a pupil, it is prudent to be sure that the previous stage of the skill being learned is so well established that the need for support is likely to be minimal and free of any need to 'grab' at the pupil in mid-air.

i   The established principles of handling and supporting should be known and applied. The supporter must be able to restrain, rotate or lift a performer as the need arises to ensure safe performance.

j   The degree of support may be gradually reduced over time as the active pupil gains in competence and consistency of performance, with the knowledge and acceptance of this by the performer.

k   'Shadow' support should be provided when physical contact by a supporter is no longer required. In this mode the supporter follows the movement in very close attendance, ready to hold a performer in the event of mis-timing or error.

l   The use of thicker weight absorbent landing mattresses or other cushioning devices may assist with the learning of some new complex movements but this does not preclude or replace the need for physical support whenever this is appropriate.

m   The use of devices for supporting, such as belts or rigs, should only be undertaken by persons trained and competent in their function and use in the particular activity.

n   The return of a pupil following absence or illness may require the provision of support, even where that pupil had previously attained a level of performance where support was no longer needed.

o   ONLY WHEN A MOVEMENT FOR WHICH A PUPIL NEEDS SUPPORT HAS BEEN MASTERED AND CONSOLIDATED WITH CORRECT TECHNIQUE IN A CONSISTENT AND CONFIDENT MANNER SHOULD SUPPORT AND SHADOW SUPPORT BE REMOVED ALTOGETHER.

4: RISK MANAGEMENT

4.1   Risk Management in Practice

4.1.1   Risk assessment is a legal requirement under the 'Management of Health and Safety at Work Regulations 1992'. In the context of education it requires a careful examination of what could harm pupils, colleagues or others in the teaching and learning situation. Risk control then requires the identification and implementation of precautions to minimise or prevent harm. The legislation serves to underpin existing good practice, where forethought and sound planning are integral to the delivery of physical education at all stages of the learning process.

4.1.2   Regular risk assessment should be used to identify hazards and calculate the related risks in the facilities, equipment, activities, procedures, transport and staffing for physical education. A hazard is anything that may cause harm (a slippery surface or equipment at the wrong height), while a risk is the chance that someone may be harmed by the hazard. The role of responsible staff is to decide whether a risk is significant and, if so, to determine and implement the precautions necessary to eliminate or minimise the risks presented.

SIGNIFICANT RISK:

A risk that will probably or almost certainly result in serious injury needing hospital treatment, or resulting in disablement or death. Such risks need to be minimised as quickly as possible. This action is called risk control.

4.1.3   The process of risk management is largely one of logic and common sense:

a   Decide whether you will complete a risk assessment for each activity or for each facility with consideration given to the range of activities which would occur in each facility.

b   Then, consider the total event or activity before it takes place, break this down into phases and then identify the foreseeable hazards.

c   Establish who is at risk - usually the pupils, but other staff and visitors may also be affected.

d   Evaluate the risks - how likely is the hazard to cause injury and how severe might these injuries be? Take into account existing procedures and precautions provided. These may be documented, possibly in the subject handbook or by posters, and need to be consistently applied. The risk may already be minimal because of existing practice.

e   Having identified the risks, decide whether any further precautions are needed and take steps to ensure that these are implemented to control the risks.

f   Keep a brief record of the assessment and any further action needed to control the risks.

g   Share the process with other adults involved in the activity and the ensuing information with all participants - both adults and pupils - through discussion, posters, notices or redrafted procedures.

4.1.4   Risk assessment should include a considered response to the following questions:

♦   What potential hazards can be reasonably foreseen?

♦   Is the risk controlled for each foreseeable hazard?

♦   Is further action necessary?

♦   How do we inform others if any changes in procedure are necessary?

4.1.5   It is not necessary to show how an assessment is made, simply that the action was carried out, that the precautions are reasonable and that a proper check took place. There is no set format for records, but good examples can be found in the reference given at the end of this section.

4.1.6   When reviewing the hazards and risks it is worthwhile to consider implications arising from:

♦   any special educational needs, medical considerations, age-related or specific group issues;

♦   changing procedures;

♦   movement or travel to the working area;

♦   fire regulations;

♦   first aid arrangements;

- working areas;

- lesson organisation;

- the activity;

- equipment;

- staffing;

- emergency action.

4.1.7   The likelihood and severity of risk may be reduced to an acceptable level quite simply. If concerns exist these may be controlled by:

- Making the activity safe:

    such as   - teaching progressive practices thoroughly;
               - explaining any inherent risks;
               - changing the way the activity is carried out;
               - using a safer alternative.

- Making the facility or equipment safe:

    such as   - periodic inspections;
               - place warning notices where risks persist;
               - amend how the equipment is used;
               - teach how to use the facility or equipment.

- Making people work safely by giving proper attention to:

               - well qualified, trained, experienced staff;
               - devising appropriate working procedures;
               - discipline and control;
               - appropriate supervision.

4.1.8   The risk assessment record should be regularly reviewed and a note made of any hazard, risk or action which should additionally be included in the revised risk assessment. This should be retained for future reference and to save time when the event or activity is repeated.

4.1.9   It is good practice to involve other adults in the assessment as it helps raise awareness of possible risks, establishes collective expertise and ensures that all understand the organisational requirements of the activity.

4.1.10   Pupils should be involved in day-to-day assessment of risk at the beginning and during lessons, according to their age and ability. Such involvement makes them aware of potential harm and contributes towards their being able to take greater responsibility for their activity.

4.1.11   It is the responsibility of the governors and the headteacher to ensure that risk assessment is carried out.   Advice may be obtained from the local education authority advisory service or health and safety officer.

4.1.12   Risk management has a very obvious application in the planning and organisation of educational journeys and visits. In this context consideration would be given also to transportation; transitional stops; residential accommodation (including emergency arrangements); the structured activities programme; seasonal considerations; use of informal time; medical services and arrangements through the night in case of emergencies, for example a child falling ill.

4.1.13   Risk management applies to any activity which forms a part of the physical education programme, particularly those aspects where hazards are readily apparent such as in trampolining. The process of risk assessment should, therefore, form an integral part of schemes of work and lesson planning.

4.2   Reference List

"School Health and Safety Management" (Croner, 1994);

"Risk Assessment in Physical Education" (Cornwall LEA, 1997);

"Managing Risk Assessment" (NAHT, 1996);

"Policy into Practice, Key Stages 1 & 2 (Dudley LEA, 1995).

5: ENVIRONMENT & EQUIPMENT

5.1   The Physical Education Environment

5.1.1   Physical education teachers at primary and secondary levels can greatly improve their policy and safe practice in physical education if they examine very carefully all the working environments in which they place themselves and their pupils. This should remove or significantly reduce the incidence of accidents through the effective management of potential hazards.

5.1.2   The main working areas where physical education is regularly practised in schools are the:

♦   gymnasium or school hall;

♦   dance studio;

♦   sports hall;

♦   fitness room;

♦   swimming pool;

♦   playground and other hard play areas, e.g. tennis courts;

♦   games field, including all-weather surfaces.

Adventure centres and the outdoor environment are also used for activities by many schools.

5.2   The Gymnasium/Sports Hall/Dance Studio/School Hall

Experience has shown that there is a long history of accidents occurring in indoor working areas, particularly gymnasia. Regrettably some of these were foreseeable. Attention on the following points will serve to reduce the incidence of accident and injury:

5.2.1   **Floor**

a   Floors should be kept clean. Dust is a daily threat to the foot/ floor purchase when travelling if the floor is not swept regularly. Economies in floor sweeping arrangements will allow dust to remain on the floor.

b   Cleaning or polishing should not leave a slippery finish.

c   Control is necessary of patches of early morning condensation which may occur, especially early in winter mornings or during actual lesson time, and of the residual wet mopping after school meals.

d   Synthetic floors may have a very high moisture absorbency which can result in bonding breakdown, when there is a real risk of the floor collapsing.

e   Loose boards, splintering, cracking and lifting edges often occur with heavy use, making for an irregular surface level which requires attention.

5.2.2   Natural and Artificial Lighting

a   Apparatus and activities should be arranged so that there is no risk of children losing visual focus when in the working area. In the early spring and late autumn in particular, there may be a risk of pupils being dazzled by sunlight coming through side windows. Apparatus and activities should be arranged so that there is no risk of pupils losing visual focus when in the workshop.

b   Glazing can be a problem. Glass should be reinforced and resistant to impact fracture; less resilient glass should not be used. If a pane is cracked it should be replaced urgently to eliminate the risk of glass slivers falling into the working area.

c   If doors are glazed around hand pushing height there should be wooden push battens across the door on both sides.

d   Artificial lighting should be in protective cages or the units made from unbreakable materials.

e   Strip-lighting should avoid those systems which produce a flickering or stroboscopic effect. This impairs visual focus and, with some people, can induce disorientation to a dangerous level.

5.2.3   Walls

a   Walls in working areas should be smooth to avoid friction injury should body contact occur.

b   Protection must be provided where there are sharp edges on walls in working areas.

c   Essential features other than physical education apparatus should be positioned well above working height whenever possible, or recessed where this requirement cannot be met.

5.2.4   Doors

a   Main access doors should have some system of closure control. This is especially important on exposed or windy sites so that the risk of doors slamming unexpectedly is minimised.

b   Glass doors can be hazardous. Where they are necessary, the glass used should be smoked or coloured for visibility, and should be unbreakable.

5.2.5   Heating

a   The heating system should provide for an adequate working temperature and should be adjustable to meet varying local conditions.

b   It should be designed so that there is no danger of any pupil being adversely affected by burns, fumes or other hazards to health, or of wooden equipment being warped by the systems used.

c   A heating system located high up will normally require greater output or need to operate for longer periods to influence the temperature at working level.

d   A regular inspection and maintenance programme of the heating system is necessary.

5.2.6   Large Portable and Fixed Equipment

a   Equipment inevitably wears with regular use. As it wears it may become dangerous. Inspection is therefore vital.

b   It should be inspected at least once a year by professional equipment engineers who should leave the school with certificates of 'safe usage' when the work is completed. This certification should specifically state that, after examination and with reasonable care and usage, items are considered safe for a further twelve months, or until the next inspection is due.

c   Those items in need of replacement or repair should be listed, and any items which are beyond reasonable repair should be marked accordingly and disposed of so that they are no longer available for use.

d   In addition, teachers should set up a school's system of daily monitoring where teachers and pupils carry out a working check when getting equipment out for use. Work should not begin until such procedures have been completed.

e   The safest school system has a further built-in check where pupils particularly, and teachers, react immediately to changes which occur whilst equipment is being used and put it right in a safe way. Mats which move slightly and fixings which slacken are two examples of this.

5.2.7   Showers and Changing Rooms

a   Wet floors can produce unexpected slips. Tiles in shower areas should be non-slip.

b   Pupils should be encouraged to dry their bodies thoroughly after showering before proceeding to the changing area.

c   Broken wall tiles can be razor sharp. They should be replaced urgently.

d   Shower water mixer valves should be regulated by one control key which should be positioned out of the reach of children to reduce any risk of scalding.

e   Mixer valves should be checked and cleaned at regular intervals to remove lime scale.

f   Foot baths, where provided, can be hazardous to the movement of pupils in shower areas and care is necessary.

g   Pegs in changing rooms and lockers should be free from the risks of bending and dangerous distortion.

h   The use of aerosol or other sprays for personal hygiene requires care through minimum application and adequate ventilation.

5.2.8   Equipment Storage and Management

a   Whatever the means used for storing equipment, the arrangements should leave the items reasonably secure from easy interference by pupils.

b   It is advisable to have a storage system for mats which meets the requirements of fire prevention. Advice from the appropriate fire service authority may be sought in this regard.

c   Fire exits should never be blocked.

d   The equipment storage system should not place pupils at risk from tripping over or falling from high piles of equipment or be so disposed that pupils cannot withdraw and replace items safely.

5.2.9   Pupils Handling Equipment

a   All pupils should be involved in handling gymnastic equipment as a part of their physical education programme.

b   Schools should have a system designed to enable pupils to learn how to handle equipment safely according to their age and strength. Early lessons should focus particularly on appropriate handling.

5.3   Fitness Rooms

5.3.1   Fitness rooms may be equipped with free weights, with weight stations or multigyms, or with a combination of both. Great care needs to be taken whatever their disposition.

a   The equipment should be positioned so that adequate space is always maintained between working areas.

b   Where free weights are used, mats may need to cover the floor for protection. They should provide a firm and stable working surface.

c   Free weights should be stored carefully on purpose-built stands and not allowed to remain loose on the floor.

d   The collars on free weights should have a device which locks the discs firmly in position when in use.

e   Wedge-shaped floor bases used to enable the correct positions of the feet for leg squats exercises should be fixed or sufficiently weighted to prevent slipping.

f   Weights stations and multigyms should be subject to the same regular inspection and repair programme by a recognised specialist firm as with other physical education apparatus.

g   Equipment with frayed wires should not be used until the defective parts have been replaced.

h   Notices on safe procedures for weight-training should be clearly posted.

i   Care must be taken not to obstruct emergency fire exit doors through the inappropriate positioning of equipment.

j   The fitness room should be lockable to prevent unauthorised use.

k   The system should not allow users to work without a proper induction.

5.4   Swimming Pools

5.4.1   Where schools use public swimming facilities it is reasonable to expect that owners of the pool will provide a safe working environment for users under the Occupier's Liability Acts, 1957 and 1984. However, teachers accompanying pupils, together with instructors, will need to ensure they know and implement the normal operating procedures and the emergency action plan for the facility being used. Teachers have a duty to react to any unacceptable changes in the pool environment and to protect their pupils accordingly.

Examples include

◆   seasonal overcrowding by the public;

◆   unruly or even dangerous behaviour by other swimmers;

◆   lack of poolside attendants and life-saving cover;

◆   inadequate supervision of changing rooms;

◆   lack of lifebelts and other essential emergency recovery equipment;

◆   poor water clarity.

In addition, in school pools

a   The principles of safe practice recommended by the Health and Safety Executive for public pools are the same.

b   The school should operate a system where water temperature and chemical levels are monitored at the beginning of the day and at regular times throughout the day.

c   At no time should chemicals be added to water directly when swimmers are present.

d   If a teacher suspects water contamination and health risks such as irritation to the eyes, pupils should be taken from the pool and the matter reported for further investigation.

e   The school must engage a cleaning system which meets acceptable hygiene practices.

f   There must be a competent teacher/instructor present to guarantee retrieval of pupils from the water in the event of an emergency.

g   There must be adequate life-saving equipment readily available in known locations, with staff (and pupils as appropriate) trained in its use.

h   Clear signs should be posted relating to water depths and behavioural practice conducive to user safety.

i   The pool surround should be kept clear at all times. Pool equipment such as floatation aids, emergency equipment and lane markers should, therefore, be stored appropriately, taking into account the need for safe access to and from the pool.

Pool comfort

j   Achieving pool comfort in school pools involves attention not only to water temperature and water clarity but also to other factors such as water purity which can affect safety.

k   There should be a pool logbook, regularly completed by the pool manager, which is available to teachers.

l   Teachers should be sure that the chemical balance of the water is appropriate. This is important at the start of each day but particularly so on Monday mornings when variations may have occurred over the weekend.

m   Public pools, because of their large size, do not present the same urgency of problem and it is the pool manager's responsibility to ensure that pool comfort is right. If children's eyes react to excessive irritant in the water, a request should be made to the management for the figures to be checked.

Sump outlet pipes

Those responsible for the management of pools should ensure that outlet pipes at the bottom of pools have a grille in place and are securely fastened. Holes in grilles should not be large enough for children's fingers to become trapped.

Schools using municipal, private or other pools would be advised to obtain assurance that appropriate action has been taken. These grilles have been known to entrap long hair. Swimming hats are the surest protection against this hazard.

5.5   Playgrounds and Other Play Areas

a   Limitations of space create most problems in playgrounds.

b   Play activities should be so arranged and controlled that the dispersal of pupils is promoted and crowding-collisions are eliminated.

c   Activities involving balls should take place well away from glass windows.

d   Play spaces should be sited to prevent the risk of running into walls or other obstacles.

e   Playground surfaces should be in good condition with no loose materials present in the playing area.

f   The presence of oil can sometimes cause early disintegration of playground surfaces.

g   Reasonable steps should be taken to avoid vehicular intrusion on playgrounds. Where this is not possible, close and careful monitoring by responsible adults is essential. Car parking areas should be separate from those used for pupil play.

h   Surround netting should be maintained in good condition.

5.6   Playing Fields, Including All-weather Surfaces

a   Safety on playing fields can be affected adversely by the aftermath of trespass. Broken glass, cans and rubbish generally deposited on these sites create serious risks to children.

b   It is advisable that all games lessons should be preceded with a visual sweep of the playing area before the lesson commences, during which time all hazardous objects should be removed or made safe.

c   Deposits of faeces by dogs or cats infected by Toxocara (roundworm) can cause toxocariasis in humans, with symptoms which include blindness, asthma, epilepsy and general aches and pains. All practical measures should be taken to keep animals off playing surfaces and to encourage owners to remove any offending deposits immediately.

d   Surfaces vary according to weather. Rain, snow and frost need to be assessed and reacted to according to degree. Where there is a real risk of injury, games should not be played.

e   Pitches should be marked out safely so that the surfaces are, and remain, level. No corrosive substances should be used.

f   As in playgrounds the spaces should be adequate to accommodate the game(s) being played and the sizes of the pupils playing. Games posts should be securely fitted in keeping with regular good practice.

g   The improvised use of equipment for which it was not primarily designed should only take place with great forethought and care. Improvised equipment is not recommended if safe practice may be compromised.

h   Playing surfaces should be regularly maintained to a satisfactory standard for safe play.

i   Safety margins should allow for adequate run-off areas.

5.7   Safe Environments Away From School Premises

5.7.1   With the growing practice of taking children away from the school premises to unfamiliar locations for adventurous activities, some of a relatively high risk nature, teachers must be alert and active in ensuring that their pupils are safe from foreseeable risks. In all these activities the Department for Education and Employment, together with other relevant agencies, produce updated statements on safety in outdoor activity centres. No headteacher should allow their schools to take part in any ventures of this kind without reference to the most updated guidance available and the production of the school's own considered action to ensure safety. Centres should be requested to provide evidence of appropriate accreditation by a recognised body and/or operate to the code of practice of the Activity Centre Advisory Committee (ACAS). Whatever the venture proposed, there are common elements to be considered. Physical education teachers and any other teachers involved should make sure that the following points are thoroughly addressed:

a   The centre chosen for any activities to be followed can deliver a safe and reliable service.

b   The staff who lead activities are competent and qualified to recognised standards. This is particularly pertinent to all higher risk activities.

c   Where a school uses a centre for the first time, further and more detailed advice than that provided in a brochure should be obtained.

d   The insurance arrangements are approved and accepted by the LEA's or governing body's insurance advisers.

e   Accommodation facilities are checked for fire protection systems.

f   For each separate venture, find out and assess the risk factors on the terrain at the location and maintain vigilance for the duration of the visit.

g   Be sure that transport arrangements comply with expected standards, including insurance.

h   Arrange that staff supervision will provide 24 hours round the clock in loco parentis cover for the pupils. Being on a visit described as a holiday in no way relaxes this obligation on the teachers involved.

i   Plan thoroughly and in good time.

j   Share planning and management ideas with parents and pupils so that they are partners in accepting the arrangements.

k   Notify the LEA or governing body of the venture in good time and be sure to have approval in writing from that authority.

l   Ensure that participating pupils are able to meet the fitness and personal and group responsibility requirements of the venture so that their safety is not compromised.

m   Be sure that the party can meet first-aid requirements at any time.

n   Establish the arrangements for doctor and hospital coverage at the location, especially abroad and have an emergency two-way contact system with the school at home.

o   Pupils and parents should be clear on the behavioural expectations of them whilst teachers are in loco parentis. These should be explained to both pupils and their parents, and accepted by them in writing before the venture commences (refer appendix 6).

5.7.2   The Adventure Activities Licensing Authority provides a helpful self-assessment guidance pack for schools with their own centres who wish to consider safe practice in line with the statutory licensing regulations.

5.8 Physical Education Equipment

5.8.1 Physical education equipment should conform with the appropriate standards of manufacture and performance as provided by the British Standards Institute (BSI) or the British Standards European Norm (BS EN). This is an important consideration to ensure safety and quality when new equipment is to be purchased or existing equipment replaced. Purchasers should make careful enquiries and be satisfied that these standards apply to the items they obtain.

5.9 Gymnastics Apparatus

5.9.1 Gymnastics apparatus in schools consists largely of fixed and portable items comprising climbing frames, ropes, benches, boxes, trestles, ladders, poles, nesting tables, movement tables, planks and wall bars. In the primary school some portable equipment, when not in use, is normally positioned in a store room attached to the hall with the remainder, plus fixed equipment, located at points around the perimeter of the working area. It is important that the following points related to safe practice are considered:

a   The equipment should be stored so that it is reasonably accessible for use.

b   Apparatus should be assembled and dismantled systematically. It should be checked immediately before use, adequately spaced out and adjusted to meet the needs of individuals. Pupils are able to participate in this process at all stages of their education and they should be encouraged to check for safety and to report any wrong adjustments or loose fittings immediately.

c   After use, equipment should be returned to its usual place so that users become familiar with its position. In its stored position it must be stable.

d   The equipment should be suitable for handling and management by the pupils following appropriate training under the direction of the teacher.

e   Any equipment deemed unsafe for use should be clearly labelled and removed from the working area until it has been repaired or replaced.

f   All large fixed and portable apparatus should be subject to a regular annual inspection and maintenance programme.

g   Only apparatus that has been officially provided or approved should normally be used for gymnastics. Improvised apparatus should be checked and approved for suitability by an appropriate specialist adviser. The use of chairs for gymnastics purposes is not recommended.

h   Apparatus should conform to British Standards or British Standards European Norms.

5.10   Check List for Faults

Teachers may find the following information helpful in their regular inspection of assembled gymnastics equipment for use by their classes:

5.10 1   Hinged type apparatus fixed to a wall.

Check that:

a   bracing wires are taut and stable and are not fraying at points of frictional contact;

b   castors are running smoothly and the contact surface is free from grit;

c   sockets in the floor are free from sweeping compounds and other dirt;

d   locking nuts are secure;

e   securing bolts are firmly fixed to their base and engage properly with the appropriate floor fitment;

f   any securing bolts that fix the apparatus to the wall have not worked loose;

g   wooden components are free from cracks or splinters.

5.10.2   Single and double beams.

Ensure that:

a   the hauling cables are free-running and not frayed;

b   the trackway is oiled occasionally so that the upright post runs smoothly;

c   the wooden beams have no cracks and shackle pins are firmly located on the hauling wires;

d   there are sufficient pins and wedges;

  e   floor sockets are free from obstructions and the bolts locate fully and lock;

  f   the beams move smoothly when hauled.

5.10.3 Climbing ropes and other suspended apparatus.

Check that:

  a   drag lines are not worn and there is a securing cleat on the wall to stabilise the ropes when fully extended;

  b   the runway operates smoothly;

  c   ropes are free of knots;

  d   the caps at the base of the ropes are not worn or missing and stitching is not working loose;

  e   the securing nuts are tight.

5.10.4 Portable freestanding apparatus (trestles).

Check that:

  a   the horizontal stays are sufficiently wide apart to avoid the risk of a hand or foot getting trapped;

  b   all securing pins are fully engaged.

5.10.5 Vaulting apparatus.

Ensure that:

  a   the wood is free from splinters and the covers are free from tears.
      (Leather covers should be rough and not highly polished through age or excessive use);

  b   there are no cracks or loose screws;

  c   fitted height adjustment mechanisms work smoothly;

  d   all rubber stops are firmly fixed and in good condition and no screws are in contact with the floor;

  e   where sections interlock, the angular interlocking surfaces are not rounded through use, allowing dangerous movement in the apparatus when struck during a vault;

f   wheeling system works efficiently, with wheels clear of the floor when the equipment is in use.

5.10.6   **Benches (and planks).**

Check that:

a   the timber is not warped and the rubber buffers are in place. These should make contact with the floor when the bench is inverted;

b   the fixing-hooks are covered with leather or plastic and the screws are firm;

c   the bracing brackets on the legs are firm;

d   there are no splinters;

e   the rubber pads on the base are in good condition and free of any build-up of dirt or polish;

f   the hinged fixing hooks on benches are laid flat when the apparatus is used in the inverted position.

5.10.7   **Beating boards and springboards.**

Check that:

a   there are no cracks in the boards or supports;

b   the take-off surface is non-slip and free from splinters.

5.10.8   **Scrambling nets.**

Check that:

a   the ropes are not worn, and all fixing devices are secure;

b   the nets are stabilised so there is no unexpected movement.

5.10.9   **Trampolines (and trampettes as appropriate).**

Ensure that:

a   all the leg braces have been properly fitted and the hinge units are securely housed;

b   all adjustments are tight;

c   the hooks of the springs/rubber cables are properly attached, with the hooks pointing down;

d   the springs/cables are all in good condition;

e   the safety pads are fitted and entirely cover the springs/cables;

f   if present, allen screws are tight;

g   the trampoline/trampette bed is clean;

h   the wheeling devices are operating smoothly and the pivotal housing on the frame holds the hub of the wheeling mechanism at right angles without any movement of the hub and the housing;

i   where safety mattresses are used, they are of sufficient size and weight absorbency to meet the requirements of body impact.

When the equipment is in position ready for use.

Check that:

j   the trampoline is placed well away from any overhead obstruction (hanging beams, lights). There should be an overhead clearance of at least 5 metres from the floor to the lowest hanging object (some trampolines may require even greater clearance);

k   removed wheel units are placed carefully in a storage position well clear of the working area;

l   the space is clear under and around the trampoline.

Unfolding the trampoline.

Ensure that:

m   peoples' feet are kept well away from the wheels;

n   the trampoline is angled and lowered carefully, and the lower leg section is held firmly so that it does not crash to the floor;

o   the frame sections are opened with a firm continuous movement, with steady force applied and maintained to prevent them springing back;

p   fingers, elbows and wrists are kept clear of all hinges.

Folding the trampoline.

Take care that:

q   the wheels are securely housed;

r   the frame sections are closed using a firm, continuous movement with steady force applied and maintained to resist the tension of the springs or cables;

s   fingers, elbows and wrists are kept clear of all hinges;

t   feet are kept well away from the wheels;

u   the lower frame and leg sections are positioned inside the upper frame and leg sections as the trampoline is rotated from the horizontal to the vertical;

v   when folded, the trampoline is locked to prevent unauthorised use. This can be achieved by locking together two links of one of the leg chains. Trampettes should also be 'disabled' when not in use to prevent their unauthorised usage.

(Note: Pupils should be taught how to unfold and fold the trampoline under direct supervision. This is a highly disciplined activity. Pupils should never pull the trampoline towards them or walk underneath it.)

Trampolining support rigs.

w   where provided, these should be supplied and fitted by a recognised specialist manufacturer and engineer. On no account should improvised rigs be used. Training in the proper use of rigs is essential.

5.11   The Use of Mats in Physical Education

5.11.1   Teachers should understand the structure and uses of mats. In many court cases involving physical education, the way mats have been used or abused has featured very prominently.

5.11.2   The use of mats to absorb landings is a feature of the physical education programme. They should be seen as equipment designed to cope with planned and foreseen landings. When used in this deliberate way, mats should eliminate or greatly reduce impact shock and associated injuries. Children should be taught to recognise the need to use mats in a disciplined way.

5.11.3 Over the years there has been considerable development in the design and specification of mats and these improvements have brought about a greater level of safety. It is important that teachers should know whether any special type of mat is more appropriate for the activity being practised, e.g. high jumping or advanced gymnastics. Schools should seek advice on the appropriate density of mats required to avoid 'bottoming out', i.e. feeling the floor surface through the mat on impact. The British Gymnastics Federation will advise on high impact thicker mattresses to be used in specific gymnastics situations, and similar advice on landing areas for athletics may be obtained from the British Athletics Federation. Reputable manufacturers of mats will also supply information for other activities. Those who buy mats for school use should check with the retailer that the mats conform to the appropriate British Standards European Norms.

5.11.4 Mats should therefore be selected with care in order to meet the needs of the child and the activity being followed. Whenever the opportunity is presented, it is helpful if young people are guided as to why certain mats are used in particular activities and how their placing can enhance safety. Pupils should be protected against a false sense of security in the way mats offer them protection. The following points will help to increase understanding:

5.11.5 **Gymnastics**

a   The placing of mats is very important. They should be used where it is expected that children will need to cushion deliberate landings. They should not be placed around profusely and indiscriminately as they can produce real danger to young people accidentally tripping over them and falling.

b   Teachers should be wary of placing mats where it is considered there is a high probability of a child falling off the apparatus. It would be better to arrange the apparatus and the demands on the child so that there is a high expectation of safe performance rather than that the child will fall.

c   The need to provide mats in the prescribed way is vital where landing impact cannot be accommodated by the body. There are times, however, when gymnasts become so skilful in their movements that they can manage and absorb their body momentum without the need for mats.

d   Teachers may be aware from past experience and knowledge of their work that a mat or mats may be required by inexperienced pupils in the very early stages of traversing apparatus at a height, such as a ladder or bar suspended between trestles. Once pupils have developed sufficient shoulder strength to avoid the need to drop down, then the mats may be dispensed with.

e   Where several mats on top of and to the side of each other are provided to give greater absorption cover, as in jumping from high apparatus, care should be taken not to leave gaps into which young people might land and thereby injure themselves.

f   When children are challenged with new tasks, care should be taken to ensure safe working conditions which reflect the capabilities and developmental stages of all the pupils.

g   It is sound practice to teach children to be aware of and to readjust mats which may have moved slightly in use.

h   The general purpose mat of approximately 25 mm thickness is adequate to meet most landing needs inherent in the usual level of school gymnastics.

i   If the force of a child's landing is increased by such factors as the weight of that child, the height of flight and the speed of the activity, then thicker mats may be necessary.

j   Mats should be light enough for children to handle easily. In general, it is better for at least two children to carry a mat; this prevents folding and subsequent damage to the core of the mat.

k   Mats should be checked by the children and the teacher to make sure that no pin, stone, or other dangerous object is concealed in the fabric.

l   Mats should always be checked to make sure that the core substances are not disintegrating to the point where there is a risk of a child 'bottoming out' when using them.

m   Mats should not be folded as this can cause cracks and damage to the core.

n   Where landings may be of high impact, thick landing mattresses of 10cm depth and upward may be more appropriate than the 25mm mats.

o   Thick landing mattresses should not be relied upon to absorb any kind of landing and to prevent injury. Physical support may be needed to ensure that a performer will land feet first and in control during the progressive stages of learning a prescribed skill, particularly when high momentum is generated or rotation is involved.

5.11.6 High jump landing modules.

a   When using high jump landing modules, particularly in outdoor practices where a running approach is used, there should be adequate breadth, width and depth of landing modules to accommodate the needs of every participating athlete. Multiple modules must be locked firmly together and this is best accomplished by the use of a coverall pad. Athletes should be trained to check the landing areas for themselves.

b   The use of high jump landing modules for other physical education purposes requires very careful consideration. The equipment can produce a secondary recoil action and can also give a child a misleading sense of what is possible and useful in gymnastics.

5.11.7 Indoor Long Jump.

a   The use of gymnastics mats for indoor long jump with a run-up is not recommended.

5.11.8 Maintenance.

a   Mats should be covered with material which is easy to clean and have a base which is very stable when in contact with the floor.

b   Mats should be free of holes or tears.

c   Cleaning the underside of mats may be necessary from time to time.

d   As with other physical education apparatus, mats should be subject to annual inspection and repair/replacement. Mats deemed unserviceable should be marked accordingly and subsequently removed from use.

e   Newly purchased mats should meet current fire regulations and schools should take advice from the appropriate fire service authority. This will ensure satisfactory storage arrangements and fire alarm provision should there be the need.

5.12   Freestanding Goal Posts

5.12.1   The use of freestanding goal posts for soccer, five-a-side football and other (sometimes improvised) team games is common practice, particularly when storage, portability and flexibility of placement are factors for consideration. Such posts are often of metal construction with folding side sections and are relatively light to facilitate transportation by hand.

5.12.2   Accidents to young people, including several fatalities, have highlighted the need for great care in the use of freestanding goals. The advantages of portability and lightness are countered by a very real danger that the posts may lack stability and topple over unless measures are taken to promote their safe usage.

5.12.3   The following guidance will help minimise or prevent the possibility of accidents involving freestanding goal posts:

a   Freestanding goal posts should be obtained from recognised sports equipment manufacturers.

b   There should be no sharp edges on the apparatus.

c   They should be regularly inspected and maintained, and assembled for use in accordance with the instructions from the manufacturer.

d   They should be properly stabilised when in use so that they do not topple or fall when forcefully contacted.

e   Netting should be well fitted and should not extend beyond the area covered by the base of the posts.

f   Safe lifting and carrying techniques should be employed in the moving and positioning of freestanding goal posts.

g   Pupils should be made aware of the dangers of misusing the equipment.

h   Under no circumstances should young people be allowed to climb or to swing on freestanding goal posts.

i   When not in use, freestanding goal posts should be secured through being anchored on their storage positions, or locked away.

6: MANAGEMENT & ADMINISTRATION

6.1 Introduction

6.1.1 The management of safe practice is an important issue for all subject leaders. It involves the development of clear procedures and standards which need to be consistently applied and met by staff, pupils and visitors for the benefit of themselves and those with whom they work.

6.1.2 The Health and Safety at Work Act, 1974, requires employers to ensure that establishments have:

- A written policy for health and safety.
- Procedures to implement the policy.
- A specified person to ensure that the procedures are put into practice.

6.1.3 Due regard to health and safety is thus important. This is usually through the development and regular review of policies, the consistent implementation of whole school procedures, regular risk assessments and effective subject management.

6.1.4 Whilst these health and safety requirements are at a whole school level it is clear that the subject structure of the curriculum indicates that some form of co-ordinated subject contributions to these whole school issues is wise. As a practical subject based on a premise of appropriate challenge within an acceptable level of risk it is natural that physical education will make a significant contribution to whole school developments in health and safety.

6.1.5 All teachers and other adults involved with physical education are required by the Health and Safety at Work Act 1974 and by common law to teach safely. The Education Act 1996 sets out a national curriculum which involves the teaching of safety. In addition, teachers' pay and conditions expect teachers to maintain good order and discipline, indicating the need for class control. The principle of anticipating foreseeable events indicates a need for teachers of physical education to have sound observation skills also. It would be helpful for the consistent application of procedures and standards for subject leaders to consider how these principles may be developed.

6.2 Safety Policies

6.2.1 Whole school and departmental policies which are consistent with Health and Safety at Work requirements and those of the LEA and governing body need to be effectively in place.

6.2.2   Policy development should be a team exercise and may involve governors, pupils and other stakeholders in an appropriate way. Regular review should be built in. This is achieved typically by ensuring that safety issues are a standard agenda item for meetings at least once each year and, preferably, more regularly.

6.2.3   The purpose of a policy for safe practice is to contribute to physical education being offered within a well-managed, safe and educational context. Common codes of practice for teachers and pupils and common administrative procedures may then be established. Statutory requirements and other national guidance, such as that in codes of practice and this BAALPE document, are also more easily followed.

6.3   Guidelines

6.3.1   Documentation which sets out the procedures to be followed by staff, pupils and visitors are often referred to as subject guidelines. These are most effectively developed as a staff or departmental exercise as the sharing of ideas and expertise helps set a common standard of practice and provides a valuable form of professional development for some colleagues. Reference to relevant issues contained in this document "Safe Practice in Physical Education" would then helpfully reinforce or add to the brainstorming aspect of the exercise. The guidelines would form part of the subject handbook containing all the information relevant to the work of the department.

6.3.2   Many important procedures may be set out within the subject guidelines. These may include staffing roles and responsibilities, accident procedures, registration of pupils, clothing and jewellery requirements, apparatus handling, arrangements for particular groups of pupils, risk management.

6.3.3   There is no definitive list of what procedures should be documented. Many will be common to most schools but some issues may be specific to particular schools or departments. The importance of setting out in writing the procedures to be followed is to establish consistent standards of safe practice and to enable anyone working within the subject area - student, supply teacher or new teacher - to easily maintain consistent practice.

6.4   Curriculum Standards

6.4.1   The national curriculum statutory requirements for physical education set out expectations for pupils' planning, performance and evaluation of a range of issues including aspects of safe practice. It is important that these are delivered through schemes of work, consistently applied procedures and, where appropriate, other strategies such as the placing of notices. In this way a significant contribution may be made to an individual ultimately becoming independently active.

6.5   Subject Development/Improvement Plan

6.5.1   The education agenda is about improving pupil attainment. To this end school or subject development plans are commonly now called Improvement Plans.

6.5.2   Every school is required to have a development or improvement plan. This should reflect the priorities the school has identified to bring about improvement. According to school policy, subject areas may be required to set out their improvement plans only in relation to the school's identified priorities; they may be allowed to identify only specific subject priorities or a combination of both school and subject needs may be encouraged. Whichever format is used safe practice should feature as a high priority in any subject improvement plan.

6.5.3   Improvement plans should indicate the tasks necessary to achieve the improvement, the estimated costs, the monitoring strategies planned to ensure that progress is being made and the success criteria to indicate the improvement has been achieved. These should be written in a way which reflects the impact on pupils, such as in the ways in which improved safe practice impinges on their work. Estimated costing for the inspection, repair and replacement of all major items of equipment should be included and especially for those where the annual departmental financial allocation is insufficient.

6.6   Informing Staff, Pupils and Parents

6.6.1   Many subject leaders, in primary, secondary and special schools, produce a handbook containing relevant information to enable anyone teaching the subject to follow required procedures and programmes. This will include schemes of work, a safety policy and any procedural arrangements to be followed, such as taking a register at the beginning of a lesson or always locking a trampoline when it is stored to prevent unauthorised use. A handbook is a valuable tool in enabling such information to be readily available and known by those to whom it is relevant, including support and supply staff and students on teaching practice. It should be reviewed regularly and the contents updated as necessary.

6.6.2   Periodic risk assessment as a team exercise will result in some form of record. This should be reviewed annually or more frequently if the circumstances change. The record may be kept in the handbook for wider awareness or it may be filed for future reference.

6.6.3   Safety issues may arise at any time. They should be addressed as soon as possible. Meetings of staff, either on a whole-school basis in primary schools or as a department in secondary schools, should provide a regular opportunity to raise and discuss safety matters.

The sharing of information is a vital first step in raising awareness which in turn can lead to more informed and, therefore, better practice.

6.6.4   Periodic monitoring and review of hazards, probability of harm, consequences and control, should be established. This is an important aspect of managing risk. Monitoring may be carried out in a number of ways - by peer observation of lessons, checking planning against schemes of work, pupil records, accident report forms and discussion at staff meetings.

Reactive management involves the review of risks and controls following incidents by collecting and collating information on injuries and near-misses. Pro-active management may involve such considerations as an annual safety audit, brief but regular reviews of policy, organisation, records, facilities, equipment, systems or procedures. Post-event reviews with a note of possible modification for future occasions is also good practice. Most important, a regular agenda item for staff meetings which considers the causes of injuries and near misses will lead to open, consistent and sound practice. Colleagues should be informed adequately of the outcomes of any monitoring and review.

6.6.5   Brief statements in the school prospectus about physical education routines and activities go a long way to keeping parents informed. Other mechanisms, such as letters, newsletters and brochures are also effective in keeping parents informed of the activities and related arrangements for good, safe practice in physical education.

6.6.6   Extra-curricular activities are popular and many parents or carers would like to know where their child is, where they are going, what they are doing, when they will be back, when and how they will be getting home. In practical terms, whilst the dissemination of this information is important, there may be difficulties in informing all parents of all details, especially when arrangements can change at very short notice.

6.6.7   It is helpful if in the school prospectus it states that it is likely that at some time most children will be involved in extra-curricular sporting activities. When this opportunity to participate arises parents could be kept informed by a range of strategies which may include:

♦   A fixture list for each sport.

♦   A practice schedule for after school activities at the start of each term.

♦   For exceptional circumstances, such as a visit to an international match, written confirmation may be required for those children taking part and consent required.

The information could also be made available to the main school office so that parents who are unsure of arrangements can contact the school for confirmation.

6.7 Community Use of Physical Education Facilities

6.7.1 Arrangements for the community use of physical education facilities should ensure that user groups are co-ordinated with consistent procedures and standards across the different groups. Written safety policies of the establishment should be developed with and made known to community user groups with due regard being given to liability and insurance matters. The inclusion of specific safety requirements in written letting agreements, such as staffing levels, qualifications or procedures, is good practice.

6.8 Responsibilities

6.8.1 All staff at a school carry responsibilities for safety.

6.8.2 Class teachers should follow given policy and guidelines. They should check that work areas and equipment are safe with protective equipment used where stipulated. It is advisable that they participate in inspections and risk assessments. Where staff become aware of a hazard they have a duty to take appropriate remedial action as soon as is appropriate to eliminate or to minimise the risk, albeit as a temporary measure. This could be, for example, arranging for an area of wet flooring in the hall or gymnasium to be dried off or for that part of the area to be cordoned off to prevent use or even to decide not to use the area on that occasion. They also have a duty to report any safety-related circumstances to a line manager or senior manager for further attention as necessary.

6.8.3 Subject leaders are usually considered to have day to day management of health and safety in relation to schools and subject policies. They should establish regular review procedures to ensure safe working environments and safe systems of work, carrying out regular inspections and risk assessments. They should also check that appropriate action is taken to safeguard pupils, visitors and other staff as required, informing senior management of any relevant issues. Many subject leaders also make appropriate arrangements for staff training in safety. Where procedures are established or modified subject leaders should ensure that those affected are informed effectively.

6.8.4   The headteacher is responsible for the day to day management of all health and safety matters. She/he should ensure that regular inspections, risk assessments and adequate actions are carried out, submitting reports to the governors, LEA or other agencies as appropriate. It is the headteacher's responsibility to ensure that health and safety information is passed to the appropriate people. The responsibility for carrying out particular tasks may be delegated to others but the headteacher always maintains the overall day to day management responsibility.

6.8.5   The employer is legally responsible for health and safety. This may be the governors or the LEA. Where the LEA is responsible, delegation for day to day responsibility for health and safety is often given to the governors.

7: CLOTHING, PERSONAL EFFECTS & PROTECTION

7.1   Personal Clothing

7.1.1   Clothing is an important aspect to safety in physical activity. It serves to insulate the body during the warm up phase and may be reduced to maintain an equitable working state during the main part of a lesson. It should be well suited to its function, neither too loose to flap around nor too tight to restrict movement.

7.1.2   A change of clothing is important for physical education, partly for reasons of hygiene but also to ensure that the clothing is suited to the physical activity. Schools are advised to have a written policy on clothing for physical education, ensuring both pupils and their parents are informed on acceptable wear and to promote consistency across all classes in a school.

7.1.3   Fashion inevitably has an impact on what young people may choose to wear for physical activity and this requires careful assessment. A trend in games for boots to be worn with laces only halfway engaged and tongues flopping is clearly hazardous and should not be allowed. Where fashion in clothing may compromise safety, it is important that awareness is raised and that pupils understand the limits which must be applied to ensure their own well-being and that of others during participation in physical activity.

7.1.4   Consideration of developments in fibres and the impact on physical education clothing is necessary. The criteria for usage should be focused on the suitability of materials and design of clothing for physical activity, with no foreseeable hazards presented to the wearer or to other participants.

7.1.5   Some cultures require the wearing of certain clothing to conform with their religious traditions and beliefs. This should be recognised and discussed with the leadership of the groups concerned, and satisfactory arrangements made for the wearing of suitable garments by young people to enable their safe participation in physical education.

7.1.6   Clothing removed during physical activity should be placed so that it will present no risk to participants tripping, sliding or falling over.

7.2 Specialist Clothing

7.2.1 Some activities require specialist clothing to be worn, with clear implications for safety. Helmets for climbing and caving are examples. It is important that teachers have a clear understanding of the requirements and that all participants are appropriately attired prior to engaging in these activities. Specialist clothing which pupils may provide for their own use should always be carefully checked by a teacher in good time to make any necessary adjustments.

7.2.2 Points that will help to ensure safe practice include:

a Clothing which is provided must be suited in size or adjustment to the wearer.

b Young people should be fitted with specialised clothing or individual equipment that they will need. They should be informed on the correct usage of such items when they are first issued, together with any constraints which may apply.

c Bright clothing or reflective strips should be made available when visual factors apply, for example: when a walk takes place during the evening or when cycling on roads.

d Systematic arrangements should be made for the replacement of any item which becomes unusable or unsafe.

e All specialist clothing should be regularly checked and repaired or replaced when necessary. Defective clothing or individual equipment must be removed from the allocation system.

7.3 Personal Effects

7.3.1 Pupils often wear personal items which will constitute a hazard if worn for physical activity. Watches, rings, chains, bracelets and other adornments should all be removed before the physical education lesson and a system instituted where this becomes part of the regular routine for changing and the registration of attendance. Pupils should be consistently reminded of this requirement and a check carried out to ensure compliance before activity begins.

7.3.2 Some schools operate a policy where the wearing of such personal items is discouraged or minimised and this can reduce the problems which otherwise arise. It is important that parents are made aware of the policy of the school on the wearing of jewellery or other personal adornments by pupils, on why the policy is in place and on the requirements for physical education in this regard.

7.3.3   There may be some occasions where a personal adornment cannot reasonably be removed. In such circumstances, consideration should be given to making the wearing of the item 'safe' for the activities concerned, both for the wearer and other participants. If this is not possible, then the pupil should 'sit out' for those activities where safety may be compromised and be involved in the lesson in ways which exclude direct physical participation. This is a measure of last resort. Where the situation persists, resolution should be sought through parent consultation and co-operation.

7.4   Personal Protection

7.4.1   The use of protection will vary with the nature of the predicted hazards and the levels of performance. Activities may need to be conditioned or modified to reduce risks to acceptable levels.

7.4.2   Protective devices for individual participants have developed to a significant extent in recent times, largely as a result of technological and design progress. These items enable wearers to engage in physical activity at less risk than was previously possible. An example is the body armour worn by goalkeepers in hockey, where almost all of the body is now much better protected. Teachers should keep abreast of these developments, and such items as are applicable in schools should be made known to pupils and be made available for use.

7.4.3   The wearing of tracksuit bottoms and long sleeved shirts may be necessary when playing on artificial plastic or sand filled surfaces where there is a likely risk of friction burns from falls. Such injuries can be very painful and long lasting and preventative measures are strongly advised.

7.4.4   Specific requirements for particular activities should be noted under the appropriate chapter headings in part 2 of this book.

7.5 Exposure to Sun

7.5.1 Recent climatic changes are now believed to have a detrimental effect on the world's Ozone layer. One of the issues of the thinning of this layer is that it allows the easier passage of ultra violet light into the atmosphere immediately around pupils who may be working outside during physical education lessons. There are two bands of ultra violet light that can be problematic for some people. Both bands are believed to pose a threat of skin cancer as well as other changes in the skin.

7.5.2 This now accepted phenomenon seems to suggest that the duty of care, which teachers manage for their pupils, would be better if it registered some concern for this new kind of risk; especially when taking pupils out in strong sunshine in games lessons. Cricket and athletics meetings may cause the pupils to be working in unacceptable levels of ultra violet light for unusually long periods. The following common-sense precautions are advised:

a Do not allow the children to be exposed to too much direct sunlight. A little is good for them; but dis-abuse them of the pursuit of tanned bodies.

b Teach the children to know when and how to cover their bodies with loose fitting, lightly woven material that will screen them from the sun. Such clothing should not be so loose as to be endangering to the performer.

c Be particularly vigilant with fair skinned children, their skins react quickly to sun burn. This same reaction potential is true of very young children.

d Encourage the wearing of hats wherever possible and practicable. Wide brimmed hats are better, they screen necks and lips more effectively.

e As with all safe practice, it is better to consolidate the pupils' understanding of the issues by repetition of the facts. They should be told regularly about the dangers of excessive sunbathing. Such sun bathing is best done at home under the direct supervision and guidance of the parents which might choose to add the benefit of protective creams to this particular practice of deliberate and extended exposure directly to the sun.

f Pupils should also be advised that it is helpful to wear good sun glasses when sunbathing.

g Be aware of the vulnerability of children with lots of freckles and moles on their skin. Set up a sensible system of checking and helping children to check for themselves without engendering neurotics.

8: PUPILS WITH SPECIAL EDUCATIONAL NEEDS OR MEDICAL NEEDS

8.1 Special Educational Needs

8.1.1 For many years, physical education has made a unique contribution to the physical, social and intellectual development of children in special schools.

8.1.2 The Education Act of 1981 placed a duty on LEAs, subject to certain conditions, to integrate children with special educational needs (SEN) into mainstream schools; thus primary and secondary teachers may find such pupils in their classes.

8.1.3 The SEN Code of Practice (1994) defines models for SEN provision. It is essential that any teacher concerned with the teaching of pupils with special educational needs consults with the school's SEN co-ordinator to ensure effective educational, pastoral and managerial policies are followed.

8.1.4 The following chapter aims to build on the excellent safe practice developed in the special education field to present material for both special schools and for those teachers concerned with SEN work in mainstream schools.

8.2 Philosophy

8.2.1 The statement "it is the ability not the disability that counts", should ensure that all pupils with special educational needs, whether in special or mainstream schools, are presented with a physical education programme that is as near normal as possible.

8.2.2 Children with mild forms of some of the disabilities in this section, for example asthma, epilepsy, diabetes, have been attending mainstream schools for many years. It would be prudent to re-assess teaching practices to ensure a safe environment.

8.2.3 All young people with SEN should take part in regular physical education; it is vital to their growth and development. Such children need more, rather than less, physical education.

8.2.4 In SEN physical education, a special kind of teaching expertise and the right degree of care is required. Just as typical parents will devote extra care to children with these needs, so then should teachers. Yet at the same time, children should not be protected to the point of stifling development.

8.2.5   For children with special educational needs, the way to a free and independent life is not only through being well cared for but also through learning to care for themselves.

8.2.6   The effectiveness of any programmes of study will be influenced by the involvement of the young people concerned. Children should be encouraged to participate in the decision making process and should, where possible, be educated to understand and take some personal responsibility for their own specific safety.

8.3   Consultation

8.3.1   Prior to any child with special educational needs being exposed to a programme of physical education, there must be consultation and discussion between teacher, parent(s) and professionals from other disciplines - doctor, physiotherapist, school nurse. Children should be involved in the discussion wherever practical. These discussions should result in a medical profile and may cover such items as:

- Personal health care equipment, for example inhalers, syringes, incontinence pads;

- body splints and aids;

- 'valves' and 'shunts';

- administration of drugs;

- incontinence;

- mobility aids;

- daily living aid;

- 'care' assistance.

8.3.2   Medical profiles should also identify any activities that the medical profession have stated to be contra-indicative in relation to disability.

8.4   Prior Consultation

8.4.1   Teachers in charge of a pupil with special educational needs must:

    a   know the nature of a child's learning problem, disability, emotional or behavioural disorder;

    b   be aware of any constraints on physical activities as a result of the disability or the regime of medication;

    c   be able to provide the emergency treatment necessary if physical activities exacerbate the disability.

8.4.2   Be prepared for problems such as:

- poor co-ordination;

- lack of spatial concept or perception;

- slow reaction time;

- variable levels of concentration;

- a short span of concentration;

- cardiovascular inhibition;

- muscle spasm;

- sensory loss;

- poor fine/gross motor skills.

8.4.3   Have examined the need for:

- mobility aids;

- dependence on non-teaching assistants;

- special handling;

- toileting and waste disposal;

- special requirements for showering;

- special resources;

- special/adapted equipment.

8.4.4   Have determined that they:

♦   have sufficient background knowledge about a child;

♦   are confident in their approach to teaching pupils with special educational needs;

♦   have the knowledge and technique necessary for safe teaching.

8.4.5   Where the teacher finds there is insufficient information to hand to ensure safe practice he/she must refer back to the various people listed in paragraph 8.3.1.

8.5   Children in Wheelchairs

8.5.1   It is important that children who depend on wheelchairs for mobility should be able to control them and make the necessary adjustments to body positions. Wheelchair skills need to be taught and assessed. The ROSPA Wheelchair Proficiency Award is one such assessment example.

Most children who use wheelchairs are very safety conscious but those with spatial problems will require constant reminders about safe practice. Teachers, non-teaching assistants and helpers should understand the problems associated with the use of wheelchairs.

8.5.2   The following points should be considered:

General

a   Regular maintenance is essential. Schools should determine who is responsible for prime maintenance: home, agency or school and act accordingly.

b   Tyres, wheels and brakes should be subject to regular checks and repairs.

c   Footrests should be at the correct level so that the feet are well supported and neither feet nor legs are at risk from other chairs.

d   A strap of webbing or leather at least 5 centimetres wide should be attached to each of the telescopic uprights of the footrest. This strap should be positioned in such a way as to ensure that the feet cannot slide off, touch the ground or get caught in the wheels.

e   Cushions, where used, should be well fitted and not affect the balance of a child nor impede the movement of the chair.

f   Teachers and helpers should be aware of the individual needs of a child when getting into and out of the wheelchair and they should be able to help as necessary.

g   A child should not stand on the footrests.

h   Consideration should be given to ensuring that the wheelchair does not become a hazard for other pupils.

(Note: Lifting and carrying a disabled pupil requires specialist training to ensure that hurt to either a child or a handler is avoided. The advice of a physiotherapist should be sought in the acquisition of these techniques.)

Sporting Activities

Sports and racing wheelchairs should be:

i   adapted to each individual;

j   specific to the demands of the activity;

k   checked for stability;

l   inspected to ensure that they are mechanically safe and sound.

Athletics

m   Calf straps should be used when racing.

n   During throwing events, chairs should be anchored below a child's centre of gravity by a holding device.

o   If this is not feasible, the chair should be held by an experienced adult whilst a throw is executed.

Swimming

p   Children must not be strapped into wheelchairs whilst at the side of the pool.

q   Chairs should be stripped of cushions prior to entering the pool area.

r   Children in the wheelchairs should not be left unattended whilst in the pool area.

Games

s   Deliberate 'blocking' by using the wheelchair should be discouraged.

t   Legs need to be secured.

Training

u   Efficient training is the most effective way to ensure safe practice in wheelchairs. This should be based on the ROSPA Wheelchair Proficiency Scheme.

8.6   Disabling Conditions and their Implications for Physical Education

Arthritis (Still's Disease)

8.6.1   Still's Disease is a progressive condition which in the main affects the joints but sometimes influences other body systems. Rheumatoid arthritis causes inflammation of the joints, which become swollen and tender. The surrounding tissues become thickened and mobility is impaired. The pain and stiffness may vary from day to day but it is likely to be most severe early in the morning. Some children affected by arthritis have to wear splints on their wrists and ankles.

8.6.2   Specific Safety Factors

a   It is essential that advice is sought from parents and a child's physiotherapist before any physical activity is undertaken.

b   Jumping activities should be very limited and jumping from a height avoided.

c   Gripping can cause problems, for example in the gymnasium or in some games skills.

d   Because of pain and stiffness in the joints, a child may require more time for general movement.

e   General clumsiness may be evident.

f   Swimming is very beneficial since there is no weight bearing.

Asthma

8.6.3   Asthma is a common ailment which appears to be increasingly prevalent in young people. The condition narrows or restricts the air passages of the lungs.

The most noticeable symptoms of asthma are shortness of breath, wheezing and coughing. The severity of an attack may vary considerably from mild, which may need no special treatment, to severe, which will require prompt medical assistance.

8.6.4   Specific Safety Factors

    a   Children with asthma should be encouraged to take part in physical education. Reluctance to participate should be discussed with the parent(s).

    b   A thorough warm up is essential. Attacks can often be prevented by using a bronchiodilator inhaler. Asthmatic children for whom these have been prescribed should be encouraged to carry one with them. Alternative treatment requires the taking of a tablet about twenty minutes before the lesson. The use of appropriate drugs will usually allow asthma sufferers to participate normally.

    c   Exhaling should be emphasised in the event of an attack.

    d   Pupils with asthma may participate in all physical activities but care should be taken to avoid prolonged strenuous exercise.

    e   Swimming is particularly beneficial. Endurance work should be avoided.

Behavioural Difficulties

8.6.5   Many children displaying severe behavioural difficulties attend day and residential special schools. They derive great benefit from physical education designed to meet their specific needs. Mainstream schools are not likely to be able to support such pupils. However, there are some behaviourally disturbed children who can cope with the corporate school ethos and, given sensitive teaching support and an appropriate physical education programme, they can both contribute to and benefit from their participation.

8.6.6   Generally, these pupils will present an aggressive stance towards physical education, either by verbal or physical means or by simply opting out. Many children with severe behavioural problems have a poor self-image and consequently poor esteem. The teacher's main task will be to improve the former in order to enhance the latter.

8.6.7   Specific Safety Factors

    a   Some of the pupils will cope well with team games but many will have difficulty in coping with peer relationships. Therefore individual and small group activities should be explored in depth prior to the larger team games.

    b   Swimming, basic trampolining, simple challenge gymnastics, small group games and stamina focused circuit training can be followed with care.

    c   Teaching groups should be small to ensure that there is suitable and satisfactory supervision.

d   Where the class includes children with unpredictable aggressive behaviour there will be a need for extra teaching support staff. In extreme cases it may be necessary to consider exclusion in order to ensure the safety of other members in the class.

Brittle Bones (Osteogenesis Imperfecta)

8.6.8   Brittle bones is a condition which is usually inherited and is the result of an abnormality of the protein structure of the bones which causes them to break more easily than normal. Joints are often more mobile than is generally the case. Occasionally, hearing may be impaired.

8.6.9   In some children, fractures may occur without warning and for no apparent reason but nevertheless it is important not to overprotect them. In more severe cases, children are small and the bones are twisted as a result of frequent fractures. These children can rarely join in class activities physically but enjoy taking responsibilities as judges or umpires.

8.6.10   Children with this condition usually require regular physiotherapy. More severely affected children use special wheelchairs for safety and support. Those with lesser impairment may use sticks and crutches. Most children with brittle bones have severely restricted mobility.

8.6.11   Specific Safety Factors

a   Because of the nature of this condition, many forms of physical education, especially contact activities, are not suitable. However, some exercise is essential for general fitness.

b   Swimming is ideal, as are other non-weight bearing activities.

c   Care must be taken in getting in and out of swimming baths and in the general handling of these children.

d   Consultation with parents, doctors and physiotherapists must take place before any physical exercise is undertaken. Evidence of this consultation should be obtained prior to pupils participating in physical education.

e   Crowded corridors, changing rooms and playgrounds need to be avoided to minimise the risk of bumping and knocking. Children with brittle bones need to be given space. Careful planning and selection of appropriate material is essential.

Cardiac Conditions and Congenital Heart Disease

8.6.12   Generalisations should not be made about heart conditions. The teacher must seek expert advice from a child's parents and physician about the advisability of participation in physical activity and the degree of that involvement.

8.6.13   Congenital heart disease signifies that a heart defect has been present from birth. In some cases, the condition may be very mild and needs no treatment. The most common condition is called a hole in the heart. Children awaiting surgery and those whose condition cannot be completely cured need special consideration but some may be able to join in certain aspects of the physical education curriculum.

8.6.14   Specific Safety Factors

   a   Some children with heart disease can lead normal lives and should be allowed to participate in physical education.

   b   Where heart disease causes circulatory problems, these may be evident in breathlessness, blueness of the lips and nail beds. Children will tire very quickly when active.

   c   Special consideration should be given to the temperature of the water when swimming; also to safety aspects and procedures in case children should become exhausted in the water.

   d   Teachers must consult parents and receive the correct medical advice about the appropriate levels of activity and capabilities of children.

Cerebral Palsy

8.6.15   There are three main forms of cerebral palsy: spasticity, atherosis and ataxia.

8.6.16   Cerebral palsy is caused by damage to, or lack of development of, the part of the brain which controls movement.

   The effects of cerebral palsy vary widely, from slight disability such as unsteady gait to severe multiple disabilities.

8.6.17   Specific Safety Factors

   a   Spatial and/or perception difficulties are common.

   b   Some children have poor motor organisation. Careful attention to correct sequencing is necessary.

c   Holding and supporting is often difficult and care is needed in climbing activities.

d   Swimming in warm water can be of great importance to help with relaxation. Children suffering from spasticity should normally be introduced in the water using the 'face upwards' (supine) position. They often have difficulty in exhaling, therefore the importance of controlled breathing and reverting to the supine position should be stressed. After swimming, care must be taken to return the child gradually to normal body and air temperature. Severe chilling can induce spasms.

e   Some children may have problems with balance and may be more prone to falling over than other children.

f   Dressing and undressing may be difficult. Allow children sufficient time.

g   Tiredness may set in more easily for children with an appreciable disability because they need to use more energy to achieve the same goals.

Clumsiness (Dyspraxia) Developmental Co-ordination Difficulties

8.6.18   Clumsiness (minimal motor dysfunction) is relative. This section is concerned with those children who appear to be clumsy in attempting most physical tasks, lack co-ordination of their physical movements and frequently display behavioural disorders.

8.6.19   There is no one example of the typically clumsy child and the condition is not necessarily related to intelligence. It is important that clumsiness is identified early and that all persons dealing with a child understand the problems and work together towards the remedy.

8.6.20   Specific Safety Factors

a   A carefully constructed physical education programme can aid the development of clumsy children.

b   Activities where children are responding to tasks at their own level of ability will be helpful. Effort and success should be acknowledged and praised.

c   Gross and fine motor skills will usually need to be broken down into the simplest stages of progression.

d   Spatial and perceptual difficulties are common.

e   Poor motor organisation may be evident. Care is required in climbing activities.

f   The 'buddy' system (working with a friend or peer) may be appropriate.

Coeliac Condition

8.6.21   Coeliac condition is caused by a sensitivity to the protein gluten. The condition can cause damage to the small intestine and/or a skin condition of small irritating blisters. It may develop at any stage. It is treated by strict dietary means.

8.6.22   Specific Safety Factors

♦   Absolute compliance with diet is necessary.

♦   Care is needed on 'out of school' activities, such as day trips, and excursions.

Cystic Fibrosis

8.6.23   This is a genetically determined disorder which causes thickening of the mucus secreted by the body, leading to reduced breathing efficiency of the lungs. Regular respiratory education and physiotherapy, together with modern drugs and diet supplements, have greatly improved the survival rate and lifestyles of children with the disorder.

8.6.24   Children with this condition cough a lot and this helps clear the lungs. Teachers should look out for excessive coughing, breathlessness, blueness around the lips and over-tiredness. In such circumstances, the children must rest.

8.6.25   Specific Safety Factors

a   Co-operation with parents and medical advisers (particularly the child's physiotherapist) is essential for all teachers.

b   Exercise is helpful and for some children it is essential. Shorter bursts of energy may be more beneficial than endurance activities such as cross country running. Otherwise these children should be able to participate in all aspects of physical education.

c   At secondary school level, these children should know how much they can reasonably do and know when to rest or to withdraw to clear the lungs.

d   In the primary school, the teachers' awareness of the associated problems is more critical.

e   Teachers need to be aware of any special prescribed inhalants to be used by children.

f   Swimming is very beneficial. Racing, which may demand too much from children, should not be encouraged.

g   In hot weather, excessive perspiring will cause loss of salt from the body; this can be detrimental to the condition.

Diabetes

8.6.26   Diabetes is a condition in which the body, owing to the lack of the hormone insulin, is not able to absorb sugar and starch properly. Treatment is usually by means of injections of insulin and/or a controlled diet.

8.6.27   Specific Safety Factors

a   Children with diabetes can normally participate in most physical education activities. However, because exercise can use up sugar in the blood quickly, they may need to have a suitable snack such as sugar, biscuits or chocolate before exercise and, sometimes, afterwards.

b   Strenuous activities should be supervised by an informed member of staff.

c   The teacher should be aware of the symptoms of hypoglycaemia and react accordingly. The symptoms are drowsiness, untypical behaviour, excessive sweating or vomiting.

d   The likelihood of the need for extra sugar should be established by consultation with a child's doctor and parent(s). It is useful for the teacher to ensure that a supply of sugar is available in case the listed symptoms occur. Children should also be encouraged to carry sugar in case it is needed.

Down's Syndrome

8.6.28   Down's Syndrome is a congenital condition in which the baby is born with a chromosome irregularity. A child may have unusual features and may be mentally retarded. Additional disabilities such as hearing loss, poor eyesight and heart defects may also be present.

8.6.29   Atlanto-axial instability may also affect a small minority of these children. In this condition, the two upper cervical vertebrae of the spine are more mobile than normal. In such cases, severe pressure can produce dislocation, or may even cause the spinal cord to sever. These children may need special care (see 8.6.30(c) below). Some Down's Syndrome children attend mainstream schools, particularly primary schools.

8.6.30   Specific Safety Factors

    a   Most Down's Syndrome children are able to participate in all physical education activities.

    b   Down's Syndrome children present a wide range of physical abilities. Some will be well co-ordinated and able; others will be flat-footed, overweight and clumsy.

    c   For pupils with atlanto-axial instability the following activities must be avoided:

        ◆   in the gymnasium: rolling activities, high level gymnastics, trampolining;

        ◆   in the swimming pool: diving, butterfly stroke, breast stroke;

        ◆   in games and athletics: martial arts, boxing, high jump;

        ◆   in high level contact activities: scrummaging or tackling in rugby.

    d   If additional disabilities are present, these must be taken into account *(see the sections on the relevant conditions for further information).*

    e   Some children will have a very short span of concentration; reinforcement and perseverance are vital. Most children will respond to constant encouragement and praise.

Eczema

8.6.31   This is an itchy, sore and sometimes very unpleasant skin condition. It is not infectious.

8.6.32   Specific Safety Factors

    a   At times joints become stiff and sore and children may find physical education difficult.

    b   Children should be protected from extremes of temperature.

    c   Some children will be sensitive to chlorinated water. Discussion with parent(s) should take place prior to participation in the swimming programme.

Epider Molysis Bullosa

8.6.33   Epider molysis bullosa occurs when the collagen fibres between the layers of skin misfunction and blisters form between these layers.

8.6.34   Specific Safety Factors

a   Gentle exercise is needed to keep the skin, muscles and joints in good condition.

b   Body contact should be avoided.

c   Team games where contact can occur are generally unsuitable.

d   Swimming is beneficial but medical approval should first be sought.

Epilepsy

8.6.35   Epilepsy is a symptom of a disorder of the nervous system which shows itself in the form of an epileptic seizure (fit or attack). There are three types of attack and the teacher should ascertain from medical or school records whether a child suffers from a grand mal, petit mal or temporal lobe epilepsy.

8.6.36   Grand Mal

This is a major attack in which children may make a strange cry, fall suddenly, stiffen and then relax, before lapsing into convulsive movements. After several minutes they should recover consciousness, although they will feel dazed and confused. This condition is often controlled by drugs and rarely happens at school.

8.6.37   Petit Mal

This is manifested by brief interruptions of consciousness and may be difficult to detect. Although brief, the absences can be frequent.

8.6.38   Temporal lobe epilepsy

This results in partial seizures taking the form of a period of partial consciousness in which abnormal behaviour such as lip smacking, head turning, and plucking at clothes may occur. These signs can be mistaken for silliness or psychological disturbance.

8.6.39   Specific Safety Factors

a   Advice from parents and doctors should be sought. However, children with epilepsy are normally able to participate in all physical education activities.

b   During swimming activities, children should normally be partnered with strong swimmers using the 'buddy' system.

c   There should be a person on the bath side whose primary duty is to watch epileptic children.

d   If a fit should occur in the water, it is essential that the 'buddy' or the person on the bath side is capable of holding a child's head above water.

e   Working at high levels in the gymnasium or participating in activities with elements of danger such as rock climbing or sailing should be undertaken with extra caution (especially if children are taking drugs and if attacks are not uncommon). As well as checking with parents and doctors, it would be a wise precaution for the teacher to ensure that children always work with responsible partners.

f   Procedures for coping with an attack must be fully understood by the teacher:

♦   allow the fit to take its course;

♦   cushion the head and do not restrain;

♦   do not give a drink;

♦   carefully loosen the clothing around the neck;

♦   call an ambulance only if a child does not regain consciousness after 15 minutes; standard procedure for summoning an ambulance should be written, displayed and known to all staff;

♦   after the fit, place a child in the recovery position and allow time to rest.

g   Careful consideration should be given to the wearing of distinctive coloured caps for ease of identification whilst in the swimming situation.

Freidrich's Ataxia

8.6.40   This is an inherited disease of the central nervous system which causes a progressive deterioration of co-ordination and muscle control.

8.6.41   Specific Safety Factors

a   Regular exercise is needed.

b   The programme of work should be designed in association with a physiotherapist.

c   There is a need to keep children mobile for as long as possible.

Haemophilia

8.6.42   Haemophilia is an inherited condition where there is a lifelong deficiency in clotting factor in the blood. Pupils with haemophilia may bleed for much longer than normal after injury and may suffer frequent pain due to stiffness in the joints.

8.6.43   Teachers should check whether normal first aid is appropriate for small cuts. Also, in such circumstances, teachers should pay due regard to the procedures advised by the Department for Education and Employment, the local health authority and the local education authority in respect of possible contact with the AIDS virus. Consultation with parent(s) over procedures for treatment following an injury or accident is essential. These children must receive prompt, correct assistance.

8.6.44   Specific Safety Factors

a   Most children with this condition can participate to some extent in physical education activities and restrictions should be kept to a minimum.

b   Contact sports such as rugby, soccer and basket ball should be avoided.

c   Teachers should check with parents about the extent of participation.

d   The likelihood of damage to the tissues is reduced by general fitness; swimming usually provides one of the best forms of exercise.

Hearing Impairment

8.6.45   There are two basic types of hearing impairment: conductive deafness and sensori-neural deafness.

8.6.46   Conductive deafness affects the outer and middle ear and can result from obstruction or malformation.

8.6.47   Sensori-neural deafness affects the inner ear. It results from malfunction in either the inner ear or the auditory nerve and prevents the proper transmission of sounds to the brain. Hearing loss may be permanent and severe but in some cases may be alleviated by the use of hearing aids. Mixed conductive and sensori-neural deafness may occur in some children.

8.6.48   Specific Safety Factors

a   Children with partial hearing are generally allowed to participate in all activities and this should be encouraged. However, it may be necessary to restrict certain activities such as swimming if there is a middle ear infection, a perforated eardrum or a post-operative condition.

b Children should be able to see the teacher's face easily, as lip-reading will be used. As far as possible, the teacher should endeavour to:

- be near to a child;

- be still when speaking and look towards a child;

- face the light so that the face is not in shadow;

- avoid shouting and use normal rhythm and intonation;

- be at the same horizontal level as a child.

c When hearing aids are worn, teachers must remember that:

- no hearing aids are to be worn when swimming;

- hearing aids tend to amplify background noise and do not make speech clearer.

d Communication problems between a deaf child and the teacher can be a source of frustration to both. It is useful to devise signals whereby a child can alert the teacher to the fact that an instruction or task has not been understood.

e Normal audio warning signals may not be heard. Visual signals may be necessary especially in the swimming pool. Another child may be designated to ensure that a hearing-impaired child is aware of the warning (the 'buddy' system).

f Peripatetic teachers of the deaf are a valuable source of help and information.

Hydrocephalus

8.6.49 *(See Sections 8.6.67 to 8.6.70 on Spina Bifida and Hydrocephalus.)*

Kidney Disorders

8.6.50 There are two main types of problem related to kidney function; severe kidney infection, which usually responds to treatment, and kidney failure which results in the need for an organ transplant or for regular dialysis. Anaemia and associated fatigue are common. Children can become irritable and/or confused.

8.6.51 Specific Safety Factors

a Consultation with the child's doctor and parent(s) will be necessary to ascertain the appropriate physical education programme for both categories.

b   As there is strict dietary control for renal failure, care will be needed to meet the requirements during out of school activities.

c   Children on dialysis could be involved in day trips where the programme is not too physically demanding.

Loss of Limb

8.6.52   Children may be born without, or lose through an accident, a limb or partial limb. Artificial limbs encourage the development of muscle strength and patterns of movement.

8.6.53   Specific Safety Factors

a   Consult with the parent(s) and physiotherapist about removal of the artificial limb.

b   The development and maintenance of physical fitness, including muscle strength, is essential.

c   Children with lower limb loss will need extra work on body balance.

d   Control of wheelchairs, through lack of balance, can be a problem.

e   Consult with the physiotherapist on the special exercise programmes which may be needed.

Moderate Learning Difficulties

8.6.54   Many children with moderate learning difficulties are educated in special schools but an increasing percentage are benefiting from mainstream education. This condition is not an illness or a disease; it is an intellectual impairment usually caused by genetic factors, or sometimes the result of an illness or accident. However many children will have perceptual and co-ordination difficulties and their skill level, both physically and cognitively, should be assessed prior to activity.

8.6.55   Specific Safety Factors

a   These children should be able to participate in all activities, although some forms of activity may need to be modified.

b   Many of these children have difficulties in activities involving co-operation.

Muscular Dystrophy

8.6.56   There are several forms, all of which are progressive. Either gender may generally be affected. The essential characteristic is a progressive breakdown of muscle fibre, resulting in the gradual weakening in all muscle groups. It first affects the extensor muscles of the hips, knees and shoulder girdle.

8.6.57   At about eight to ten years of age children will start to use a manual wheelchair and as the arms weaken an electric chair will be needed. Splints on the ankles and a body brace to keep the spine as straight as possible will probably be worn. At this stage children will become prone to chest infections.

8.6.58   Children with muscular dystrophy should be encouraged to use all the movement they have for as long as possible. Medical advance is extending their life expectancy.

8.6.59   Specific Safety Factors

a   As children age, a gradual reduction in mobility levels should be anticipated. However, these children should be included in all aspects of physical education for as long as possible.

b   Teachers should appreciate that the condition will cause children to tire easily.

c   Adaptations to work and equipment will need to be introduced gradually and carefully to avoid frustration.

d   Because of the weakness of the muscles in the shoulder girdle, children can rarely use sticks or rollators.

e   Swimming in warm water is one activity which can be maintained for a relatively long time. However, a close watch should be kept for tipping the body over and immersing the head because the child may not be able to return to an upright position unassisted.

f   Consultation with the parent(s) and physiotherapist is essential. The physiotherapist will be able to advise on an appropriate exercise programme to maintain fitness as long as possible; also on lifting and handling techniques.

g   Children will need assistance from an aide or teacher for many activities, for example dressing and undressing and getting in an out of the swimming pool. Because of the weakness of the shoulder girdle, particular care is needed.

    ♦   do not attempt to lift by holding arms; a child will slip through your grasp;

◆ do not hold the hands in order to pull a child up;

◆ ask a physiotherapist to demonstrate correct lifting procedures.

Poliomyelitis

8.6.60 The disease injures the nerve circuit between the spinal cord and the peripheral nerve endings of muscles. This results in non-functioning or partially inactive flaccid muscles.

Large or small areas of the body can be affected, leaving a variety of disabilities which may vary from affecting the muscles of just one limb to those of all four limbs and the trunk.

There will be a loss of muscle tone and unequal muscle strengths, leading to an imbalance of the body. The deformities of some limbs may require children to wear splints, callipers or body braces. Poor circulation in affected limbs is usual.

Intellectual functioning is not impaired.

8.6.61 Specific Safety Factors

a Depending on the severity of the condition, a child will be able to participate in most physical education activities; however, some modifications and adaptations may be necessary.

b Swimming in warm water is particularly beneficial. A pupil should not be allowed to become cold. If the legs are affected, the supine position should be adopted first as flaccid limbs float more easily.

c An individual with balancing problems may be prone to falling over easily. The use of aids such as callipers, sticks or body braces many overcome this problem to a degree. The physiotherapist should be able to indicate if the brace aids may be taken off for physical education.

d A child with this disability will tire easily.

e Advice should be sought from parent(s) and a child's doctor and physiotherapist.

Raynaud's Disease

8.6.62 Raynaud's is a condition in which the blood supply to the fingers and toes and sometimes the ears and nose is temporarily slowed down because the blood vessels go into spasm and restrict the flow of blood.

Symptoms are usually worse in winter but a slight change of temperature during other times of the year can initiate an attack.

During an attack the hands take on a white, wax like appearance and feel dead and useless. They may turn blue/ purple and then red when the blood starts to flow back. This can be accompanied by considerable pain and numbness.

8.6.63   Specific Safety Factors

a   Take heed of the child's knowledge about their capacity to withstand cold. However physical activity is good for children with Raynaud's.

b   They need to keep warm by wearing suitable clothes. Consult with parents regarding thermal underwear, tracksuits, gloves, hat.

c   An attack of Raynaud's could result in 'loss of grip'. This is critical in climbing activities.

d   Consultation between PE staff and parents is essential prior to any inclusion in a swimming programme.

Short Stature

8.6.64   Short stature can be divided into two main categories:

   ◆   proportionate short stature where the whole of the body growth is restricted. This condition can usually be treated if there is early diagnosis;

   ◆   disproportionate short stature which is an abnormality of some aspect of bone and cartilage development and cannot be treated.

8.6.65   Specific Safety Factors

a   These children usually have good health.

b   They tend to be robust but are more prone to tiredness than their peers.

c   They should be encouraged to participate in the full physical education programme with the exception of contact sports.

d   Swimming is good and should be encouraged.

e   Where children are eager to participate in a more intensive programme of physical activity, medical advice should be sought.

Sickle Cell Disease

8.6.66 Sickle cell disease is an inherited disability affecting the haemoglobin factors in the blood. The sickle cells create blockages in small blood vessels. This is known as 'sickling' or a 'sickle cell crisis'.

8.6.67 Specific Safety Factors

a Medical advice should be sought about the extent and limitations of the physical education programme.

b 'Sickling' can be brought on by strenuous exercise.

c Children can usually take part in normal physical education but prolonged and strenuous exercise should not be attempted.

d Children know their limitations and should be allowed to rest if they become fatigued.

Spina Bifida and Hydrocephalus

8.6.68 These are two conditions which often occur together but which may occur independently. Eye defects and epilepsy are sometimes associated with spina bifida.

Spina Bifida

8.6.69 This is a congenital condition where the bones of the spine (vertebrae) are incomplete and the spinal cord is exposed. The physical consequences depend on the amount of damage to the spinal cord. The resulting paralysis can range from minimal to complete.

Hydrocephalus

8.6.70 Hydrocephalus is caused by a build-up of fluid which may exert pressure on the brain. Where this does not drain of its own accord, a device known as a 'shunt' is implanted to serve this purpose. Usually this will work very well but some children will have problems with a shunt which occasionally becomes blocked.

8.6.71 Specific Safety Factors

a Children with more severe forms of spina bifida are usually paralysed in the lower parts of the body. They move around with the aid of a wheelchair, sticks or crutches. Risk assessment will be necessary.

b The child may wear special boots or callipers. If long-leg callipers are worn, advice on taking them on and off should be sought from a physiotherapist. If the callipers are the type worn below the knee only, most children can manage by themselves. Boots and the ferrules of sticks and rollators should be regularly examined for wear.

c   Damage to the spinal cord may cause lack of sensation to pain, temperature and touch, also poor circulation to lower limbs. The following precautions should be observed by the teacher:

- ◆   during sliding activities the legs and feet should be covered to avoid friction burns;

- ◆   pressure on one part of the body over a sustained period (for example the bottom when sitting) could cause bruising and pressure sores;

- ◆   impact on the floor, apparatus or the sides of the swimming bath could cause fractures;

- ◆   children should be reminded to take care of the position of their legs in all activities to avoid accidental damage.

d   Exercise is vital to all children using wheelchairs and other aids to mobility. They should be encouraged to participate as far as they are able, in order to keep fit and healthy. Physical exercise aids circulation and improves muscle tone, as well as helping the functioning of the many organs of the body. The child's physiotherapist should be consulted for advice on the forms of physical education which will give maximum therapeutic benefit.

e   Activities which strengthen the upper body are generally considered valuable.

f   Swimming is generally considered to be beneficial. Children who are paralysed in the lower limbs will often 'ride high' in the water; it is therefore recommended that they should start in a semi-sitting supine position. Great care of the limbs should be exercised when entering and leaving the water to avoid scrapes and bangs. The water in the pool should be warm.

g   Incontinence of the bowel and/or bladder may be a problem for children with the more severe form of spina bifida.

h   Advice on special hygiene arrangements should be sought before proceeding with any physical activity.

i   Time, privacy and perhaps assistance will be needed. Some children will be able to manage their toilet arrangements quite independently but it may be necessary to provide a private changing area.

j   Children with hydrocephalus may have slightly enlarged heads which will be quite heavy, so extra care should be taken with movement and they should not be rushed.

k   Special considerations, modifications and adaptations to the physical education programme may be necessary. However, many children with spina bifida, hydrocephalus, or both conditions in combination are able to participate satisfactorily in most physical education activities.

l   Medical assistance is required immediately if the child develops a high temperature or severe headache, becomes drowsy or vomits.

m   It is helpful to have a full length mirror available in the changing area so that pupils can check visually that their clothing is not disarranged.

Visual Impairment

8.6.72   Functional loss of vision may be considered in two categories:

♦   problems with focus;

♦   problems with the field of vision - peripheral vision.

8.6.73   Peripheral vision is important for mobility and for the perception of moving objects. It is used for scanning the environment and detecting moving objects.

8.6.74   Specific Safety Factors

a   Apart from the more obvious implications, eye defects are variously responsible for difficulties in co-ordination, orientation, position in space, object identification and tracking.

b   Spectacles should be worn in physical education lessons if the child finds that they are helpful. They should have shatterproof lenses and should be secured.

c   Good light is important.

d   Safe practice in all activities should be fully understood by children. The teacher must be aware that partially-sighted children will not necessarily see dangerous situations or stray missiles.

e   The placement of apparatus and equipment should be as constant as possible. Any changes from the normal practice should be made clear to visually impaired children. Unnecessary equipment must be tidied away and not left lying about in a haphazard fashion.

f   Partially-sighted children need to be as independent as possible but it is often useful to designate friends to assist them without taking away their confidence.

g   For swimming:

◆   where the wearing of spectacles poses a problem children should be well informed of the geography of the pool; the depth, width, length, points of entry and exit, rails and troughs;

◆   orientation is easier in the prone than in the supine position;

◆   the teacher should obtain medical approval before allowing children to enter chlorinated water.

h   If appropriate teachers should seek to obtain advice on suitable strategies for assisting the partially-sighted child in physical education.

8.7   Reference - Appendices

8.7.1   The school/department check list which appears as appendix 1 at the back of this book is an important point of reference for teachers with children who have special educational needs.

8.8   Acknowledgements

8.8.1   The following publications have provided valuable points of reference:

◆   The Educational Implications of Disability, by J. Male and C. Thompson. Published by the Royal Association for Disability and Rehabilitation (RADAR) 1985.

◆   Physical Education for Children with Physical Handicap by Sheila Jowsey. Published by Northamptonshire County Council 1984.

8.9   Supporting Pupils with Medical Needs

Policy.

8.9.1   It is the responsibility of local education authorities, schools and governing bodies to formulate their own policies, relating to pupils with medical needs, in the light of their statutory responsibilities.

8.9.2   The employer of teachers, generally the school governing body or the LEA, is responsible under the Health and Safety at Work Act 1974 for ensuring that a school has a health and safety policy. This should include the procedures for supporting pupils with medical needs including the management of medication.

8.9.3   The headteacher should ensure that all parents/guardians are aware of the School's policy and procedures.

8.9.4   Further guidance on policy and procedures can be found in "Supporting Pupils with Medical Needs" which is issued jointly by the DfEE and the Department of Health.

Teachers Supporting Pupils

8.9.5   There is no legal duty or condition of service that requires a teacher to administer medication. It is a voluntary role.

8.9.6   Those members of staff who agree to administer prescribed medicines should;

- have a clear understanding of their legal responsibilities;

- have the 'protection' of a sound and effective system of management;

- be adequately trained to ensure that they have understanding, expertise and confidence;

- be familiar with normal precautions for avoiding infections;

- be provided with written confirmation of insurance cover to provide specific medical support.

Management of the Policy

8.9.7   An effective management system for safe practice should ensure that the following areas are addressed within the school policy and guidelines:

- consultation process to include parents/guardians, school health service, general practitioner etc.;

- adequate training programme for involved staff;

- system for the administration of medication;

- documentation of pupils and their needs;

- 'health care plans' for pupils with needs;

- storage and access to medication;

- emergency procedures.

Risk Assessment

8.9.8 Schools should be aware that the entry into school of a child/children with medical needs will require a re-examination of their existing risk assessment.

9: ACCIDENTS, FIRST AID AND HIV/AIDS

9.1 Accidents

9.1.1　　Wherever there is a risk, accidents are a possibility. To attempt to eliminate accidents entirely would involve reducing the activities in which people engage to an unacceptable degree. In addition, some accidents may not be foreseeable and their prevention is thereby inhibited. The advice in this book is intended to minimise the incidence of such occurrences in physical education. However it is important to acknowledge that no matter how carefully programmes may be planned and implemented and risks assessed and managed, accidents will inevitably occur from time to time.

9.1.2.　　Accidents will vary in their severity, from the trivial to the life-threatening. Procedures must be laid down and implemented in all educational establishments to ensure that all reasonable measures are taken to deal promptly and effectively with any accidents other than those of a trivial nature. This will apply equally to incidents during activities away from the main premises but which are school initiated or related.

9.1.3　　Accidents may result from young people being in situations where they are unable to cope because of insufficient strength, skill, endurance or reaction. Often, several factors occurring together will be the underlying cause. In all cases, it is important that accidents are reported to the headteacher and recorded by the school, whether or not injuries are sustained. Subsequent investigation may point the way to measures which will prevent a recurrence. Recording will help with the requirements of any liability that may arise and with reporting to governors. The discussion of near misses and the sharing of the circumstances and implications with colleagues will also prove useful. Wherever possible the causes of injuries should be identified.

9.1.4　　When major injuries or death are caused by accidents, legislation under the 'Reporting of Injuries, Diseases and Dangerous Occurrences Regulations 1995' (RIDDOR) applies. The requirements cover workplace or work related accidents to pupils and to teachers as employees.

　　　◆　　A reportable accident is defined as any resulting in death or any injury requiring hospital treatment for any length of time.

　　　◆　　Major injuries include fractures (other than to the bones of the hands and feet), unconsciousness resulting from electric shock or lack of oxygen and acute illness caused by a pathogen, a substance or infected material.

- Dangerous occurrences may be the result of the unintentional collapsing or fall of structures (such as walls, floors or equipment), pressurised vessels exploding, or the accidental release of substances or pathogens which severely threaten health.

- The list of reportable diseases is unlikely to apply to any extent in schools, other than possibly hepatitis caused by exposure to human blood or secretions and occupational asthma resulting from work with epoxy resins or animals.

9.1.5   RIDDOR requires that notifiable accidents are reported to the Health and Safety Executive by telephone and, within seven days, in writing using the form F2508. Some local education authorities carry out this function for schools for which they have responsibility but in many instances it will be the individual institutions which must ensure that the correct procedures are in place and are systematically followed.

The information required will include:

9.1.6   Location of accident; time of accident; name and status of injured party; nature and site of injury; names of those involved; names of witnesses; activity during which the accident was sustained by the injured party; circumstances of the accident, including any environmental factors; protective measures in operation (if applicable); the training of the injured person for the activity; the supervision at the time; and any design or facility fault which may have contributed to the accident.

9.1.7   Failure to comply with the reporting requirements may result in prosecution.

9.1.8   The Regulations apply equally to accidents off-site as well as on-site.

9.2   Managing Injury

9.2.1   It will be expected that the school will have a realistic first aid system which is readily available and efficient for dealing with injury if it should occur. Managing injury means being able to call urgently upon skilled medical assistance and hospital transport when needed and arranging for the attendance of the parents to the injured child as soon as reasonably possible.

9.2.2   Procedures to address the needs of the injured child and the remainder of the group should be anticipated in order to fulfil the duty of in loco parentis. This aspect requires extra thorough planning when the pupils are away from the school on visits, including attention to pupil/teacher ratios and to group sizes generally.

9.3   First Aid

(Note: The following information has been written with reference to the Health and Safety Executive (HSE) Guidance to the Health and Safety (First Aid) Regulations 1981 and the Revised Approved Code of Practice 1997.)

9.3.1   First aid in educational establishments is subject to the Health and Safety (First Aid) Regulations 1981 and Guidance and to subsequent revisions as approved by the Health and Safety Commission.

9.3.2.   First aid is defined as the immediate attention needed to prevent minor injuries becoming major. It excludes giving tablets or medicines to treat illness.

9.3.3.   The minimum requirements for schools' first aid provisions are to have an appropriate number of suitably stocked, identifiable and easily accessible first aid containers, a person appointed to take charge of first aid arrangements and information for employees on first aid arrangements. There are no fixed levels or provision beyond this but the level of provision of facilities, equipment and trained staff within the school may need to be justified.

9.3.4   Schools are deemed to be low risk areas of work by the Health and Safety Commission. The guidance given for low risk areas sets out the suggested number of first aid personnel for numbers of employees. Bear in mind that pupils are visitors, not employees. Typically, one person qualified to emergency aid level should be available where less than fifty are employed; at least one first-aider where fifty to one hundred are employed and an additional first aider for every additional one hundred employees.

9.3.5.   Assessment of first aid need should arise from a risk assessment. The greater the risk the greater the specialist provision such as when leading groups in remote areas. Past accident records are helpful when considering levels of need.

9.3.6   Provision for those working off-site needs to be made. The provision of a travelling first aid kit and clear, effective procedures for contacting the emergency services would be deemed to be minimal provision.

9.3.7   First aiders should be appropriately trained in the techniques relevant to the circumstances of the undertaking. It is advisable that all teachers of physical education should receive first aid training appropriate to their teaching responsibilities with young people.

9.3.8   It is good practice to keep records of incidents requiring aid to be
            given.

9.4   First Aid Training Recognised by the Health and Safety Executive

9.4.1   The following subjects should be included in the syllabus for teachers
            appointed as first aiders:

  ◆   resuscitation;

  ◆   treatment and control of bleeding;

  ◆   treatment of shock;

  ◆   management of the unconscious casualty;

  ◆   contents of first-aid boxes and their use;

  ◆   purchasing of first-aid supplies;

  ◆   transport of casualties;

  ◆   recognition of illness;

  ◆   treatment of injuries to bones, muscles and joints;

  ◆   treatment of minor injuries;

  ◆   treatment of burns and scalds;

  ◆   eye irrigation;

  ◆   poisons;

  ◆   simple record keeping;

  ◆   personal hygiene in treating wounds: reference to hepatitis B
      and human immuno-deficiency virus (HIV) with regard to
      first-aiders;

  ◆   communication and delegation in an emergency.

            (Note: Where teachers are involved with activities where specific
            hazards are possible, additional training should be included, for
            example treatment for hypothermia where activities take place in
            mountainous areas or in or on water.)

9.4.2   Certificates of qualification in first aid will be valid for such a
            period of time as the Health and Safety Executive directs (presently
            three years), after which time a refresher course and examination will
            be required for re-certification.

9.5 First Aid Boxes and Kits

a   First aid boxes and travelling first aid kits should contain a sufficient quantity of suitable first aid materials and nothing else.

b   Contents of the boxes and kits should be replenished as soon as possible after use in order to ensure that there is always an adequate supply of materials. Items should not be used after the expiry date shown on the packets. It is therefore essential that first aid equipment is checked frequently to make sure there are sufficient quantities and that all the items are usable.

c   First aid boxes should be made of suitable material designed to protect the contents from damp and dust and should be clearly identified as first aid containers; the marking used should be a white cross on a green background in accordance with the Safety Signs Regulations 1980.

d   First aid boxes which are to form part of an establishment's permanent first aid provision should contain those items determined by a risk assessment.

e   Sufficient quantities of each item should always be available in every first aid box or container. In most cases these will be:

   ◆   one guidance card;

   ◆   twenty individually wrapped sterile adhesive dressings (assorted sizes) appropriate to the work environment;

   ◆   two sterile eye pads, with attachment;

   ◆   four individually wrapped triangular bandages;

   ◆   six safety pins;

   ◆   six medium sized individually wrapped sterile unmedicated wound dressings (approx. 10 cm x 8 cm);

   ◆   two large sterile individually wrapped unmedicated wound dressings (approx. 13 cm x 9 cm);

   ◆   1 pair of sterile disposable gloves.

Where mains tap water is not readily available for eye irrigation, sterile water or sterile normal saline (0.9%) in sealed disposable containers should be provided. Each container should hold at least 300 ml and should not be re-used once the sterile seal is broken. At least 900 ml should be provided. Eye baths, eye cups or refillable containers should not be used for eye irrigation.

f   Soap and water and disposable drying materials should be provided for first aid purposes. Alternatively, wrapped moist cleaning wipes which are not impregnated with alcohol may be used.

g   Sterile first aid dressings should be packaged in such a way as to allow the user to apply a dressing to the wound without touching the part which is to come into direct contact with the wound.

h   That part of the dressing which comes into contact with a wound should be absorbent. There should be a bandage or other fixture attached to the dressings and consequently there is no reason to keep scissors in the first aid box. Dressings, including adhesive ones, should be of a design and type which is appropriate for their use.

i   Where an employee has received additional training in the treatment of specific hazards which require the use of special antidotes or special equipment, these may be stored near the hazard area or may be kept in the first aid box.

9.6   Travelling First Aid Kits

a   The contents of travelling first aid kits should be appropriate for the circumstances in which they are to be used. At least the following should be included:

- card giving the general first-aid guidance;

- six individually wrapped sterile adhesive dressing;

- one large sterile unmedicated dressing;

- two triangular bandages;

- two safety pins;

- individually wrapped moist cleaning wipes.

b   Polythene survival bags to treat exposure are useful extra items for activities in open country.

c   Teachers undertaking ventures with young people into remote areas should consider acquainting themselves with the St. John Ambulance mountain first aid course, which includes practice in the use of inflatable splints.

Supplementary equipment

d   Where an establishment covers a large area or is divided into a number of separate and self-contained working areas, it may be necessary to provide suitable carrying equipment for the transportation of casualties.

e   It is recommended that where blankets are provided, they should be stored alongside the equipment and in such a way as to keep them free from dust and damp.

f   Disposable plastic gloves and aprons and suitable protective equipment should be provided near the first aid materials and should be properly stored and regularly checked to ensure that they remain in good condition.

g   Blunt-ended stainless steel scissors (minimum length 12.70cm) should be kept where there is a possibility that clothing might have to be cut away. These should be kept along with the items of protective clothing and equipment.

h   Plastic disposable bags for soiled or used first aid dressings should be provided. Employers should ensure that such items as used dressings are safely disposed of in sealed bags. Local authorities should be contacted for guidance on disposal.

9.7   HIV and AIDS

The information below is in accordance with advice received from the Department for Education and Employment (DfEE).

Children with HIV and AIDS

9.7.1   Since on all present evidence the risk of transmitting HIV in the school setting is minimal and since the benefits to a child with HIV or AIDS of attending school and enjoying normal social relationships far outweigh the risks of him or her acquiring harmful infections, such children should be allowed to attend school freely and be treated in the same way as other pupils.

9.7.2   It follows from this that the fact of HIV infection or AIDS should not, in the Department's view, be a factor taken into account by local education authorities, governing bodies and headteachers in discharging either their various duties concerning school admissions, transfers and attendance (in respect of an infected child or otherwise), or their powers of exclusion from school.

DfEE Guide for the Education Service - HIV and AIDS

9.7.3   In respect of sports and outdoor adventurous activities:

a   These may be freely allowed, provided that in the case of an infected child there is no other medical condition that prevents the child from participating.

b   Swimming pools and splash pools should be chlorinated or suitably treated according to standard practice. Normal precautions should be taken.

c   Barefoot work presents no risks.

d   Bleeding due to accidents should be dealt with immediately. Those offering first aid should wear disposable waterproof gloves and rinse wounds with water only.

First Aid

9.7.4   No cases are recorded of HIV infection having been transmitted as a result of direct mouth to mouth resuscitation, although there is a theoretical risk where there are bleeding cuts or sores in the mouth. In an emergency, direct mouth to mouth resuscitation should not therefore be withheld. Rigid airways for resuscitation may only be used by first aiders who have special training in their use.

9.8   Some Further Reading

♦   The British Red Cross and St. John Ambulance publications.

♦   First Aid in Education Establishments, HMSO 1985.

♦   The DfEE leaflet 'First Aid Provision in Schools and Colleges' first issued in 1987.

Further copies or updated information available from:

Pupils' Safety and Appeals Division, Room 06A, DfEE, Mowden Hall, Staindrop Road, Darlington DL3 9BG.

♦   The Health Education Authority booklet 'Sport and HIV' published in 1992 and available from the Health Education Authority, Hamilton House, Mabledon Arch, London WC1H 9TX.

10:   INSURANCE

10.1   Introduction

10.1.1   Insurance is an area where misconceptions abound. It is too important to be left to chance and those involved with schools (teachers, pupils and parents) need to be sure of the nature and level of cover which is provided, both according to statutory requirements and that which may be additionally obtained on a voluntary basis through premium payments.

10.1.2   The following advice will help clarify some of the many queries which are raised, though it does not replace the need for individuals to seek information on insurance from their LEA, school or professional association which is pertinent to their own circumstances.

10.2   Personal

10.2.1   The teacher, in common with all other employed persons, is covered against industrial injuries by the weekly contribution which must be paid during employment. In addition, all employed persons have a possible claim against their employer if they sustain any bodily injury by accident arising out of, or in the course of, their employment. Such claims can only be substantiated where injury can be proved to be through negligence of the employer or another employee (Employers Liability).

10.2.2   In respect of pupils, schools have a legal duty to take care of the well-being and safety of young people. Where there is a breach of this responsibility a claim for compensation may be brought.

10.2.3   There is no requirement for schools to make provision for loss through personal injury as the result of an accident where no blame may be attached (as in the case of Van Oppen-v-Bedford School Trustees). Personal accident insurance cover for pupils is a matter for the parents to arrange, though schools may wish to inform parents of relevant schemes which are or which become available.

10.2.4   It is appropriate to advise parents through the school prospectus of what insurance cover is provided. Parents then have the choice as to whether to take out some form of cover or whether to increase the levels of cover beyond any which may or may not be provided through school sources.

10.3 Indemnity

10.3.1 Arrangements may vary so it is important that teachers make enquiries and are aware of any situations where cover may not be in place. This particularly applies when teachers are acting as an agent for an association external to their school, for example a district or county sports association.

10.3.2 The written consent of parents should always be obtained by the school for the participation of pupils in any activity out of school or outside the planned curriculum. Schools should have appropriate forms available for this purpose.

10.3.3 Consent forms indicate a parent or carer's agreement for a child to participate in an event and do not indemnify a teacher from responsibility. It is a signed statement that the parent is aware of what the event involves and the organisation to minimise risks, an agreement to comply with safety rules and procedures and an agreement for the pupil to participate in the event.

10.4 Insurance Provision

10.4.1 Teachers should be aware of the LEA or school provision for insurance. Arrangements may vary so it is important that teachers make enquiries and are aware of any situations where cover may be limited or not in place.

10.4.2 Public liability insurance is provided by an employer in case of a legal claim being made by someone other than an employee for injury or damage caused by a defect in the premises or equipment which it is the employer's responsibility to maintain. This cover, often called third party liability, also applies to any injury or damage to a party other than an employee as a result of an activity organised by or involving employees or approved volunteers. This may include the provision of poor professional advice to another party within the remit of one's contract.

10.4.3 Letting agreements by the agent of a school, such as the governing body, should state clearly that all independent users hiring premises must have their own public liability cover. Parent-teacher associations and other school-related bodies such as former student groups are very likely to be considered to be independent hirers and clarification as to any public liability should be sought.

10.4.4 Extra-curricular activities within a school are normally included in the insurance arrangements whether they take place after school, at weekends or during holidays providing they have been sanctioned by the headteacher. With ever changing legislation and arrangements for insurance it is for individual teachers to check the extent of any public/third party liability provided by their employer or professional association.

10.4.5   Arrangements vary for teachers involved with sports beyond their LEA remit - such as with district, county or national sports associations. It is important that the individual teacher involved at these levels clarifies with his/her employer as to whether the employer's public liability cover extends to this additional work. Some LEAs include such work, others do not. It is advisable to obtain written confirmation from one's employer as to whether the teacher is covered for this work or whether some form of independent public liability insurance needs to be obtained for any administrative or technical involvement with district, county or national schools associations.

10.4.6   All involved with the delivery of physical education and sport should make enquiries as to whether they have or need:

♦   Personal accident insurance in case of injury incurred during an activity.

♦   Public liability insurance in case of injury, loss or damage involving a third party.

♦   Professional indemnity against poor advice or management within one's work.

♦   Transport insurance (see Chapter 1) when carrying pupils in the school's transport or one's own car.

10.5   Adults Other than Teachers

10.5.1   The use of voluntary helpers in schools is common. These may include parents,sports coaches, retired teachers, national governing body coaches, activity centre staff or other adults who are not teachers at the establishment to which the pupils have been placed by their parents. These people carry a duty of care for those they work with but do not act in loco parentis. Insurance arrangements for voluntary helpers may differ from one establishment or authority to another. In many instances voluntary helpers would benefit from public liability cover by the LEA or school but would not have personal accident provision. It is important that the subject leader understands the precise insurance arrangements under which any voluntary helpers work within or without the school and shares this knowledge with the volunteer so that they may make alternative arrangements should they so wish.

10.6　Additional cover for Outdoor and Adventurous Activities

10.6.1　Staff arranging outdoor activity events being undertaken by community/maintained schools should clarify with their local authority what insurance provision exists and what additional cover may need to be taken out.　Other schools, for example self governing foundation schools, will need to investigate and make satisfactory arrangements of their own.

10.6.2　Special arrangements may be necessary to obtain insurance for activities abroad.

10.6.3　It is difficult to give advice on insurance cover since practice varies about standard policies which cover the following aspects.　However, regardless of access to an LEA policy, organisers of visits should satisfy themselves that they are covered for:

- ◆　third party liability covering claims against the authority or school and its employees;

- ◆　personal accident cover for leaders, voluntary helpers and party members;

- ◆　medical treatment;

- ◆　transport and passenger liability;

- ◆　high risk activities (often excluded from standard policies);

- ◆　damage to or loss of personal or hired equipment;

- ◆　programmed as well as non-programmed activities;

- ◆　transport and accommodation expenses in case of emergency;

- ◆　compensation against cancellation or delay;

- ◆　compensation for loss of baggage and effects;

- ◆　legal assistance in the recovery of claims;

- ◆　failure or bankruptcy of the centre or travel company.

10.6.4　Cover arrangements for personal accident or injury to pupil participants in outdoor and adventurous activities may need to be considered separately.　Parents should be informed of the cover provided.　They may then take out additional insurance independently if they so wish.

10.6.5   For visits involving extensive travel, either in the UK or abroad, organisers will also need to arrange appropriate cover for third party risks when using vehicles in the European Community and other countries. Where foreign travel is planned, organisers should scrutinise carefully the list of exclusions in their policy.

10.6.6   School staff should check the existing cover provided by the employer and this is best done through the employer.

11:   SOME QUESTIONS AND ANSWERS

This section has been included because it provides the opportunity to highlight safety issues in physical education which arise most frequently or which have been the subject of litigation. The questions are practically founded and it is hoped that they will provide useful information on which teachers may base their own practice in schools. It is helpful to identify questions on topics relevant to you and read these along with the appropriate sections of the book.

Qu 1   **I teach reception children in an infants school. The children do not have a specific PE kit. Should I be taking them outside in vest and pants?**

Ans   Schools are advised to have a written policy on clothing for physical education. A change of clothing is important for a number of reasons. Children should have the opportunity to play games in a variety of indoor and outdoor settings.   Clothing serves to insulate the body in the initial stages of the lesson. Children should be encouraged to have something warm, which can then be removed if necessary.

Qu 2   **The large apparatus that we use for gymnastics in the school hall has to be stored around the perimeter of that area, owing to a lack of storage space. Is this acceptable?**

Ans   It is common practice in many primary school halls to store large gymnastic apparatus at points around the hall. Care should be taken to ensure that the apparatus so positioned is well spaced, stable and accessible, that carrying distances are minimised and that passage ways and emergency exits are not blocked. It is helpful if the equipment is always returned to the same safe place after use.

Qu 3   **A child in my Y4 class has difficulty in controlling his behaviour and will often interfere with or impede other pupils when working on apparatus in gymnastics. What action should be taken?**

Ans   It is clearly unacceptable that any child should put the safety of themselves or others at risk through unsociable behaviour.

Preventative steps to be considered include:

- ♦   monitoring the child very closely and guiding positively in physical education and other lessons;
- ♦   restricting the activities of the child until such time as a positive behavioural response is expected;

- involving the parent(s) with the child in the formulation of a 'sanctions contract' to foster good behaviour in school and at home, which is reviewed at agreed intervals.

Where the problem persists, it may be necessary to seek further advice for example from the school psychologist. The involvement of parents from the earliest stage is essential.

Qu 4   **Some children in my Y6 class take unacceptable risks when working on the climbing apparatus in gymnastics lessons such that they probably will fall. Would it be appropriate to provide a thick weight absorbent mattress in case this should happen?**

Ans   All children should receive, and be able to understand, guidance on the use and management of mats. A mat or mats should be provided where it is anticipated that landings will occur and need to be cushioned, not where it is expected that a child will fall.

If a young person is performing an action where a fall is thought to be likely, then the task should be modified by the teacher to reduce the risk to an acceptable level.

On some occasions, where a child is performing an action at or near to the threshold of movement ability for which it is ready and having experienced the progressive stages leading up to it, individual support may be provided by the teacher to enable the action to be practised safely by the performer. This support may be reduced and later removed over time as the pupil develops the individual capability to perform the movement correctly and consistently.

Qu 5   **Some money raised at my primary school has been allocated for the purchase of an additional piece of physical education equipment and it has been suggested that a trampette or a thick weight absorbent mattress should be bought. Is either suitable apparatus for use by primary pupils?**

Ans   Both pieces of apparatus referred to are best suited to a secondary gymnastics programme.

A trampette is a specialised piece of equipment which requires very careful management and use. It is potentially hazardous and there are recorded cases of very severe injuries resulting from trampette accidents.

Any teacher using this apparatus would be expected to have undertaken a course in rebound activities and be fully conversant with the techniques and progressive stages of those activities. Most primary teachers will not have experienced the use of this equipment as part of their training and some local education authorities prohibit such provision in their primary schools.

Likewise, the thick weight absorbent mattress is intended for use in the teaching of specialised formal gymnastics where high momentum is generated. It is more appropriate for use in the secondary school where landings may require the increased cushioning that this apparatus provides.

Qu 6   **The primary school where I teach is very well equipped for gymnastics but the hall space is not sufficiently large to accommodate the use of all the available apparatus at any one time. How may this problem be resolved?**

Ans   It is desirable that primary schools have a sufficient variety and quantity of gymnastics apparatus to enable pupils to experience and develop a broad range of body management skills. However, it is most unlikely that all the apparatus available will be appropriate for use in a single lesson.

The teacher should relate the apparatus to be used to the theme or task(s) of the lesson or preferably to a related series of lessons, selecting those items either singly or in combination which best enable the focused areas for skills development to be practised. In addition, it is important that the arrangement of apparatus allows sufficient space between pieces and away from the walls or equipment stored at the sides for activities to be undertaken safely. This will determine the total number of separate items or combinations of apparatus to be used at any one time.

Qu 7   **I am a newly qualified teacher in a primary school and I am concerned that my initial teacher training and experience has not equipped me with the skills and knowledge to confidently teach gymnastics in the curriculum with my class. I am particularly worried about using apparatus. What should I do?**

Ans   Current initial teacher training courses in primary education sometimes do not provide sufficient time to meet entirely the training needs of their students and there are many new teachers who express similar concern. In view of the safety element, it would be wise for you to raise this matter with the headteacher.

Arrangements should be made with the local education authority for you to receive in-service training in primary gymnastics at the earliest possible date. Until then, it will be necessary for you to modify your lessons to include those activities which you feel competent and able to manage. A possible alternative is to arrange for an experienced teacher to take the lead, providing a type of 'on the job' in-service training.

You would be wise to seek the help, assessment and approval of the local education authority advisory service on completion of any training which you undertake.

Qu 8   **The primary school where I teach has stage blocks stored at one end of the hall. Would it be acceptable to use these items during the apparatus section of the gymnastics lesson with my class?**

Ans   The improvised use of apparatus for purposes other than that for which it has been designed and provided requires great care and forethought.

The key criteria will be centred on the suitability of the equipment for the activities to be undertaken and the nature of the hazards and attendant risks.

If these matters can be satisfactorily resolved, then the use of the stage blocks for gymnastics should be acceptable.

Qu 9   **There are times when the school field becomes waterlogged and I am forced to take my primary class on the playground for games teaching. Is this acceptable?**

Ans   Provided that the surface is in good condition, reasonably even and free of loose grit, then teaching games on the playground is common and acceptable practice.

It is necessary to modify the programme to exclude those activities which are likely to result in pupils falling, for example physical contact as in tackling, which would be acceptable on a softer grass surface.

Racing activities such as relay games should be very carefully assessed for risk and modified as necessary to reduce foreseeable hazard.

It is important that pupils are made aware of when they are neither racing nor competing.

Qu 10   I intend to take a group of forty Y6 pupils (boys and girls) with three other teaching staff on a three-day summer residential youth hostelling and walking venture in the Peak District of Derbyshire. I have already visited the area and planned the routes in discussion with the youth hostel warden. Is the venture viable? What general advice do you have on teacher/ pupil ratios for such visits?

Ans   With the widespread publicity which inevitably accompanies outdoor activity ventures when something goes tragically wrong, it is not surprising that this question has arisen. In this case, the leader has prepared the activity with a visit to the location and, by discussing the walking itinerary with the hostel warden, has benefited from local expertise.

Four staff should be more than adequate to meet an emergency. An even split of male and female staff would enable an equitable sharing of duties, particularly in meeting an emergency through the night when in hostel residence. At least one member of the staff should be capable of administering first aid.

It would be necessary for governors to have sight of the complete planning schedule, including a risk assessment, before finally giving their approval. The written consent of all the parents of participating pupils would need to be obtained.

Teacher/pupil ratios will vary with the nature of an activity and the young people involved. For a walk in the countryside, in well-known safe terrain where no traffic will be encountered, 1 to 20 may be acceptable. There may be occasions when the risk factor increases and the pupil-teacher ratio will need to be adjusted accordingly. The involvement of pupils with special educational needs will require additional staffing consideration, perhaps even 1 to 1 (using a responsible adult) for some individual cases.

There is a minimum staffing requirement of two. This could be a teacher plus a carefully chosen responsible adult. With a party of boys and girls, the minimum staffing should be one male and one female.

Qu 11   As a male member of staff, I run an outdoor games club for pupils in Y5 and Y6 at my school one lunchtime and one evening after school. It has proved very popular with both girls and boys and about sixty pupils attend on a regular basis. This number presents organisational difficulties but I am anxious not to turn anyone away. What advice do you have?

Ans   It would be unwise to accept responsibility for a group greater in number than the usual class size.

In the case of high level competition where close refereeing may be required, the numbers should be such that control can be realistically effected.

You might consider splitting the total number in two, with half attending at lunchtime and the other half after normal school hours. These two groups could be switched round at suitable intervals, for example each half term. Another possibility is to split by gender but here you will need to weigh up the benefits or otherwise of operating single sex activities. It may be advisable to share the activity sessions after normal school hours with a female colleague or adult helper, to provide responsible support in case of an emergency.

Qu 12   **When should support or 'standing-by' be provided in gymnastics?**

Ans   In meeting the challenge of some prescribed gymnastics and the progressive lead-up practices which are used, the provision of support either by the teacher or by pupils trained in the accepted methods, should be an integral part of the system.

At such times, there should be clear understanding between the performer and the supporter(s) of the activity and the method of assistance to be provided.

This support should be continued on a gradually reducing basis over time, until the performing pupil is able confidently to replicate the correct action under control on every occasion without any physical assistance. At this stage the supporting individual(s) should 'stand-by' in a close position to the action, ready to give support only in the event of a mistake by the performer which requires retrieval.

The ultimate aim should be for the performance to be so sure and safe that the performer opts to perform freely. That moment should be decided jointly by the teacher and the performer. It is not possible to apply a scale of successful stand-by attempts before moving to the freely executed move; this will vary from pupil to pupil but no young performer should be allowed to take this decision unilaterally.

It follows that before embarking on a supporting procedure, a teacher must be confident that a performing pupil has the necessary ability to learn the action. Also the teacher must have the essential knowledge of the movement and the skill techniques to provide the physical help which is needed. Pupils should only support or stand-by when they have the maturity, knowledge and training to assist as required in a particular situation.

(Note: Care should be taken to ensure that supporting accords with the advice given in DfEE Circular number 10/95 'Protecting Children from Abuse: The Role of the Education Service'.)

Qu 13 **In gymnastics, is it reasonable to allow pupils learning a recognised rotational vault to perform unassisted so long as a thick weight absorbent mattress is provided to receive their body weight when landing?**

Ans   The aim of any formal vault or other formal rotational action involving flight is to develop the orientation and motion necessary so as to perform the action correctly and to land, under control, on the feet after completing the flight phase.

The stages leading up to this level of performance may require physical support as described in the answer to Q12 above.

When the action has been practised and consolidated successfully to the extent that a feet-first landing under control by the performer can confidently be expected at each attempt, support may be reduced to standing-by and eventually removed.

The thick weight absorbent mattress may be the most suitable means for receiving the body momentum generated but can never replace the requirement for support during the learning phase, nor can it be guaranteed to eliminate injury.

Qu 14 **I am a secondary teacher involved with the teaching of rugby and on occasions I take a team away to play against other schools. At such times, I am often the only teacher present from my school. Is this a satisfactory arrangement?**

Ans   You would need to consider what you would do if one of the players from your team was injured and required medical treatment part-way through the game. Clearly you would have a duty of care for all of the pupils in your charge and your position of sole-responsibility would place you in a dilemma. If you were to take the injured pupil for treatment, the other pupils would be left unattended.

It may be possible for a teacher from the host school to assist in what would be an emergency but this would not be entirely satisfactory and could in no way be expected unless an agreement had been entered into beforehand. One solution could be for the fixtures system to require two teams from your school, each with a member of staff, to play away at any one time. Two staff would then be present and the above injury situation could be managed. When the side plays away, an alternative would be to take a second responsible adult (a parent, perhaps), with the remit to supervise pupils if this should prove necessary. It may also be helpful to have an emergency telephone contact number with your school for use at such times.

Qu 15   **When inter-school games matches are played out of school time is it acceptable for pupils to travel independently to and from the venue?**

Ans   Pupils should not be asked to undertake difficult journeys independent of supervision unless their age, experience and maturity is sufficient to cope with the problems involved and the parents have given their agreement. It is first necessary to assess that the risks are reasonable and then to give pupil guidance on the arrangements for travel. Whenever practicable, the pupils should journey together or in groups.

Qu 16   **Am I able to use rebound equipment in my school without a national governing body award?**

Ans   Trampolines and trampettes add an exciting dimension to the gymnastics programme in many secondary schools. Serious accidents could occur. This equipment requires the utmost care if such occurrences are to be avoided. Teachers using either piece of apparatus need to be fully informed on the safe practices and techniques to be employed. They should ensure that the progressive stages of learning skills are fully implemented.

Because of the hazardous nature of rebound activities, it is recommended that teachers involved with these aspects should attend suitable courses from time to time, to keep themselves appraised and updated on developments. Some local authorities arrange and validate their own in-service courses; others rely on the relevant qualification from the national governing body. It is important that the policy of the local authority in this regard is known and followed.

If you have gained acceptable or approved experience via reputable courses, this may enable you to teach without holding a national governing body award. It is even further evidence of suitability to teach if, as well as the approved experience, you do hold the appropriate national governing body award.

Qu 17   **I understand that a thick weight absorbent mattress may be used in trampolining in two ways:**

   i.   as an aid to learning for certain activities by being pushed on to the bed for a performer to land onto, and

   ii.   as a safety measure in place of spotters when two trampolines are worked together and placed end to end, by positioning a thick weight absorbent mattress across the adjoining frames and coverall pads. Is this acceptable?

Ans   Developments in trampolining are happening all the time and the use of thick weight absorbent mattresses in the ways you describe are innovations which have taken place. If used in the right way they are acceptable. A mattress is now available which is designed with handles to enable its use as an aid for learning some trampolining skills. However, the safe use of such mattresses requires considerable skill and judgement on the part of the teacher or coach.

These new developments should only be introduced by those who have undergone appropriate training, are very experienced in the teaching of trampolining, and are working with performers who have fully mastered the basic skills.

Qu 18 **The two step count for the lay-up shot in basketball is a co-ordinated skill which many pupils find difficult. In teaching it, would it be appropriate for a bench to be so positioned that pupils jump across the bench before taking their two step count and then their lay-up shot at the basket?**

Ans By using a bench in this way an unnecessary hazard is being introduced into a skill practice which many pupils do find very challenging.

It is foreseeable that a pupil concentrating attention on receiving the ball whilst jumping across the bench might misjudge the step onto the bench and fall, causing injury.

Alternatives to the bench method should be explored.

Perhaps each pupil could start by standing in a chalk circle drawn in an appropriate position on the floor, then take their two steps forward of the circle towards the basket and shoot. This could be developed into running forward and taking the ball from someone standing in the chalk circle, then taking the two permitted step count rhythm before shooting. Whatever the methods and progression selected, the use of the bench for this practice should be avoided.

Qu 19 **Does the same duty of care apply to students in Years 12 and 13, as that for younger pupils?**

Ans Yes, whether older pupils are in school or college education, the duty of care for their well-being is a requirement on the part of any teacher who has responsibility for them, in the same way as for younger pupils.

A student in the sixth form has the right to seek redress for any allegation of negligence on the part of a teacher: though the increased level of responsibility reasonably to be expected of a pupil of this maturity, as opposed to a 'minor', might serve to mitigate any such claim.

Qu 20   **Teacher colleagues from other departments in the school are timetabled to assist with some games lessons in physical education. Is this acceptable practice?**

Ans   In general, it is better if the physical education programme is delivered by teachers with specialist training in the subject but this may not always be possible. Games is one area where teachers of other subjects may be knowledgeable and experienced and their support acceptable; provided they are familiar with the rules and are able to ensure that these are applied.

Subject leaders should satisfy themselves that such teachers are able to deliver the programme safely and effectively. This may require monitoring and assessment by specialist staff in the early stages.

The use of non-specialist staff with expertise in only one game or activity may be a significant constraint in staffing the range of activities for pupils in a given year. This should be discussed with senior management where it may impinge on safety.

As an extension of this question, assistance by non-specialist staff on 'sports days' needs very careful planning.

These personnel should be fully briefed beforehand by a specialist teacher on the technical and safety requirements, particularly for the potentially hazardous throwing and jumping events.

Qu 21   **Is it acceptable for pupils in Y11 to use local off-site sports centre facilities as part of an options programme for physical education. If so, will staffing at the centre be sufficient for supervisory purposes?**

Ans   Provided the headteacher approves, parental consent is obtained and suitable activities and arrangements can be made with the manager, the use of the sports centre may well offer useful experiences for the pupils, particularly where the specialist physical education facilities at the school are limited.

The programme should be carefully planned and agreed with the sports centre manager so that the system works well and there is no misunderstanding on either side. Pupils using the centre should be made fully aware of their responsibilities during the planning stage.

At least one specialist physical education teacher from the school should attend the sessions in loco parentis, though centre staff may work with the pupils in specific activities.

Under no circumstances should the pupils attend the centre without the member of the school staff being present.

Qu 22   Are 'tidy' store rooms an issue for safe practice?

Ans   Yes, equipment should be stored consistently where it may be expected to be located and not left lying about in a haphazard manner where it may be inadvertently stepped upon or fallen over. 'Every item in its place' is a sound maxim. It is reasonable to expect that facilities will be provided for the appropriate storage of such items.

In many schools, storage space is inadequate but the provision of appropriate wall fitments, shelving and containers will help minimise or overcome many of the difficulties encountered.

Qu 23   During a curriculum lesson in athletics the contracted agent arrived to cut the grass on the activities area. The pupils were informed to take care and to stop whatever they were doing whenever the machine came near. Unfortunately, a stone flew up from the cutting blades and struck a child, causing a wound that needed treatment. Was this an accident or would the contractor have been liable for the injury caused?

Ans   Problems associated with grass cutting and other maintenance requirements can arise. The principle must be that grass cutting constitutes a potential hazard and should not take place on areas and at times when physical education activities are in progress. Either one of two steps should have been taken which would have prevented this unfortunate occurrence:

(i)   The grass cutting should have been delayed until the athletics lesson was over; or

(ii)   the pupils and the activities should have been moved to a position well away from the grass cutting area, space and facilities permitting; or

The contract between the school and the agent should have included a clause which would have prevented grass cutting being carried out during timetabled use of the playing area. The teacher responsible for the class had a duty of care for the pupils and should have taken action to safeguard them.

The grass cutting contractor should have been approached by the teacher and a satisfactory arrangement agreed along the lines already stated. The contractor, also, should have been aware that grass cutting is hazardous when young people are in close proximity. The work should not have started until a satisfactory arrangement with the teacher had been negotiated.

In the circumstances, it is possible that liability for the injury to the pupil would have been apportioned on both the teacher (that is the school or LEA as employers) and the contractor for not taking reasonable care.

Qu 24 **How soon after eating a meal (for example sandwiches or school dinners at lunchtime) should pupils be permitted to engage in swimming?**

Ans It is wise to allow a reasonable time from ending the meal before pupils are allowed to enter the water. This will enable the process of digestion to be sufficiently advanced to minimise the hazardous possibility of vomiting during the swimming session, which could be life threatening if air tubes become blocked.

Where pupils swim in the session which follows the midday lunch break, it is advisable for them to eat lightly and as early as possible during this break period to enable the necessary time from eating to swimming to elapse.

Qu 25 **What is the need for, or value of, parental consent for pupil participation in any given activity?**

Ans Where a teacher involves pupils in an activity which is not a part of the curriculum normally offered by the school, it is advisable to inform parents and seek their consent prior to participation taking place.

This action will in no way reduce the duty of care required of the teacher, though it will prevent a parent from pleading ignorance of their child's involvement in the activity. LEA's and headteachers are experienced in this area and may be expected to provide an appropriate form for this purpose.

The legal sections of teachers' unions and professional associations may also assist with advice on the wording and format for consent forms.

Qu 26 **Following the annual inspection of gymnastics apparatus the specialist firm that carries out this work has condemned two benches and a mat and advised that these items should be replaced. Do I need to follow this advice?**

It is important that a formal inspection by a specialist firm of all large apparatus and fixed equipment used for physical education purposes should be arranged to take place annually.

Where apparatus has been condemned following inspection, this should be clearly stated in the specialist firm's written report, the equipment marked accordingly and immediate action taken to remove the designated items from all use.

Qu 27   **A playing member of the local hockey club who is also the parent of a child at this school has offered her services to assist with an extra-curricular school hockey club. Is the school able to accept this offer and are there any constraints to be considered?**

Ans   External help of this kind can be of great benefit to a school, whether it be from a parent or someone less closely associated with the establishment, provided satisfactory arrangements can be made to accommodate such assistance.

The person concerned must not have any recorded offence which would prevent her by law from working with young people and it will be helpful to produce evidence that she has prior coaching experience and/or experience of working with youngsters in addition to playing capabilities. In any case she must work to a teacher who will be in loco parentis.

The teacher will need to work closely with the helper in the early stages but this supervision can gradually be reduced as the external input develops satisfactorily over time. However, it is important that the teacher always remains on hand and available, so that in loco parentis can be seen to be in operation at all times.

It will also be important to ensure that suitable insurance cover is in place for the external helper.

Qu 28   **Is it acceptable in gymnastics to drape a mat over a bench in providing a working surface?**

Ans   This arrangement requires great care. Unless the mat used is very flexible there is a danger that the edges of the underlying bench will not be clearly defined, thereby presenting a hazard to those working on the apparatus. The arrangement should only be used when it is appropriate for the task set, the activities clearly defined and any foreseeable risks controlled.

Padded benches are produced by some recognised manufacturers of gymnastics equipment and it would be better to purchase and to use these rather than to improvise in the manner described.

Qu 29   **Am I able to use my car for transporting pupils, for example to a games fixture with another school or to hospital for treatment?**

Ans   You should first make sure through the headteacher that the governors approve this arrangement as an aspect of school policy. You should also ensure that your car insurance covers this risk. An additional premium may be payable.

You should first make sure through the headteacher that the

On no account should you ever transport more than the stated maximum number of passengers for the vehicle. Seat belts should be worn during journeys and a first-aid box carried. A second adult should be present on trips to hospital.

Qu 30   **Why is it that 'pirates' is not allowed to be played?**

Ans   'Pirates' is basically a chasing game played off the ground using gymnastics apparatus. It has proved very popular with pupils, especially as an activity at the very end of a busy term. Unfortunately, it has resulted in some very serious accidents to participants and it is now deemed too hazardous. The competitive nature of the activity has caused some pupils to over-extend themselves and to fall.

Obstacle courses similarly present hazards if pupils race against the clock or against each other. These should only be undertaken with the greatest care when the risks have been fully assessed.

All pupils should be very practised and competent in the skills required of them. The emphasis should always be on taking sufficient time to negotiate each obstacle correctly, on teamwork and on successfully completing the course under full control rather than on competing to win.

Qu 31   **When should an accident be reported?**

Ans   Health and Safety legislation required that accidents of a serious nature (broken bones for example) which result in time off school, must be reported in an approved format and a copy sent to the appropriate health and safety officer. Each school will have this information which should be made known to all staff.

Whenever a pupil has an accident which results in injury, it is advisable for this to be recorded on an official form giving the name of the injured child; the date, time and place of the accident; the names of the teacher and of any witnesses; a brief description of the occurrence and the subsequent action taken with no personal opinion expressed. Teachers are advised not to express any opinion as to cause or effect of the accident at this early stage.

The report should be completed and sent to the headteacher as soon as possible after the occurrence. This procedure will apply equally to accidents which occur on school visits.

If teachers have any doubts they should seek advice from their professional association.

'Near misses' are also of interest and significance. Although there is no requirement for these to be reported, sharing such incidents with colleagues can be useful in raising awareness and minimising a repeat or similar occurrence at some other time.

Qu 32 **I am a primary school teacher with no specialist P.E. background. After reading your book, 'Safe Practice in Physical Education', I am perplexed by one particular aspect of your comments on mats used in Educational Gymnastics whilst the children are working on agility equipment.**
In 5.11.5.b of the book (Millennium edition) I am told not to place mats where I think that a child might fall from the apparatus. Does this guidance tell me that I am wrong to place a mat where I think that the foreseeable probability is that a child runs a high level of risk of falling from the equipment?

Ans   What matters in every Physical Education lesson which you teach is the kind of judgement which you exercise in deciding the content of your lesson and the apparatus set up which you choose for your children. This is because you are 'in loco parentis', owing a duty of care to all pupils in that class.

That judgement must be seen to be wise and founded on physical education schemes and practices which have been approved and accepted by employers and training agencies throughout the schools in this country. All teachers are expected to arrange their lessons so that all foreseeable hazards are eliminated and consequent accidents avoided. Regular and approved practice does accept however that there will always be the unforeseeable accident, against which no teacher can legislate.

If, therefore, you in your assessment of what you are asking the children to do in your P.E. lesson, identify a situation where unacceptable levels of risk are foreseeable; your employers would expect you to so arrange your lesson content that the children are protected from that foreseeable accident.

Our advice, conditioned by experience in how the Courts have dealt with such cases, is that placing a mat to accommodate a foreseeable fall from apparatus would not be deemed good practice. Teachers would be expected to modify the task set for the children; perhaps by modifying the height of the apparatus or the degree of challenge in the movement so that the children and you are confident that they will complete the task successfully without involuntarily falling off the equipment.

One particularly difficult example might be where a child is making its first attempt to traverse, by hand, a long ladder or pole which may be suspended between two trestles at a height. In this the child might well be caught out by the sudden and unexpected onset of muscle fatigue. During these early attempts, the teacher should be prepared to support the beginner if the need arises.

In this situation, a mattress might well be placed at a point between the trestles and on the floor below the trestles. This mattress should be used in this planned way so that the child can be taught to release from the bar or pole and make a controlled landing on two feet on the mat whilst the teacher supports. But it could be dangerous and misleading for the child if it were left to experience a random fall from the equipment.

Qu 33   **Recently I was asked to supervise the work of an AOTT who, through the local football club, was assigned to help with my class's football lesson. Feelings flared a little when I told him that I wanted my class to spend most of their time working on basic skills rather than just playing 5-a-side. He told me that he would decide what they would do since he was an FA Coach. My class is a mixture of seven and eight year olds. Should I have given way to the AOTT?**

Ans   There is a strong, but not at first evident, element of 'Safe Management' here. Whatever claim to football skill the AOTT may have in excess of yours, the legal fact is that you, the teacher, are the person 'in loco parentis' and you would be the person held to be responsible for the well being of your pupils. You would know better than he whether it was totally safe for such young children to be encouraged to play the team game rather than simple skills practices and consolidation before setting up small side games, (not necessarily 5-a-side competitions). You would be expected to know and to decide whether every pupil was sufficiently mature to be involved in sophisticated 'grown up' type games playing. You would be the one aware of the dangers of mis-matched children and what might happen to them in the hurly-burly of full games. In this instance, therefore, you would be right to oversee the games experience.

Qu 34   **The school is taking a few senior pupils away to an Outdoor Adventure Centre for a character-development week. Last year, on the same type of course, I felt that the children were being exposed to challenges unreasonably beyond their capabilities. The Centre is a well established one and all their Instructors are professionally qualified, according to their brochure. I feel that I should have intervened to have the pupils' level of challenge modified to meet their needs but was uncertain of my authority since this was a professionally-run establishment. If the same thing happens this year, what should I do?**

Ans   Long before you attend the centre, there is a lot of work to be done in checking all sorts of issues and you would do well to read the advice elsewhere in this booklet (Section 5.7) All these checks are expressions of the school's duty of care towards its pupils so that they are not confronted by unreasonable hazards. When all these checks have been carried out, it still remains the duty of the school to see that the expectations of the checks are being realised. In the event of your being unsure whilst on the spot, you must intervene to protect the pupils, even if it means your over-riding the non-teacher instructors. May we quote the example of a centre abroad which assured the school that all its instructors were qualified? In truth many of them turned out to be student-teachers in their last year who were totally lacking in real experience of teaching children in the activities they professed to be qualified to teach. Had you been faced with such a situation you would have been expected to step in and put the matter right.

Qu 35 **A girl in my class came to me to announce that, as she had her navel pierced so that she could sport a gold safety pin, she should not do Physical Education in case she was damaged by the pin being knocked. I tried to persuade her to remove the pin so that she could benefit from some health giving exercise but she was adamantly defiant. What can I do if I meet this again in the future?**

Ans   This is an extension of the problems of wearing jewellery in physical education. That problem has gone on for years and no one has found a general answer. Each case has to find its own solution. The constant factor seems to be that the school has a right to insist that its prescribed curriculum is followed by all its pupils so long as they are free of any 'special need' adaptation. No education experience should be followed where the pupil is exposed to foreseeable injury. To eliminate that danger, the pupil should be asked to remove the jewellery in order to conform with reasonable school rules. The parents should be asked to support the school's expectations in this matter. If that fails, then padding or concealing jewellery in a safe manner should be pursued. Where this is not possible it may be expedient to give the child its own PE programme, suitably modified so that there is no risk of offending jewellery becoming a hazard during the modified PE work.

(Editor's note. This is a very new phenomenon in the jewellery irritant. I am not aware of any court case where this issue has been tried but I would be curious to know about it. As with tattooing, there is a minimum age for such piercing to be done to minors. I would be keen to involve the welfare agencies looking after children in my area and I would hope that the school's counselling of its pupils would make available to children all the advice and guidance they might need, at an early age, to cope with this problem).

Qu 36   My Headteacher has designated me as party-leader in charge of a skiing party to Italy in this year's programme. I am happy to accept this but am not happy about including two of the pupils who have applied to go. The Headteacher has told me that their names must stay on the list. I feel strongly that they should be excluded. Where is the way forward on this?

Ans   Solving this problem will test your best endeavours as a professional educator and could blight your management of safe practice if you fail. Once the school party leaves the premises to start the trip, and until you arrive back at the school at the end, you are acting on behalf of the Headteacher and will be answerable to the parents, the school governors and the Headteacher for all that happens to the party whilst you are away.

If the two questionable pupils start the trip then you must protect them just as well as all the other pupils against foreseeable risks. You should, therefore, leave the Headteacher in no doubt about your real anxieties and you should be ready to demonstrate clearly the reasons for your concerns.

Every force available should be brought to bear on the pupils before you set out so that they know exactly what you expect of them and why, whilst they are in your care. They must also understand clearly the consequences of their failing to conform with your expectations of them. Well before your departure date, if you feel that their chances of succeeding to conform are not good enough, you should tell the Head that, in your opinion, their continuing as members of the party will prejudice the safety and well-being of everyone and hope that the Head will accept your assessment. If he does not and if you are still certain of your judgement, you should suggest that someone else becomes the party leader. YOU CANNOT PROCEED WHERE YOUR PROFESSIONAL JUDGEMENT IS COMPROMISED, ESPECIALLY IN THE MATTER OF SAFETY.

Qu 37   At a Governors' meeting the matter of the hall-floor being used for physical education lessons was criticised. It was alleged this practice was unsafe because the floor was not a sprung, wooden floor and the children's legs were likely to be injured. How should I deal with this problem?

Ans   If this allegation were wholly true, then thousands of schools would also be guilty of unsafe practice in physical education lessons. Fortunately, it is not and they are not. In growing children, there is a slight risk that long bones in the leg might react painfully to the incidental jarring effects of repeated, high-impact landings, (shin-splints), on hard floors. Sprung wooden floors are kinder than hard floors but you would have to be following a very vigorous running and jumping regime for such consequences to impact on your pupils' health. It would be very surprising to find a school following such an inappropriate scheme of physical education. This challenge from your Governors would seem to be ill-founded and extreme.

Qu 38   I am the Head of a large primary school with a governing body which would like to install an impact absorbing surface (IAS) beneath our outdoor agility equipment. They have introduced a great deal of anxiety amongst the staff, by implying that without a matting cover it is not safe for pupils to use this equipment. Could you please advise me on this whole business of outdoor agility equipment and its use, with and without IAS, in schools?

Ans   This is not an easy question to answer but this Association has already given advice on this matter. Our guidance was based on 'regular and approved practice' as perceived in schools using this type of outdoor equipment without an impact absorbing surface. This has been going on since just after the second world war. Reacting to that long and relatively accident free experience, we stated our position along the following lines.

a   This Association traced back the history of a committee which, just after the war, was convened by the then equivalent of the B.S.I. Agency. That committee was seeking to set up guidance on safe play on outdoor agility equipment. This initial committee was split into two sections: one to establish a system for use in parks; largely, it seemed, because as early as the late 1940's, it was recognised that there would be no adult supervision of the users in parks. The other section of that initial committee was to set up their system for use in schools. The scheme which the schools' group established reflected the professional awareness and expertise of teachers who had long experience of working within the prescription of the teacher's duty of care so that 'in loco parentis' was an active element of their system. After a few years, the schools' section of this Committee was disbanded because they seemed to have produced an acceptably safe system. The parks' section of the Committee still meets because their system is a troubled one, proving to be not reasonable, in safety terms. It was through their anxiety that they promoted the idea of an impact absorbing surface. We believe it would have been better for their users had they promoted the practice of better child supervision by adults.

b   The schools' system of managing this equipment without using an 'impact absorbing surface', was different and safer than the system used in public parks. The 'IAS' idea seems to have sprung from the parks' section, following some research which has seemed, in some respects, not to have tackled the real issues appropriately. The schools' system was, and is, superior and safer for the following reasons:-

1   Play was under the direction of professionally trained supervisors.

2   Such supervision was direct, in so far as, during school-time the pupils were in the reasonable purview of the supervisors and operated on the equipment in a much more contained and self-controlled system than there was or is in the parks.

3   In the school curriculum sessions, the children brought with them a collection of previously developed and practised movement skills and awarenesses which removed the haphazard exposure which they might experience in the parks system. These real instruments of self management and disciplined self-conformity virtually removed the random acts of movement, from which the foreseeable accidents which plague the Parks system, usually spring.

4   Well-trained staff supervising these school apparatus sessions are well versed in the proper manner of monitoring and modifying the way children use this equipment, thus controlling wild 'horseplay' and reckless actions.

5   Children thereby do not risk moving into unknown patterns of movement wilfully. Where their own curiosity moves them that way they are trained to ask for guidance from a supervisor.

6   Children are trained not to interfere with other performers, not to touch them, not to move into occupied space or space which is the focus of another child's immediate attention.

7   The equipment installed is much more user-friendly in design than much of that which is seen in parks. It is more regularly checked by understanding staff and, in most schools, even the children are trained to react to the condition and stability of the apparatus.

Further and Better Thoughts

a   We believe that the advice in our book 'Safe Practice in Physical Education' is reasonable and would be acceptable to the average, reasonable parent if they were aware of its intention and asked to approve it. We therefore believe that it is reliable in support of the requirements of a teacher's duty of care towards the pupils.

b   We have evidence which shows that an impact absorbing surface introduces some risks as well as the slight benefit which there is. They bring alterations in the smoothness and regularity of the surface. This can cause accidents. Vandals will continue to damage these surfaces, thereby creating a negation of the surface function. Dogs and cats particularly can threaten the well-being of children by fouling the area. With some children 'IAS' can produce an unreal notion that they will be all right if they fall on an impact absorbing mat. They are thereby lured into a false sense of security.

c   It is our considered opinion that WHERE THERE IS UNSUPERVISED AND UNSTRUCTURED PLAY BY CHILDREN ON OUTSIDE AGILITY EQUIPMENT IT IS BETTER TO PROVIDE IAS. It should be appreciated that 'IAS' will not reduce the number of accidents nor significantly lessen the degree of injury where the impact is high, no matter from what height the child falls. However, in some cases, 'IAS' may reduce the degree of injury if the impact force is low.

d   Recently, one of our Officers was involved as an 'expert witness' in what, so far as we know, is the very first claim against a primary school for negligence whilst one of its pupils, during school time, was injured by falling onto the floor under a climbing frame which had no impact absorbing surface. We were encouraged in our advice to schools by the fact that the claims of the pupil against the school were rejected by the Judge. The case was "thrown out".

N.B. In particular, we would urge all schools with outdoor agility units to assess their pattern of use. IN PARTICULAR, ALL HEADTEACHERS SHOULD ENSURE THAT THEIR SYSTEM OF SUPERVISION IS WORKING SAFELY. Where any school makes its equipment available, OUTSIDE CURRICULUM TIME, to outside users; that school should consider its legal position with regard to the application of the 'Occupiers Liability Act'. We believe that where such community use is or may operate in the future, the school apparatus would more safely serve the needs of outside users if an impact absorbing surface were provided. Better still, it would be useful to insist that such users have an acceptable system of adult supervision. Headteachers should approach their LEA's for guidance in this particular context to make sure that they approve the equipment and what is happening on it.

Qu 39   **My Headteacher has forbidden us to allow some of the pupils (Down's Syndrome) to perform any agility work in physical education because of 'joint hyper luxation' as he put to us at a staff meeting recently. What is my position because my pupils take part in a limited programme of agility work and I believe he is not totally wise in this case?**

Ans   As it is probably part of your contract with your employers to do as you are reasonably asked by your Headteacher, (His reasonableness!), you would be at risk if you disobeyed. However, it well may be that his stance does not reflect total reasonableness and it would seem better if, because you feel sufficiently strongly about it, you asked him for an opportunity to discuss this matter more fully with him. If he agrees, you should, at the right time and in the right place, point out to him the following:

a   Hyper luxation occurs in different degrees with these pupils and each case requires particular study.

b   Not all agility activities involve those 'joints at risk'. (The most common area is the cervical spine).

c   It is safer for the school if any pupil thought to be at risk is defined by the school's doctor. S/he should also be asked to give some indication of activity limitation.

d   All staff concerned should know that any agility which puts these joints under excessive stress, especially any kind of roll involving pressure on the neck whether on mats or trampoline bed, at speed, should be avoided.

e   When the school decides its policy with regard to these pupils, the parents should be informed of that policy and agree to the pupils working in this way.

If the Headteacher, at the end of this, still feels it best not to allow agility work for them you would be wise to accept his regulation in this matter.

Qu 40   In former times, this school accepted appropriate responsibility for guiding college students on their P.E. teaching practice. What we did seemed to conform with previous guidance given in this book. Now, however, it seems to me that many student/AOTT helpers are involved in teaching the children and that we, as the class teachers, need to be even more concerned to see that the children are not left in the care of inexperienced or unqualified teachers. I worry about my position in this changing scenario and would appreciate some guidelines to strengthen my position vis a vis my class in the P.E. lesson.

Ans   This is a timely request which assumes ever increasing importance as 'under-qualified-teaching' help is more evident in schools. The following major points are offered as guid lines for your inclusion in your own system. Please note that there may be other factors which are very peculiar to your own school and you should identify any of those which need to be included in YOUR system.

1   Whatever the arrangement, the named, **qualified** teacher in charge of the class and the lesson, is the parents' agent standing 'in loco parentis' to the children in that class for that lesson.

2   That teacher is the main agent in the setting up of, and the reliable discharge of, a duty of care which the parent would accept as reasonable.

3   This would mean in practice that the class teacher must be satisfied that all the lessons proceed within bounds which conform to reasonable and well established previous practice. More importantly, the class teacher would have to satisfy her or himself that any student teacher or AOTT is not attempting work which is not within reasonable compass of the children.

Hence you would have to have sight of any scheme of work which the 'helper' proposes to follow. In real terms, the school, in the period prior to any such work being done should ask for written evidence of what the helper proposes to do so that any unacceptable detail can be corrected.

4   When all this has been done it will still devolve upon the teacher to see that, during the lesson, no circumstance develops which can harm the children. (For example, if the class management and discipline deteriorate to the point that the work and the safety of the pupils are threatened then the teacher must intervene).

5   In practical terms, this means that you must always be in reasonable contact with what is happening to the children working with the 'helper'; preferably visually, so that you can immediately influence deteriorating circumstance.

6   Be ready to make some assessment of the work done, discuss it with the helper and make sure that you keep the Headteacher informed of your assessment of how much the children have benefited from the presence of the helper.

7   Be ready to ask questions of the helper so far as his/her scheme of work is concerned and, where there is apparatus involved, especially gymnastic and athletics apparatus. Make sure for yourself that the helper is reliably familiar with the apparatus in your school, especially gymnastic apparatus which can be very varied in design.

Observance of these suggestions will go a long way to show that there was no dereliction of your previously well-established duty of care to your pupils.

Qu 41   **I am afraid to use gymnastic equipment in any improvised way, following an accident which seemed to arise out of such improvised apparatus set-up. Would you please comment on improvisation?**

Ans   There was a time in schools' P.E. when the lack of appropriate equipment made it necessary to use one's wits so that essential experience could be provided for the children. Happily, there is now a lot less need to resort to such improvisation because most schools have equipment designed and manufactured to work safely whilst pupils are using it.

Good equipment has design which provides such adaptation in its structure that improvisation is virtually redundant. Even so, there may be the odd situation where improvisation is appropriate but, IT MUST BE SAFE! If you improvise, you must foresee the full situations in its use, so that no pupil is caught out by lack of forethought.

A recent example we have met was in the use of mats being placed over benches to provide padding. Where such provision masks totally the outline of the benches and where the pupils will need to be clearly and perhaps quickly aware of just where the benches are underneath the matting: then, in our opinion, such improvised apparatus arrangement is potentially hostile to the pupils' well-being and the teacher would be well advised to find a better way of accommodating the pupils' needs.

The safest advice would be that if there is equipment which has been professionally designed to do the job which you want doing; try to get it provided through official sources and be ultra careful if you improvise.

PART 2:

ACTIVITIES

12: ATHLETICS

12.1   Introduction

Athletics embraces a range of both track and field events. It is a sport where constant and maximum effort is being used by individual participants under the stress of competition and where a variety of separate events; running, jumping and throwing may be taking place at the same time. Throwing events present the greatest hazard, though all aspects of athletics require careful planning. Sound management and vigilance is necessary to avoid the dangers which can arise, whether the involvement is with teaching, training or competition.

12.2   Responsibility for Safety

12.2.1   Responsibility for safety is a matter for all involved with the activities. Clear written guidelines and established routines based on good practice will help to ensure that all those in positions of authority or leadership are aware of their roles for specific aspects of safety.

12.2.2   The groups which may be identified are:

- those who plan the layout of facilities;

- the grounds staff;

- the organising officials;

- teachers and coaches;

- the athletes.

12.3   Teaching and Training Athletics

Facilities for Training

12.3.1   Facilities should be maintained in good condition through regular attention to maintenance, particularly prior to and during the athletics season. At all times when athletics facilities are used, a check should first be made to ensure that the intended activities may take place safely.

The training area should be level and the layout free from danger zones, that is spaces where activities overlap or into which pupils might inadvertently wander. There should be adequate space overall and throwing zones must be positioned in a defined area set aside for the purpose.

12.3.2   Responsibility rests with the teacher to decide when the facilities for teaching or training are suitable and safe.

The Teaching and Coaching of Athletics

12.3.3   The elements of greatest importance in teaching athletics safely are concerned with good class control, organisation and supervision. The development of responsibility and self-discipline by the pupils is essential. Teachers must be confident that pupils are able to exercise such control before the most hazardous (throwing) activities are introduced. The assessment and management of risks by the teacher and the sharing of these with pupils is an important feature.

12.3.4   Secondary schools present the greatest potential for danger. Teaching a mixed ability class on a school playing field is potentially more hazardous than coaching specialist athletes using properly prepared facilities with full backup resources at an athletics stadium.

12.3.5   Safe methods must be taught from the outset and the teacher must ensure that the training in which the young athletes engage follows a carefully graduated programme which meets the following criteria:

a   The athletes must be sufficiently mature, fit and skilled to tackle each new event. National governing body recommendations should be used as a guide to events and distances that are suitable for pupils at different ages and stages of development, particularly in the primary school.

b   Serious training in athletics should not begin too early, although excellent preparatory work may be possible in running, jumping and throwing. The metabolism of children aged 9 to 13 years works mainly aerobically and is therefore suited to endurance type activities and the learning of basic athletic skills. Specialised and technical training for 'explosive' athletic activities should only begin at the secondary school stage.

c   All pupils must be taught to be safe participants and safe spectators. Sweets or gum should never be chewed while actively participating.

d   Special vigilance and control is needed when standards are being recorded (judging, measuring, time-keeping, photographing and so forth). Spectators should be allocated to specific safe zones and should never crowd around the edges of the track or field event areas.

e	Teachers should remain in direct control of group events with beginners. Mistakes and a wide variation in standards should be anticipated and allowed for when working with novices.

f	Care must be taken in all events when the ground is wet. Throwing and hurdling are particularly hazardous in wet weather.

## 12.4	Field Events

12.4.1	All field events, especially the throws, involve obvious hazards. The activities must be introduced gradually into the programme, one event at a time. They must be under the direct control of a qualified teacher during the early learning stages.

12.4.2	The following points should be noted with regard to safe practice:

Throwing Activities

12.4.3	Good preliminary work can be done under class instruction and by using demonstration and practice. More detailed coaching requires smaller groups. Working space must at all times be adequate. The teacher must judge when pupils may be ready to work on their own.

12.4.4	The routine of lining up, throwing and retrieving must be strictly enforced along the following lines:

a	Throwers waiting to throw should stand well behind the circle or scratch line until ready to move forward. They should be well spaced and all eyes should be on the thrower(s) in action.

b	The teacher and the thrower(s) must always check that the predicted line(s) of flight and the adjacent area are clear of pupils. A wide margin of error should be allowed for.

c	Throwers must always remain behind the circle or scratch line after throwing. Their implements must be retrieved only after instruction to do so by the teacher, then carried back by the taught method, walking to the circle or scratch line. On no account should implements ever be thrown back.

d	Left-handed throwers should work together at one end (on the throwers' left) of the scratch line.

e	Where space is limited, only one pupil at a time should be allowed to throw.

f	Footwear must provide a firm foothold.

g Implements should never be used if they are cracked or damaged in any way; if the ground is wet they should be dried off after each throw.

Javelin

12.4.5 Younger children or beginners should be introduced to throwing for technique, control, accuracy and distance using balls and/or foam javelin shapes.

The metal javelin is potentially lethal and should only be used when basic throwing skills have been mastered and then only at the secondary stage.

12.4.6 The following points will promote safe practice:

a If possible, javelins should be carried in portable storage stands which can be taken from the store room to the practice or competition area.

b An athlete or carrier must never run with a javelin except when throwing.

c When a single javelin is being moved to the throwing site, both ends should be covered with a block of cork or some other protective material.

d Javelins should never be stuck in the ground at a dangerous angle. At the throwing assembly point, they should be maintained in a vertical position, either in the ground or in storage racks.

e Before a thrown javelin is removed from the ground, it should first be levered into a vertical position. It should then be carried in the same vertical position with the point as near to the ground as possible.

f Whenever possible, a surfaced area should be provided for the javelin run up, since this gives a firmer foothold than grass.

Discus

12.4.7 Children can begin by using a foam or small rubber practice discus which is less weighty, less hazardous and easier to control than the metal rimmed version.

The same care should be taken as with the proper implement, as it is important to inculcate the right procedures in readiness for the transition to throwing the regulation model.

12.4.8   The following safety points should be observed:

   a   A discus with cracks, worn rims or projecting rivet heads should never be used.

   b   Practice throwing should be confined to a safe area in which there are no other activities taking place.

   c   Waiting throwers should stand well back from the throw line.

   d   Control should be developed from the initial use of standing throws which, when accomplished, may be followed by movement to add momentum. Turning should then be introduced once these progressions have been learned and consolidated.

   e   A collected discus should be carried firmly and never rolled.

   f   In restricted areas and for higher level competitions, safety nets or cages should always be provided.

Shot Putt

12.4.9   The early introduction to the action of putting the shot can make use of foam shot shapes and/or cricket and rounders balls. These implements provide some weight against which to push and provide good opportunities for technique to be taught and acquired.

12.4.10   Points for safe practice include:

   a   Pupils should never be allowed to play around with the shot.

   b   Each implement should be carried securely in two hands held close to the body and placed carefully on the ground (never dropped) on arrival at the shot putt area.

   c   The putt should be learned from a side-on still position. Movement should only be introduced when the standing putt has been accomplished successfully.

   d   Rotational methods should be introduced at a late stage and only when very good control and technique have been achieved in prior stages.

Hammer

12.4.11   Hammer throwing is arguably the most hazardous and physically demanding of all the throwing events. It requires great technical skill and co-ordination. In the early stages, it may best be improvised using a quoit and rope or a tennis ball inside a nylon tight or stocking.

12.4.12   Safety is at a premium and the following points should be carefully noted and implemented:

    a   Hammer throwing must always be strictly controlled, with rules and procedures that are clearly understood and applied.

    b   Only purpose-made hammers should be used. The spindle must be free to rotate. Bent, worn or rusty wires are dangerous.

    c   Protective cages are essential. The frame must be fixed firmly in the ground. The cage may be of wire mesh or suspended fibre netting which must not be rigid. Any guy lines must be well clear of the throwing sector lines.

    d   The throwing sector must be roped off, at a wider angle than the sector itself, to prevent danger from access to the landing area and its immediate surrounds.

    e   A system of auditory and visual ready and response signalling should be used when preparing for throws.

    f   Hammers must at all times be carried when being returned to the circle after a throw has taken place.

Jumping Activities

12.4.13   Sandpit landing areas for the high jump and pole vault are safe only for low heights where the jumpers land on their feet. For more advanced training and competitions, a soft landing area is required.

12.4.14   If the edges of the sandpit landing area are lined with wood or concrete, they should be flush with the ground and covered at places where a jumper is liable to contact them. A convenient and adequate cover can be made of small sacks loosely filled with cork or granular rubber chips.

12.4.15   The sand used in jumping areas should be 'sharp' (that is non-caking) and deep enough to absorb the impact of any landing without jarring. It must be free from hard or sharp objects such as metal, wire or broken glass. It should be dug and raked over frequently, both in training and competition. Digging and raking implements should never be left lying near the landing area, or with the teeth or prongs pointing upwards.

12.4.16   Jumping must never take place while the landing area is being dug or raked.

12.4.17   **Long Jump and Triple Jump**

    a   Separate runways and landing areas should be provided for long jump and triple jump. If only one runway is available, it should be wide enough for staggered boards.

b   Runways should be repacked and rolled when they become so worn that the edge of the take-off board is no longer level with the surface of the runway.

c   If grass is used as a runway surface, spikes are essential.

d   Take-off boards should be of regulation size and must be firmly embedded in the runway. A loose board can cause serious injury to the instep of the take-off foot.

e   Boards should be painted in a distinguishing colour and kept clean and dry.

f   If there is only one board for the triple jump, it may not be suitably positioned for both junior and senior pupils. In this instance, additional boards should be inserted level with the runway at distances of 7 metres, 9 metres, 11 metres and 13 metres from the landing area.

High Jump and Pole Vault

12.4.18   **Landing Areas**

a   In the high jump, the athlete must be taught that the angle of approach and take-off point largely determine the landing position.

b   Round bars are recommended, especially for 'flop' styles of jumping. If 'flexi-bars' are used, the supporting stands must be secured so that they do not collapse on the jumper.

c   Flexi-bars should be colourful and strong, so that they may be clearly visible and remain still for the athlete.

d   Soft, multi-unit landing areas are essential when jumpers use styles which involve landing on the back and shoulders.

These should conform to the following minimum requirements:

◆   In training and competition, the landing area must be large enough to allow safe use by all participants, irrespective of jumping style.

◆   For competitive jumping, the area should conform to the sizes recommended by UK Athletics for the level and age range of the competition.

e   Cushioning material must be deep and dense enough to prevent 'bottoming out', (that is, the weight of landing must be completely absorbed by the material). Suppliers should be asked to provide relevant data on absorbency, which may be checked against reference tables from the British Athletic Federation.

f   Fitted coverall sheets for landing areas must be all-weather, low friction and resistant to wear from spikes. These enable units to be held firmly together to give an even cushioning effect and should also be used in practice.

g   Soft landing areas deteriorate over time and need to be regularly inspected, with appropriate maintenance and repair as necessary.

h   Dependent on their experience, athletes should take some responsibility to check that the landing area is safe and suitable.

12.4.19   Poles and Take-off Boxes

i   Fibre poles can deteriorate and snap after extensive use. They should be examined regularly and discarded if they are cracked or spiked.

j   Poles should be treated with care and contained in a box or cover when not in use.

k   Fibre poles should never be used in planting boxes which have a vertical backplate, as these do not allow the pole to achieve its full bend.

12.5   Field Events in Competition

12.5.1   Competitors should always be suitably prepared and should have reached the appropriate standard for the competition.

12.5.2   In external competitions, the regulations and recommendations of the body under whose rules the competition will run should be carefully studied and followed.

12.5.3   For school sports days or inter-school competitions, it is relevant that:

a   Throwing areas should be clearly identifiable, with sectors roped off well away from the sector lines marked on the ground to prevent casual access.

b   Implements must only be thrown from their respective circles or scratch lines, both during practice and competition. They must always be carried when returned to the starting area.

c   Circle and scratch lines must be sited so that implements thrown fairly or otherwise will not land in the vicinity of spectators or the judges and officials of other events.

d   Careful instructions should be given on the methods to be used for the retrieval and return of implements.

e   Written advice and rules should be contained on the back of boards issued to officials for recording purposes.

f   Planned audible and visual signals known to all involved with the events should be used for effective communication.

g   Officials should stand so that each successive throw or jump point is blocked until measurement and recording of the previous throw or jump has been completed.

h   The planned programme should limit the number of events that take place at any one time to manageable and safe levels.

12.6   Track Events

a   Great self-discipline and control are necessary to prevent accident and injury from spikes. Instruction on their safe use should be given at the earliest opportunity. When they are removed they should be placed with the spikes facing down in the soil.

b   When spikes are worn, numbers in events should be safely limited.

c   All races of one lap or less should be run in lanes. This rule is particularly pertinent to safety in relay races.

d   Finishing tapes should be of worsted or similar material which break easily and be held no higher than chest height for the athletes.

e   Hurdles should be of rigid construction, smooth and free from sharp or protruding edges. They must be of the correct weight and resistance as laid down in the U.K. Athletics rulebook . The legs and feet of hurdles must be at right angles to the top bar.

f   Starting blocks, hammers, nails and any other materials must be removed from the track immediately after use.

Starting Pistols

12.6.1   There is no such thing as a safe firearm.

Current legislation prohibits the possession and use of a firearm above, and including, .22 calibre by any individual not duly licensed by the police.

"Firearms" are interpreted as any pistol or revolver that can (or can be converted to) the firing of a live round of ammunition.

It is strongly recommended that no teacher or school that does not fulfil the criteria described above should use, attempt to use or procure such a pistol for athletic events.

Very small calibre 'cap' firing pistols are allowable. Ammunition for such pistols should be stored securely and separately from the firing mechanism.

If in any doubt about their position, staff should contact their local police authority,

12.6.2   Safe practice requires that:

a   A starting pistol should always be fired at arms length above the head.

b   A pistol should never be left loaded after use. The slide or magazine should be taken out, the ammunition removed and the pistol, firing mechanism and ammunition safely and separately locked away.

c   For reasons of security, all starting pistols should be marked with the name of the owner or school.

d   The loss of a starting pistol or ammunition should be reported immediately to the police.

12.7   Cross Country Running

12.7.1   **Competitions**

a   The start should be sufficiently wide to accommodate the number of runners safely.

b   There should be a long, clear approach to enable the competitors to thin out before the first obstacle. This barrier should be sufficiently wide to prevent queues or bunching.

c   First aid and casualty transport should be provided at various points on the course. The base amenities should include hot drinks, showers, washing and changing facilities.

d   Participants should be counted at the start, during the run and at the finish. Short cuts should not be permitted.

e   Courses should be graded for different abilities. The slowest runner should be tailed throughout the race so that runners injured or in distress can be located and escorted back for treatment.

f   Runners should take a shower after the race.

12.7.2 Training in Schools

a Courses should be chosen with care and should avoid busy roads.

b Distances should be appropriate to the ages and fitness of the pupils.

c Hazardous sections (for example ditches) should be marshalled or kept in view.

d A teacher or supervisory presence is essential.

e Pupils should be counted out and in. A back-marker should be nominated.

f Advice on any aspects of cross country training or competition in schools may be obtained from the English Schools' Athletics Association (ESAA).

12.8 Indoor Athletics

Many aspects of safe practice which are applied to outdoor athletics are directly transferable to work indoors. The more confined environment, however, in this form of athletics merits some specific considerations in ensuring that performers are not exposed to unnecessary risk.

a A sound surface, adequate space and clearly designated working areas remain essential and this is particularly important when running at fast speed.

b Activity should take place well away from projections and walls.

c Rebound boards can be useful in sustaining fast running in confined space, providing participants have been appropriately trained in their use. Otherwise, running events should be organised as 'run-around' activities using skittles or markers.

d Equipment should be safely stored when not in use, well away from working areas.

e Composition mats should be used to cushion landings when jumping.

f Crash mats should be avoided when landing on one foot. The teaching of sound landing technique will do much to avoid potential injury where space is limited and no specialist facilities are available.

g Approach runs should be kept to a minimum for example, 4 strides when jumping for height and distance.

h Throwing implements, such as those of foam or rubber manufacture, should be used indoors. Although such implements constitute a lesser danger than traditional implements strict rules are still applicable in regulating throwing procedure.

13: DANCE

13.1 Introduction

Dance may generally be considered as one of the safest aspects of physical education. It takes many forms, from the creative to the formal. Each dance form should be assessed for any risks which it presents to safe practice and these should be satisfactorily addressed and managed.

13.2 General Points

13.2.1   The principles which underpin safe practice in other physical activities may reasonably be applied to dance. Teachers should be qualified or experienced and should know about the structure and functioning of the human body.

Health related dance styles (aerobics, pop-mobility, step) can place heavy demands on pupils and may be harmful if incorrectly taught.

13.2.2   An adequate warm up is essential before strenuous exercise. Care must be taken to ensure that young people are properly prepared for the physical demands of the lesson.

13.2.3   Clothing should be suitable and sweets or gum should never be chewed during active participation.

Jewellery, watches and other such personal effects should be removed.

13.2.4   Attention to the following points will help to ensure safe practice:

Facilities and Equipment

a   Facilities and equipment should be maintained in good order. Dance is very often taught in facilities which are not designed for the purpose. In these circumstances great care should be taken to ensure that any modifications or adaptations meet satisfactory safety standards, such as lighting and floor surfaces.

b   Equipment may be used in an improvised manner in dance and care should be taken that any associated risks are properly assessed and managed.

c   Floors should not be slippery and the surface should preferably be yielding when high-flight and frequent landings might combine to cause discomfort in the lower limb joints. Bare-foot dance may need to be adapted to meet the needs of individuals. Appropriate footwear may be a valuable aid to the performer.

d   Any obstructions in the activity space should be removed if at all possible. If this cannot be arranged, active participants should be made aware of the presence of these obstacles and movement activity should be adjusted accordingly.

Training

e   Avoid work-rate which makes excessive demands on the main movement joints, especially on growing children. Their joint structures are vulnerable.

f   Excessive speed work may predispose such children to stress injury in joints.

g   When helping children to acquire greater suppleness beware of over-stimulation which could inhibit the protective reflexes of the main movement joints.

h   Teachers should observe pupils carefully, to check that they do not over stress themselves.

i   In the context of dance there are particular working positions which need informed handling. Such positions are:

♦   vigorous rotation of the neck;

♦   maximal and loaded arching of the spine;

♦   exercises which extend the spine under stress loads;

♦   movements which flex the hips whilst seeking to over extend straightened legs.

Work in Pairs and Small Groups

j   Care should be taken that holding, lifting, supporting, catching and lowering techniques, which are characteristic of work in pairs and small groups, satisfy the basic anatomical and mechanical principles which determine the safety of such activities. Being stable, not supporting excessive weight relative to one's own weight, building activities progressively, holding and supporting at or near to the centre of gravity, graduated practices and consolidation are fundamentals which should be incorporated into all training programmes. Please refer to the new guidance given on 'supporting' which seeks to protect against issues of abuse.

(Note: Please refer to chapter 14 for exercise related information.)

14: HEALTH RELATED EXERCISE

14.1   Health related exercise has been defined as 'exercise of the appropriate type, intensity and duration to improve and/or maintain health' (Health Education Authority). When taught within the context of physical education, it can:

◆   enhance participation in a wide range of physical activities;

◆   provide a good basis of fitness for participating in these activities;

◆   encourage commitment to a physically active lifestyle;

◆   provide the knowledge and experience base for safe involvement.

14.2   Health focused exercise may be delivered through structured programmes of exercise, with a health related knowledge base including such activities as aerobics, weight training, circuit training and jogging. It may also be delivered by applying the same knowledge base to the physical education programmes of study (games, gymnastics, dance, athletics, swimming and outdoor and adventurous activities) identified within the National Curriculum. Whatever the chosen method, the procedures and principles identified below will serve to encourage safe and responsible involvement.

14.3   Development Considerations

a   Careful thought should be given to the frequency, intensity and duration of exercise, particularly with pre-pubescent children. Factors associated with physiological immaturity and spurts of rapid body growth place limits on training overload with specific reference to stamina and muscular strength. However, work designed to enhance and maintain flexibility may be undertaken on a more regular basis and may well form part of the warm up and introductory section of most physical education lessons.

b   Three sessions per week (with a maximum of five) of approximately 20 minutes duration will answer the stamina requirements of the majority of children and adults.

c   The Multistage Fitness Test, more commonly known as the Bleep Test, requires maximum effort if the test result is to be useful. Pupils with an injury or illness should not undertake the test. It is advisable to do some light jogging and gentle stretching before starting even though the test starts very slowly and there is, therefore, a gentle warm up as the test progresses. As accidents, some very serious, have happened to pupils whilst taking part in the bleep test care should be taken to ensure that the environment is safe and that no pupil suffers from any medical condition.

d   Maximal strength training using weights is not appropriate for the pre-pubescent child and may result in musculo-skeletal injury.

e   Where children have suffered from viral infection, including the common cold or high temperature illness, exercise should be avoided until they have recovered to the stage where they feel well in themselves.

f   Advice relating to diet will need to be sensitively handled and should take account of body image problems often experienced by adolescents.

14.4   Content and Methodology

a   Clothing should be appropriate and the chewing of sweets or gum should never be allowed during activity sessions.

b   The importance of a thorough warm up before vigorous exercise should be clearly understood by all participants and should never be omitted from sessions designed to promote health focused activity.

c   Teachers will need to be well informed about the appropriateness of certain activities. Research has indicated that some 'traditional' exercises, for example straight legged sit-ups, V-sits and burpees which are designed to improve suppleness and strength using the body's own resistance may be contra-indicated for both children and adults. Such exercises may expose the lower back or other major joints to unnecessary risk and suitable alternative exercises should be used. Standing side bends, full head circles, sit and reach with legs locked and hurdle stretches are further examples of potentially unsafe exercise.

d   Physiological testing should always be undertaken with caution, particularly when involving young people. Resulting data may not always prove reliable, whilst motivational elements may encourage some pupils to extend themselves beyond reasonable expectations.

e   Circuit training is a popular method for providing vigorous indoor training, with the emphasis on muscular stamina and strength. It is essential that the physical demands made are progressive over time and they should reflect individual proficiency. Efficient technique should be constantly reinforced and teachers should be aware of the dangers inherent in spasmodic participation.

f   A readily accessible record-keeping system should be used to inform on individual levels of participation, particularly when the exercises are associated with progressive resistance and repetition.

(Note: For advice on equipment, please refer to chapter 5.)

Further guidance:

J. Harris and J. Elbourn "Warming up and Cooling Down", Loughborough University Department of Physical Education.

R. Smith "Flexibility for Sport", Crowood Press.

Fitness Leader Network "Exercise Danger."

15: GAMES

15.1 General Conduct and Supervision

15.1.1   For general comments on duty of care requirements for both curricular and extra-curricular activities, refer to Chapter 1 'Physical Education and the Law'.

15.1.2   Safe practice requires attention to the following points:

a   All activities require appropriate clothing to be worn, the removal of jewellery and other potentially hazardous personal effects and the prevention of sweets or gum being chewed during active participation.

Formal Games

b   Before any competitive play can begin, pupils should be given instruction in the rules of the game or sport to be pursued, as well as training in the basic skills involved. The teacher should be capable of refereeing to the rules.

c   Training in all sports should follow a carefully planned and graduated progression that ensures all pupils master the necessary skills at any given level of competence before progressing to the next stage.

d   Team sizes, the length of a game and the size of pitch should be appropriate to the age, stamina and ability of the players.

e   A game is safer when preceded by an adequate warm up session.

Created and Modified Games

f   Care is taken to ensure that improvised rules, skills, tactics and the use of equipment give due attention to safety.

Clothing and Equipment

g   Pupils should know and understand what constitutes a safe standard of practice and accept responsibility for meeting that standard.

h   Equipment and clothing, including footwear and protective wear, should be appropriate to the activity in practice, teaching and match play situations and are checked before activity commences.

i   Regular arrangements should be made for the inspection, repair and maintenance of equipment.

j   Games posts should be stable and of acceptable dimensions and standards.

k   Corner flags should be tall enough and sufficiently pliable to avoid impact damage and possible impalement.

l   Faulty equipment should not be used. Such equipment should be suitably marked and removed from general accessibility until repair or replacement has been effected.

m   When using games posts as markers care should be taken to ensure that pupils are not at risk from collisions or impalement.

(Note: Please refer to chapter 5 for general advice on equipment, and chapter 7 for general advice on clothing and personal effects.)

Playing Areas

15.1.3   This advice applies to grass and synthetic pitches, tennis courts and playground areas. Special care needs to be taken to avoid hazards resulting from inclement weather conditions, such as frost, on any playing surface. All debris should be removed before play commences, by a mass scour of the playing area if necessary. Playgrounds should be free of accumulations of grit.

15.1.4   Pitches should be:

♦   large enough to allow safe play without overcrowding;

♦   reasonably level;

♦   free from dangerous objects, such as stones or glass.

Discipline

15.1.5   Good discipline will be evident where:

a   Participants are aware of the need for a controlled approach to the playing of any game.

b   Players respect all other participants, officials and their decisions.

c   Players conduct themselves within both the spirit and the wording of the rules of an activity.

d   Excessive and over zealous competitiveness, loss of temper, violent conduct, personal fouls and intemperate language are not tolerated. Such occurrences should always result in appropriate action by those in positions of responsibility.

Teacher/Adult Participation

15.1.6   There are implications for the way teachers or other adults involve themselves in games in which physical contact is a feature. Legal cases which have involved accident and injury to pupils caused by physical contact with adult participants have provided clear guidance in this regard. The value of teacher participation is recognised where it is used for the purposes of keeping the game moving or of demonstrating the skills of an activity.

15.1.7   In particular, teachers must bear in mind that:

a   Their participation must not impact on their effective control of a game or of the lesson as a whole.

b   Participation in body contact games will be restricted to demonstrating the skills of a game or keeping the game moving. Demonstrations that require physical contact will require that children are matched by size, strength, experience and ability.

c   They should not participate in a game involving young people as a member of one side against another. This advice applies to all games in which physical contact is present or can be reasonably foreseen to occur. The same principles should also be applied where hard missiles are projected, for example bowling a cricket ball.

d   At times, teachers will operate in the dual role of teacher and referee. Good practice demands that this dual role does not reduce their capability to discharge adequately the duty of care to those in their charge.

15.2   Combat Games

Please refer to the general section 15.1 on 'Conduct and Supervision' at the head of this chapter.

15.2.1   Combat games comprise those activities where there is an emphasis on overcoming an opponent, often through physical contact. They include boxing, fencing, judo, martial arts, self defence and wrestling.

Boxing

15.2.2   The physical education profession continues to be concerned to minimise the risk of accidents and injuries to pupils and to exercise the necessary control which will enable this objective to be realised.

15.2.3   Some medical authorities have expressed the view that blows to the head, if delivered with force and frequency, can cause damage to the brain as well as injury to the eyes, ears, mouth and hands.

15.2.4   Where, by choice, schools and colleges wish to practise boxing then it must be established that the participants and their parents readily accept the risks.

15.2.5   Initiatives which seek to reduce the incidence of injury in boxing such as the non-contact boxing skills award Kid Gloves Scheme of the Amateur Boxing Association of England Limited and the Standards Scheme operated by the Schools Amateur Boxing Association warrant consideration by interested schools.

15.2.6   The institution has the duty to make sure that coaching is provided by responsible and qualified personnel in a safe environment. Mandatory headgear and equipment must be used. All precautionary measures, as laid down by the Schools Amateur Boxing Association must be taken.

Fencing

15.2.7   Fencing may take the form of epee, foil or sabre. The weapons used are potentially lethal. It is imperative that the correct safety measures are taken and that the rules of the activities are strictly followed at all times.

Although the risk of injury cannot be totally eliminated the following points will help minimise this possibility:

a   At no time should pupils be allowed to fence unless qualified supervision is present.

Clothing and equipment

b   The correct clothing and the right equipment must be used.

c   Fencers should never cross swords unless wearing full protective clothing comprising mask, plastron, jacket and gloves.

Mask

d   The mask should be sound and complete with bib. Masks must not be worn if the mesh shows signs of rust, displaced wire or undue denting.

e   The binding around the mesh should be in good repair and the bib which protects the throat should be sound and strongly sewn to the mask.

f   The mask must fit properly, with an effective head clip.

Jacket

g   Jackets must be of the right size and of the type approved by the Amateur Fencing Association Schools' Fencing Union.

h   They must be kept in good repair, with no tears or holes through which a blade might penetrate.

i   Where jackets have side fastenings, right handed fencers must have right handed garments with the openings on the left hand side. The opposite will apply for left handed fencers.

j   Jackets should be long enough to cover the waistband of the trousers (the official requirement is 10 cm overlap when in the 'en-garde' position).

k   In epee, it is particularly important not to use a lightweight, zipped jacket. An epee jacket should be used, made of material weighing at least 400 grams per square metre.

l   Training jackets with one arm coverage must not be used in competition.

Plastron

m   A plastron must be worn for all fencing, whether for practice or for competition.

Breeches

n   Fencing breeches are a requirement for competitions. The side opening should correspond to that of the jacket, that is, being on the opposite side to that of the sword arm.

o   Long white socks should be worn to cover the legs below the breeches.

Gloves

p   Gloves must have a gauntlet to cover the cuff of the jacket sleeve and so protect the wrist and arm.

q   The gauntlet must extend halfway up the forearm to ensure a safe overlap.

Weapons

r   Weapons must be regularly checked. Any with blades that are broken, badly bent or rusting must never be used.

s   Blades which bend and stay bent show weakness and must be condemned.

t   Well used swords can develop sharp edges around the guard circumference and must not be used.

u   Points should be covered with purpose-made protective tips.

Floors

v   Floors should be non-slip and clean. They should be checked before use.

Control of space in competition

w   The space between pistes should be a minimum of 1.5 metres and there should be a clear run-off area at both ends for the safety of competitors and spectators.

x   Spectators should sit or stand in a defined area well away from the fencing.

Emergencies

y   A first aid kit should always be available, together with the address and telephone numbers of the nearest doctor and hospital.

Judo

15.2.8   Judo is a sport which involves vigorous physical activity where two participant opponents attempt to 'throw' and to 'ground' each other. It is carefully regulated by a code which should be understood and implemented at all times.

The following points will help to promote safe practice:

Competence to teach

a   The judo grade, shown by the colour of the belt, indicates the level of proficiency in the sport but does not measure teaching ability.

b   The minimum requirement for a person with qualified teacher status to teach judo in a school is 2nd kyu of the British Judo Association.

c   The minimum qualification for an instructor in further or higher education or the youth service is a 1st dan (black belt), together with the completion of a recognised course in teaching or coaching the sport.

d   A visiting coach should hold a 1st dan (black belt) and should have completed a recognised course in teaching or coaching the sport.

e   Most courses will have been organised by the British Judo Association; otherwise referral should be made to the LEA inspector or adviser for physical education, Sport England or other national responsible bodies for further scrutiny.

Mats

f   There is a range of mats designed specifically for judo.

g   Mats must be firm and dense enough to minimise the risk of injury.

h   There should be sufficient firmness to avoid excessive sinking and drag during movement on the mat.

i   If the floor below has no resilience (if it is made of concrete, for example) then the thickness of the mats may need to be increased.

j   The individual mats comprising a judo area must be secured in position and not allowed to separate. A canvas cover should not be used. A frame for the purpose must be carefully constructed to avoid any danger from being struck by participants in the activity.

k   The mat area should measure 5.5 metres x 5.5 metres or 7.0 metres x 5.0 metres.

l   Unless the mat area is exceptionally large, no edge should be within two metres of any wall, projection or open door.

Ceiling height

m   The ceiling height should be at least 3 metres.

Clothing

n   Participants must wear judo jackets, trousers and belts.

o   Judo suits should be hygienically stored and regularly laundered.

Class organisation

p   The number of participants should be limited according to the area of the mat available.

q   In free practice (randori) it is reasonable to permit 11 square metres (approximately 3.3 metres x 3.3 metres) for each competing pair. This area may be increased for formal class teaching when there may be fewer people on the mat.

r   Figures may need to be varied according to the physical size of participants.

s   No pair should practise throwing techniques while other pairs are practising groundwork skills.

t   In judo, both gender groups can be taught together. However, boys judo is physically stronger than that for girls and some different techniques are used. For these reasons, contests between the gender groups should not take place.

Martial Arts

15.2.9   Martial arts comprise a range of different activities, each of which is characterised by particular modes of physical combat which involve elements of attack and defence, usually one versus one. Aikido, Karate and Kendo are three examples of martial arts, though there are numerous other forms, many of which may be described as variations of karate. Some require the use of weapons, some the wearing of armour, for example mask, body padding and gauntlets. Some permit full bodily contact when striking or kicking.

15.2.10   The hazardous nature of the activities makes it essential that they should only take place under the specific codes which are laid down by the respective national governing bodies and taught by instructors who hold current recognised teaching or coaching awards issued by those bodies. Progression is a key feature of the codes, usually incorporating the dan or kyu system and it is important that each stage of development is fully mastered by each participant before moving to the next.

Competence to teach

15.2.11   Only those martial arts which have a national governing body to administer and control the activity should be considered for inclusion in the curriculum or as an extra-curricular activity in schools and colleges. Teachers or instructors should hold a current recognised qualification or licence from the national governing body which is appropriate to the level of activity to be undertaken. They should carry appropriate indemnity insurance which complements the third party liability cover in force within LEA or EA schools. **Qualification in one martial art activity is not transferable to another martial art activity.**

15.2.12   The key to safe practice is to have contacted Sport England or the other national sports councils in Northern Ireland, Wales and Scotland before any appointment is made, allied to contact with the LEA or EA adviser or inspector with responsibility for physical education, to ensure close scrutiny of qualifications. Only after this thorough process should an appointment be approved.

15.2.13   Aikido

a   A loose fitting tunic is essential and the correct trousers are preferable.

b   Mats should fulfil the requirements laid down for judo.

c   Aikido can be conducted as a mixed gender activity except in competition.

d   Instruction must ensure that no dangerous locks or movements are either taught or practised.

15.2.14   Karate

a   The two styles which are mostly practised are:

   ♦   Kihon (basic technique of single kicking or punching sequences) and

   ♦   Kata (stylised, controlled, predetermined movements).

b   Only British Karate Federation constituent members should be allowed to teach karate within or outside the curriculum and all licences should bear the heading of this body.

c   An instructor's style is acceptable if graded by an association that is a member of the British Karate Federation. There are few national courses or awards organised specifically for the teaching or coaching of the sport, so the grade of an applicant is the only assessment criterion. Particular close scrutiny of these grades is advised.

d   The minimum requirement for a person with qualified teacher status to teach karate in schools in 3rd kyu. An instructor in further education or the youth service should hold at least 1st kyu.

e   A karate jacket is essential and the correct trousers are preferable. Clothing should be stored hygienically and laundered regularly.

Class organisation

f   Free fighting (jy-yu-kumite) should only take place under the direct control of the instructor and should be authorised only when participants have sufficient mastery of the techniques of attack and defence.

g   Each individual requires 3 square metres of space for basic technique and 4 square metres for kata.

h   Supplementary weapons should not be permitted.

i   An instructor should use only minimum force when correcting a pupil's position or movement.

j   Karate classes may include both genders but free fighting between girls and boys is not acceptable.

15.2.15   Kendo

a   The British Kendo Association (BKA) is the national governing body for the sport. It provides training and awards certificates at various levels.

b   The minimum grade for teaching kendo in schools, colleges and the youth service is 1st dan.

Equipment

c   The wearing of armour (mask, body padding and gauntlets) is essential for free fighting. It should be stored where it can dry naturally and hygienically.

d   The shinai (dummy sword) should be of the traditional type; it should be kept in good condition and maintained regularly.

Class organisation

e   Laido is a type of kendo that uses swords; bokker (wooden swords), iaito (specially blunted swords) or real swords. Only iaito should be used in iaido practice.

f   Instructors should be BKA approved and hold the 1st dan grade in iaido. The minimum qualification is the BKA assistant coach award.

g   Permission from the BKA should be obtained before real swords can be used for demonstration or practice. It will only be given for advanced performers.

Self Defence

15.2.16   It is becoming increasingly common for self defence classes to be organised in curriculum time and extra curriculum time. As there is no governing body for the activity, it is particularly important to scrutinise closely the qualifications of potential coaches and to have the course syllabus content vetted and approved by the LEA inspector or adviser for physical education. No-one should be appointed who has not attended the equivalent of the National Coaching Foundation course 'Working with Children'.

Wrestling

15.2.17 Olympic style wrestling is the internationally agreed freestyle form of the sport used in the Olympic games. The rules are formulated so that two wrestlers can engage in hard physical combat without pain or injury. Submission, punching, kicking, high or heavy throws, or any move that will cause pain, are not allowed.

15.2.18 The Schoolboys' Olympic Wrestling Committee controls the sport for all boys of school age on behalf of the English Olympic Wrestling Association. It also organises instructor certificate courses for teachers.

Clothing

a   Swimming trunks are ideal for training; the wearing of shorts should be discouraged. Protective armpads and kneepads should be worn.

b   For competition there is a specially designed wrestling costume which is close-fitting and has short, tight-fitting legs. There should be no loose parts which can trap an opponent's fingers. Suitable support underwear should always be worn.

c   A warm jersey or tracksuit is essential, especially for competitions.

d   Pupils should wear light shoes with smooth soles and without metal lace tags or eyelets. The basketball-type boot with high sides is suitable but pupils likely to enter competitions should wear specially designed wrestling boots with soft sides.

Facilities

e   The wrestling area should measure at least 3 metres by 3 metres.

f   Mats should fulfil the requirements laid down by the British Amateur Wrestling Association and should be suitable for use with wrestling boots.

Safe wrestling

g   A wrestling class should never be left unattended or unsupervised.

h   Wrestlers in the under-17, under-15 and under-13 years age groups are not allowed to execute any form of full-nelson or half-nelson which involves holding the chin with the other hand. Pupils under 11 years of age are not allowed to use any form of nelson or bridging.

i   Moves which put pressure on the neck or twist it are not allowed.

j   During training, teachers should watch for any illegal or potentially dangerous move and take action to prevent it.

In competitions

k   Pupils must be matched for a contest according to weight and age. Age groups are in two-year divisions and weight groups are carefully arranged within these age divisions.

l   In most competitions and championships an international pairing is used which gives each competitor at least two contests.

        No competitor under 17 years should normally be expected to take part in more than four contests in one day.

m   In a contest, supervision should be by a competent referee on the mat and by a judge and a mat chairman at the edge of the mat. They should act to stop the match immediately if they consider that any move or hold is causing pain or injury, or is likely to do so.

15.3   Invasion Games

Please refer to the general section 15.1 on 'Conduct and Supervision' at the head of this chapter and sections 5.5 and 5.6 on environment and equipment earlier in the book.

15.3.1   Invasion games is the collective term used to describe games involving two teams where the aim is to attack and defend territory with the aim of scoring, for example a goal, a basket or a try. Association football, basketball, handball, hockey, lacrosse, netball and rugby fall within this category.

Association Football

15.3.2   The risk of injury is present in any physical contact sport but many footballing injuries can be prevented if sufficient attention is given to playing conditions, clothing and equipment and playing in the spirit of the game as well as to the rules.

        Whilst a reasonable level of robust play is an inevitable and appealing part of the game, responsible teachers will use intervention and advice to promote the safety of all players.

15.3.3.   Playing surfaces and environs

a   For general safety of pitches, refer to the first section of this chapter.

b   Halls with unprotected windows or low-level mirrors should never be used.

c   Outdoor pitches should be inspected for dangerous objects such as broken glass or cans. These should be removed before play begins.

d   Materials used for marking pitches should be non-corrosive and non-toxic. Creosote is not suitable; its use can be damaging to eyes.

Equipment

e   Goal posts should be rigid and stable, with secure fixtures at the junctions of the uprights and crossbar.

f   Portable goals should be stabilised during play to prevent them falling over when contacted.

g   Items such as cricket stumps or stakes should not be used as improvised goals; plastic marker cones are suitable for this.

Footwear

h   Footwear appropriate for the playing surface in use is important, to ensure control and to prevent slipping.

i   Studded boots should be worn on grass. Nylon and metal studs should conform to size regulations. Worn studs with sharp edges should not be allowed.

j   Players should, where possible, carry their boots to and from the grass playing area if this involves walking on hard surfaces.

k   Teachers using synthetic pitches on a regular basis should seek advice on appropriate footwear from the Football Association. There is a danger of stress injury from the use of such surfaces unless boots with suitable traction are worn.

l   The use of track suit trousers and long-sleeved shirts should be considered for play on artificial surfaces to prevent friction injuries when falls occur.

m   Shin pads should be worn by all players.

Conditioned games

n   There will be occasions when games will need to be conditioned or modified to promote safe participation, especially with beginners and with groups of varying abilities. In particular, the techniques of tackling and legitimate body contact should be very carefully introduced at the appropriate stages of maturity and development in the game.

Basketball

15.3.4   Basketball is a game played at speed in a confined space and on a hard surface, often on a court surrounded by obstacles. It must be played as a non-contact sport from the very early stages of learning.

15.3.5   The points which follow will help to promote safe practice.

Court Area

a   The court surface should be even, clean, dry and non-slip.

b   Any protruding obstruction closer than 1 metre to the side or end lines should be removed or padded, particularly if behind and in line with the backboards.

c   Gymnastics or other equipment stored around the perimeter of the activity space should not impinge into the 1 metre 'safe' area.

d   When posts and backboards are erected for out of doors use it is recommended that these are permanently fixed into the ground.

Equipment

e   British Standards specifications exist for all basketball (and mini-basketball) equipment. Schools purchasing new equipment should ensure that it meets the appropriate British Standard or British Standard European Norm.

f   Where possible, backboards should have an overhang of 1.25 metres on match courts and 0.75 metres on practice courts.

g   Backboards should be fitted by specialist contractors.

h   Regulation pattern rings and baskets should be used. The 'basket' should be no deeper than 0.4 metres and be of fine nylon or cord mesh.

i   Basketballs should not be over-inflated. They should be inspected regularly for splits or other damage, in which case they should be removed from use.

Personal clothing and effects

j   Specially designed basketball boots are desirable. Players should not wear just socks or stockings.

k   Vests and other clothing should be reasonably close fitting. Loose hair should be tied back.

Gaelic Games

15.3.6   Gaelic football, hurling and camogie are fast moving contact sports. Specific advice on safety matters in these games should be obtained from:

The Gaelic Athletic Association, Croke Park, Dublin 3, Eire.

Handball

15.3.7   Goals need to be secure and checked regularly.   The area behind the goal line and to the side of goals should be free of equipment and projections.

15.3.8   During game play the attacking areas may become slippery due to perspiration from players who have made contact with the ground. Vigilance to maintain a safe floor surface is important.

15.3.9   Balls should not be over-inflated and be 'soft' to the touch or non-sting.   When played outdoors a water resistant ball is essential.

Hockey

15.3.10   The development of plastic, sand-filled and water based all-weather surfaces has done much to improve the safety of hockey. Control is greater and accidental lifting of the ball is significantly reduced. Good coaching and facilities, firm control and care of equipment can reduce potential hazards to a minimum.

Facilities

a   For general safety of pitches, refer to the sections 15.1.3 and 15.1.4 at the beginning of this chapter.

b   Grass pitches should be cut and rolled regularly to ensure that the ball runs true.

c   Goals should be kept in good order and regularly painted. Lighter portable goals should be secured to prevent them tipping over.

d   Corner flags should be between 1.2 metres and 1.5 metres high and smoothly rounded at the tops.

Control of the game

e   The rules of the game should be known and observed. They are detailed and are regularly modified.

f   In teaching and coaching, particular emphasis should be placed on those rules concerning potentially dangerous play, the use of the stick, body interference and obstruction.

g   Great care and control must be exercised in teaching and pre-game preparation when more that one ball is in use.

h   Umpires should exercise firm control but not to the extent that the flow of play is unduly affected.

i   Loss of temper, dangerous play and deliberate body contact should be penalised. Umpiring at school level should always involve an element of education.

j   Good coaching will lead to good habits. Practising skills will enable players to develop good control of the stick and ball and will reduce the chance of dangerous play.

k   Goalkeepers should always intend to remain on their feet.

Equipment and clothing

l   Footwear should be checked regularly for safety and be appropriate to the playing surface.

m   The wearing of shin pads is recommended.

n   On plastic synthetic surfaces, players should be encouraged to wear protection to knees, elbows and hands.

o   Goalkeepers must always be well protected and equipped. For matchplay they should wear adequate pads and kickers, gauntlet gloves, body and abdominal armour. A full helmet and mask should be considered.

p   Sticks must be maintained in good condition and must never be used if they become dangerous through wear, roughness, splinters or other faults.

q   The wearing of personally designed mouthguards is recommended.

Use of playground

r   The game or practice should be modified and a softer "pudding" ball used.

Roller Hockey

Facilities

a   For general safety of playing areas, refer to the section 15.1.3 and 15.1.4 at the beginning of this chapter.

b   The playing area should be non-slip and a level surface of wood, asphalt, concrete or other suitable surface.

Equipment and clothing

c   Sticks should be made of wood or plastic.

d   Wheels on skates must roll freely.

e   Appropriate protective clothing should be worn.

f   Specific advice on safety should be obtained from the National Roller Hockey Association in Hindhead, Surrey.

Ice Hockey

15.3.11   Attention should be given to the environment, clothing and equipment. Specific advice on safety matters should be obtained from the British Ice Hockey Association.

Lacrosse

Men's lacrosse

15.3.12   Men's lacrosse is a fast moving contact sport. The extent of protective clothing needed in the senior game depends on the level to which the game is played. At junior level such equipment is not compulsory but all players are advised to wear as much of it as possible.

a   Gauntlets should always be worn and should be well padded on the outside of the hand and wrist. A rigid or padded cap is desirable to protect the head and face; it should be fitted with a mask and chin strap and be properly fastened on both sides.

b   The goalkeeper should wear chest, stomach and thigh pads and an abdominal protector.

c   The wearing of all protective gear is mandatory for the international game.

Women's lacrosse

d   Women's lacrosse is a non-contact sport. The rules are specifically designed to protect players, especially around the head.

e   Players should wear gloves. These must be close fitting, with no webbing or excessive padding. Boots with metal studs must not be worn.

f   The international rules require all players to wear mouth guards. Other protection such as nose guards may be worn but field players are not allowed to wear protective headgear or face masks.

g   Goalkeepers should wear leg pads, a body pad and a helmet, and have the option of wearing a throat protector.

Pop lacrosse

h   Pop lacrosse is an ideal introduction to the game. It incorporates the basic skills and strategies of the field game but has more flexible rules which can be adapted to suit the needs of the players involved, their equipment and the playing area.

i   There is no body or stick contact in the game.

Netball

15.3.13   Netball is a non-contact game. The official rules of the All England Netball Association (AENA) which prohibit physical contact and rough play should be enforced. A simplified version of the netball rules for those working with players under-11 years is available from the AENA. The following points will help to promote safe practice.

The playing area and court

a   The court surface should be level, firm and non-slip.

b   There should be a minimum of one metre of space between the outer lines of the court and any netting, wall, kerb edging or other obstruction.

c   The space between adjacent courts should be at least two metres.

d   Indoor courts should be free from furniture or other obstructions.

Posts and rings

e   Equipment should comply with AENA rules.

f   Posts should be stable; if they are freestanding, the bases should be of metal and weighted as necessary to ensure stability.

g   The bases should not project into the court area and should be checked regularly for rust.

Clothing and hygiene

h   Fingernails should be short and clothing should allow players sufficient freedom to run and jump with safety.

i   In competition, gloves may be worn only if they are needed for medical reasons.

j   Umpires must be satisfied that gloves do not present a hazard to other players.

Rugby Union and Rugby League

15.3.14   The strenuous and physical contact nature of rugby means that safety must be given paramount importance. Direct supervision by teachers with a good knowledge of the game is required. Refereeing must be firm in upholding the laws, especially those related to scrummaging and tackling.

Clothing and protection

a   Boots should be firm-fitting with good ankle support.

b   Studs should conform to the appropriate British Standard and should be examined regularly for wear. Badly worn studs can be very dangerous for the wearer and for other players.

c   Shin guards should be worn by all players. They should be made of light material and strapped in position.

d   Shoulder padding should conform to the requirements of the International Rugby Board and consist only of light, flexible protective padding.

e   The wearing of personally designed mouthguards is recommended as a valuable means of protection. Care should be taken to ensure that they fit properly.

f   Rings, earrings and other jewellery should not be worn.

Facilities and equipment

g   There should be no dangerous obstructions close to the perimeter of the playing field.

h   Fertilisers and mixtures used for pitch markings should be free from irritants to the skin or corrosives.

i   The base of the uprights of the goalposts should be padded. So should the base of any floodlit pylons close to the touchline.

j   Corner flags should be flexible, smooth and with rounded ends.

k   The playing area should be free from stones, glass, other sharp objects or excrement.

l   Telephone communication should be available near the pitch for all games.

m   Pitches should be accessible by ambulance.

Coaching

n   The teaching of good technique particularly in the skills of scrummaging, tackling and falling on the ball will improve playing standards and make the game safer.

o   Players must be progressively taught the fundamental skills before they play the game competitively.

p   Opposing players should not be widely disparate in age and experience.

q   The teacher should have knowledge of basic first aid and expired-air resuscitation sufficient to deal with immediate injuries. Attention is drawn to the need for an appropriate knowledge of assessing neck and spinal injuries.

r   Players who are known to have suffered concussion should not train or play until given clearance.

15.4   Net / Wall and Racket Games

Please refer to the general section 15.1 on the 'Conduct and Supervision of Games' at the head of this chapter and to section 5.5 on the environment earlier in the book.

15.4.1   Net/wall and racket games, comprising badminton, fives, racketball, real tennis, squash, table tennis, volleyball and the 'mini' or 'short' versions of the games are comparatively safe, though injuries do occur, including damage to the eyes.

Many points of safe practice are common or adaptable across the various games and reference to all the sections in this chapter is recommended, especially for the games that are not covered specifically.

Accidents to players arise from:

♦   being struck by a racket, ball or shuttlecock;

♦   tripping or slipping;

♦   wearing unsuitable, damaged or improperly fitted footwear;

♦   colliding with walls or equipment in the vicinity of the playing area.

Badminton

15.4.1   Badminton is a relatively safe game but attention is necessary to the points below.

The playing environment

a   The playing environment should be free from avoidable hazard or obstruction, including removed clothing.

Players and participants should be alerted to fixed obstacles, for example pillars or radiators. They should be shown appropriate procedures to manage safe play in the condition.

b   The floor should be level and free of dust.

c   The background and lighting should permit clear visibility of the shuttle in flight.

Equipment

d   All equipment should be in a satisfactory condition. Rackets with broken strings should not be used.

e   Lighter rackets and slow flight shuttlecocks may be the most suitable for younger pupils and beginners.

f   Posts should be properly positioned and secured.

g   Nets should be in good order, pulled tight and secured flush with the posts so that there are no holes or gaps through which the shuttlecock may pass.

h   Equipment not being used should be removed from the playing area.

i   Shuttles left lying on the floor constitute a hazard.

Players and participants should:

j   Have the rules and arrangements to be implemented clearly explained to them.

k   Take extra care that there is sufficient space to accommodate group practices on court.

l   Never attempt to hit the shuttle if there is a risk of colliding with or hitting another participant.

m   Avoid crossing another court when it is in use.

Squash and Racketball

15.4.3   Squash is played in a confined area and care is needed. In particular:

a   The use of protective eye-shields designed for squash is highly recommended owing to the potential for eye injuries in the game through being struck by the ball.

b   Players should never intentionally impede an opponent.

c   Always knock on the door and wait to be admitted to a squash court.

d   Racketball is a suitable game for young players and beginners as an introduction to squash and as a game in its own right.

Tennis

15.4.4   Tennis, in common with other racket games, is a relatively safe game but it is necessary that attention should be paid to the points which follow:

Equipment

a   Lighter and shorter rackets are more suitable for younger children, for beginners and in areas where space is limited.

b   The use of sponge or other types of soft ball are recommended for use with classes or groups in restricted areas.

Playing areas

c   Lines on the floor should be flat, level and securely fixed.

d   Shale or similar non-grass courts should be watered and rolled regularly to maintain a firm, level surface.

e   When outdoor courts have been made slippery by rain or frost, then play or practice must be delayed until the surface reverts to its more normal state.

f   Games nets and surrounding fencing should be kept in good order. In particular, games nets should not be used if they have holes that will allow a ball to pass through.

g   When posts are removed, caps should cover socket holes.

h   Portable equipment should be removed from the playing area after use.

i   Broken wire-surround fencing can be particularly hazardous.

Organisation

j   Class numbers and the positioning of players needs careful planning.

k   When players are practising serving, smashing or lobbing a routine drill is needed to prevent accidents. In service practice there should be a maximum of six players behind the baseline and feeders of the ball should never be positioned directly in front of players practising the smash. Players waiting their turn should be outside the court, well spaced and alert, so that they can move quickly, if necessary, to avoid being hit.

l   Group formations should be designed to ensure that players moving backwards do not collide with other players or with the wall or fencing or any other restricting barrier.

m   The attention of all participants should be drawn to potential hazards such as permanent columns or pillars.

n   A court may be used safely by two groups for rallying purposes, each group using half the available space across the court.

o   Sufficient space must be allowed for the stroke that is being played, including allowance for any follow-through. A stroke should not be played where a player considers that striking another player with either the racket or the ball is likely.

p   A stroke should be controlled, avoiding an exaggerated back-swing or follow-through.

q   Players should never:

- Attempt to play strokes outside their own playing area.

- Enter other courts to retrieve balls while play is in progress.

- Look round at a partner who is serving.

- Jump over, climb over or duck under the net when changing ends.

- Leave balls, rackets or clothing lying on the court or in the closely adjacent floor space.

Volleyball

15.4.5   Volleyball differs from the other net/wall racket games in that it is played by teams rather than individuals or pairs of players. The arms and hands are used to play the ball in place of a racket and falling and rolling are an integral part of the strategies employed.

15.4.6   Attention to the following points in addition to those that precede this section will help to promote safe practice in the playing of the game:

a   The floor should be clean, dry and free from splinters or grit and have an even surface.

b   Any protrusion from the walls or equipment not in use should be well clear of the court boundary and all players made aware of these.

c   All lights above the court should be guarded.

d   Weighted posts should be tied back to the wall and not allowed to stand freely. Tie wires should be positioned well above head height. Bases should not protrude into the court. Free standing or weighted posts are not permitted in competition.

e   Ropes used as nets should be made clearly visible to all participants. Practice nets are advised.

f   Rules of the game should be strictly enforced, especially those covering at the net which involves smashing and blocking and possible physical contact.

g   Skills appropriate to the level of competence and experience should be used in games whether full size or modified.

h   Trainer (softer) balls should be used by beginners, to prevent injury.

i   When players are practising the smash or serve, they should be well spaced out and the ball should be aimed at an empty part of the court.

j   During a match situation where only one ball is used it should be rolled back to the other half of the court. In practice situations where both halves of the court are in use, balls should not be returned to the other half other than by carrying them.

k   Practice balls should be placed in a receptacle when not in use. Balls left rolling around the floor constitute a hazard to safety.

l   Where space is limited the numbers of players should be adjusted.

m   The improvisation of equipment not designed for volleyball, such as badminton posts, should not be used.

15.5   Striking and Fielding Games

Please refer to the general section 15.1 on 'Conduct and Supervision' at the head of this chapter and to sections 5.5 and 5.6 on the environment earlier in the book.

15.5.1   These games are characterised by activities where the ball is bowled or delivered, struck by an implement then fielded and returned for the procedure to be repeated. Games are normally played by two teams each taking turns at batting and fielding. Cricket, rounders, softball, baseball and stoolball are the games most often played in schools.

Cricket

15.5.2   When played outside with a soft ball, cricket should present few difficulties to a teacher organising class activities or a game. Softball cricket is a nationally recognised game with rules that are simple to understand and implement. It represents a relatively safe way to introduce the skills of cricket.

15.5.3   Cricket played with a hard ball requires that the teacher will give attention to issues which include the following points.

Playing area

a   The wicket (batting and bowling area) should be reasonably true and the general playing surface should be reasonably even and free from obstructions.

b   A level synthetic wicket is an acceptable alternative to a grass wicket. It is preferable where a grass surface cannot be adequately maintained but it needs to be kept in a safe and playable condition. The surface should be securely fastened and any tears in the material must be repaired before use.

c   Wickets for games should be sited to provide a reasonable boundary and to avoid the risk of balls being hit on to paths, roadways or gardens.

Nets

d   Nets should be sited so that users of adjacent areas will not be at risk from balls hit from the nets. A roof net is desirable to contain balls within the appropriate net area.

e   Netting should be inspected frequently and kept in good repair. Those practising in nets should not be in danger from the activities in adjoining nets.

f   Net practice should be organised so that all participants are fully aware of acceptable routines and safe practice. Bowlers should bowl in a controlled order and ensure that batters are ready before each delivery.

g   Balls coming to rest in a net should only be collected after all the bowlers have delivered. Where a ball ends in an adjoining net, it may be retrieved by the batter reaching with the bat under the net. Alternatively, it may be retrieved by the bowlers in that net when all the balls have been delivered. Ball retrieval should only take place when it can be done safely.

h   Players preparing for or waiting their turns to bat should do so in a safe position.

Attire and equipment

i   On grass or artificial wickets, boots or shoes with a grip on the soles are suitable footwear.

j   Protective equipment for batters and wicket keepers should be worn as appropriate.

k   Bats, balls and protective equipment should be suited to either age, size, strength and ability of participants.

Match play

l The laws of the game of cricket should be observed and implemented as appropriate.

m Teachers should be familiar with advice from the English Cricket Board. In particular, the following statement is helpful to ensure that young players are not placed in dangerous fielding positions relative to the batter on strike:

'No fielder in under-15 years or under-14 years cricket games, excepting the wicketkeeper, shall be allowed to field nearer than 8 yards to the batter (measured from the middle stump) except behind the wicket on the off side. A fielder shall be allowed to move into the restricted area to make a catch or to field a ball provided that she/he was outside the area when the stroke was made. At under-13 years level, the distance shall be 11 yards. If necessary, umpires and teachers will, under local rules, arrange for markers to be used in determining the distances referred to above. Play will not proceed with participants in unsafe positions.'

Rounders, Softball, Baseball and Stoolball

15.5.4 The games have similarities and the points below should be applied as appropriate.

a Younger players should be introduced to the games using balls which are softer and/or larger to reduce the dangers from catching or fielding balls which may cause injury before good co-ordination has been developed.

b The rounders stick should always be carried when running between bases. To throw it away after striking the ball and beginning the run to first base is hazardous.

c Players should watch the ball at all times.

d No ball should be pitched before all the fielders and the batter are entirely prepared and ready.

e Catching mitts should be worn as necessary for softball and baseball.

15.6   Target and Other Games

Please refer to the general section 15.1 on 'Conduct and Supervision' at the head of this chapter and to sections 5.5 and 5.6 on the environment and equipment earlier in the book.

15.6.1   Target games include archery and golf; 'other games' are classified here as relay races, tag games, and weight lifting. Games not specifically addressed will be able to draw from the points covered in the chapter to enable safe practice to be applied.

Archery

15.6.2   School archery should always be organised and supervised by a competent and qualified teacher. Archers must appreciate that an arrow can be lethal.

Equipment and facilities

a   For initial teaching, bows with a draw of 8 kilograms or 11 kilograms may prove most suitable, especially for younger or smaller pupils.

b   Target supports should be padded to reduce the risk of a rebound or ricochet. The use of drawing pins or other similar objects for attaching additional targets to the boss should be forbidden.

c   Beginners should use arrows of 72 centimetres in length, of which at least 2 centimetres should be seen to project in front of the arrow rest. Taller pupils may require arrows of 76 centimetres, when at least 4 centimetres (but no more than 12 centimetres) should project in front of the arrow rest. **Arrows which are too short are dangerous.**

d   Bracers should be worn during shooting. These keep the sleeves out of the way of strings and provide some measure of arm protection in the event of a bad shot.

e   Tabs are advisable in order to perform a clean loose of the arrow and to protect the shooting fingers.

f   Loose clothing may foul the string and should not be worn. Neckties should be removed.

Outside facilities

g   Where there is no bank or slope behind the targets, the range should be limited to 135 metres and the targets should be positioned inside this area with a least 45 metres clear behind them.

h   Where there is a bank or slope of adequate height behind the target, the clear area may be reduced but care must be taken to ensure that this area affords adequate protection to anyone moving behind the target.

i   The width of the range should be such that no target is positioned less that 27 metres from public road, rights of way or any areas over which the teacher has no control.

j   A shooting line should be clearly marked and a waiting line (behind which those who are not actually shooting should wait) should be positioned at least 4.5 metres behind it. These lines should remain fixed, while targets should be moved as appropriate.

k   The whole area of the range should be clearly marked and roped off wherever necessary.

l   The range should be so placed that it does not lie on the route to other playing areas and is away from buildings, walls, hedges or fences where there may be a risk of a person emerging without warning.

m   The grass should be cut short and there should be no bushes or undergrowth within the range, so that stray arrows fall safely and can be easily seen and retrieved.

n   The layout of an archery field according to the rules of the Grand National Archery Society may be obtained from that body.

Indoor facilities

o   The premises must be large enough for shooting at ranges of not less than 9 metres.

p   A suitable protective device such as a fine mesh nylon net at least 3.5 metres in height and extending the full width of the hall (or at least 6 metres on either side of the target) should be provided behind the target to act as a backdrop.

q   Entrance doors to the hall in which archery takes place should be kept locked with the key on the inside throughout the duration of the archery class.

r   Removable shutters should be provided to cover all glass panes in any doors which may be in the target area.

15.6.3   Organisation

a   The number of pupils per teacher or instructor should not exceed twelve, with no more than four pupils at a target at any one time.

b   Targets should be at least 3.5 metres apart and archers should stand at least 1.5 metres apart when on the shooting line.

c   In outdoor archery, shooting must not take place when the wind strength is such that arrows may be dangerously deflected. Shooting directly into the wind should be avoided.

d   Archery should be practised only on the archery range. Bows should be loaded only on a signal from the person in charge.

e   Archers must have their bows pointing at the target as soon as loading begins and must be in position on the shooting line.

f   A drawn bow, whether loaded or unloaded, must never be pointed at anyone.

g   Shooting should only start on a signal from the teacher or instructor.

h   The teacher or instructor is responsible for making sure that the target area and range are clear before shooting begins.

i   Only when all the archers have completed their shooting should the signal be given to advance to the target to retrieve the arrows. Archers should walk forwards with their eyes down to detect any arrows which may have fallen short.

j   All archers should understand the meaning of the command 'fast'. When this word is shouted, they must hold onto the string and lower the bow without shooting.

k   All archers should understand and act instantly on the command 'come down' which is used when a dangerous situation is developing. It means that the archer should hold onto the string, lower the bow, let it down to the undrawn position and remove the arrow from the bow.

l   When arrows are being withdrawn from the target, the archers and others should stand at the side of the target so that there is no possibility of the withdrawer or anyone else being struck as the arrow is pulled out.

m   Spectators should remain at least 4.5 metres behind the shooting line.

Golf

15.6.4   Golf requires discipline and great care and should ideally take place on a golf course or range. Where practice takes place elsewhere, even greater care should be taken. Any pupil intending to swing a club or drive a ball must have absolute regard for the presence of others in the vicinity of their actions.

IN ALL ASPECTS OF GOLF, ESPECIALLY WITH BEGINNERS, IT IS SAFER TO DEVELOP CONTROLLED POWER RATHER THAN WILD LUNGING, EXPLOSIVE FORCE.

a   For indoor lessons without a net, airflow plastic balls must be used.

Indoor lessons using hard golf balls

b   A special golf net with a fine mesh should be used. The net should be a least 2.5 metres high and should hang clear of any supports.

c   Suitable protective mats should always be used on the floor.

d   Players should be at least 3 metres apart at all times when handling clubs. During demonstrations this distance should be maintained between the demonstrator and the nearest pupil.

e   Players driving at a net should remain strictly in line.

f   No player should advance to collect balls or for any other purpose until all the balls have been struck by the other players. Balls should be retrieved only on a given signal.

g   If players are using both sides of the net at the same time, only airflow balls should be used.

h   The mesh of the net should be examined regularly for damage.

i   Players should not walk up to each other during practice.

Outdoor lessons using hard golf balls

j   Acceptable layouts for practising strokes or playing shots are:

   ♦   a straight line of players facing in one direction;

   ♦   two straight lines at least 6 metres apart and facing away from each other;

   ♦   a semi-circle facing outwards.

k   Players need to be careful and to accept responsibility for ensuring that the immediate space in front, around and behind them is clear of any person before they swing a golf club.

l   No player should play a shot of any kind if anyone is in the line of flight and might conceivably be hit.

m   No player should advance into the target area until all the balls have been hit. All balls should be collected at the same time on a given signal.

n   No player should practise out of a sand bunker if another player is near the line of flight.

Playing on golf courses

o   All players should learn and apply the rules and etiquette of golf.

p   There have been awkward incidents arising out of pupils using poorly maintained kit. Pupils need to be educated in the matter of maintaining all their kit in good condition and to check it regularly. Such things as slippery, worn grips on club handles and the use of very badly cut golf balls can contribute to lost control of shots with ensuing danger to others on the course.

Relay Races and Tag Games

15.6.5   These will often form a part of games lessons, particularly in the primary school. They are reasonably straightforward to organise, children enjoy them and they promote active participation. There is usually an element of competition involved and care needs to be taken by the teacher to ensure that:

a   The tasks set are reasonable and take account of the range of ability and experience of all the class.

b   The competitive element is kept in perspective, with successful completion of a task and 'doing it well' as a pair or a team being of importance and meriting praise.

c   Practice takes place in a non-competitive context so that the pupils are well versed in the skills involved before these are employed in a relay race or tag game.

d   The pupils are clear when racing or competition is to take place and the formations used reflect this, for example equal teams in a file.

e   Skills which are highly challenging and where it is foreseeable that children might fall, such as when running backwards or carrying a partner, should not be used for races.

f   The surface on which relay races and tag games take place is conducive to safe practice. Concrete, for example, would not be suitable.

g   Pupils share in the assessment and management of the risks involved, so that their awareness of safe practice is raised and their knowledge is applied in the activities.

h   The use of equipment is appropriate to its design and function.

i   Racing to vertical walls is not allowed as this can cause wrist injuries. It is appropriate instead to race to a line marked on the floor which is well clear of any obstruction.

j   Footwear and floor surface provide good traction.

Weightlifting

15.6.6   Weightlifting is fundamentally a test of strength and must not be confused with weight training which is concerned with the development of muscular strength and endurance in the pursuit of fitness. Weightlifting includes the two Olympic lifts, together with strength tests and other competitive work with barbells and dumbbells. Mature participants work towards their threshold of strength in the activities.

15.6.7   The sport can be hazardous for adolescent pupils where there is a particular danger of injuries to joints, including those of the spine. It must therefore be taught only by teachers who are recognised as competent. The minimum requirement for teaching weightlifting in schools is a teaching or coaching award from the British Amateur Weight Lifters' Association (BAWLA).

15.6.8   Overuse injury in young people is a very real problem. Overloading must be avoided and competitive lifting should be delayed until skeletal growth is complete. Weightlifting competitions for young adults should not involve the lifting of more than the individual's own body weight. Any competition should preferably be judged on the style of lift rather than on the sheer weight lifted.

15.6.9   Class organisation should be similar to that for weight training (see section 1) with free weights but there is a greater need to work in groups with trained and alert spotters. The emphasis in the early stages should be on skill and fitness.

16: GYMNASTICS & TRAMPOLINING

GYMNASTICS

16.1 Forms of Gymnastics

16.1.1   The essence of all gymnastics is the development of skilled movement under control. Over time a variety of different forms of gymnastics have been developed. Fundamentally they may be divided into two groups with different emphases.

16.1.2   The first group consists largely of informal activities in which tasks are set to which varied individual responses are made and for which 'support' is not generally applicable. The aim is to develop and refine a range of controlled movements in fundamental areas of skill which may be performed singly, in combination and in sequence, using the floor and apparatus.

16.1.3   The second group involves a more formal and prescriptive approach and comprises those forms recognised in competition. Olympic, rhythmic and acrobatic gymnastics are included. The provision of support in the initial stages of some activities is essential. *(Note: please refer to chapter 3, section 3.11 for advice on supporting.)*

16.1.4   The two groups are not mutually exclusive but the first group will generally be the approach which is used in the curriculum as being appropriate to all pupils. The more formal system will be better suited to those pupils with the range of skills and abilities that will enable them to benefit by choice from these more prescriptive activities and from engaging in formal competition.

16.2 Teaching Styles

16.2.1   A range of teaching styles will be evident in the effective teaching of gymnastics but there are two contrasting methods with implications for safety which need to be considered . These are the indirect and the direct approaches.

The indirect approach

16.2.2   The indirect approach serves the needs and abilities of all pupils in gymnastics and allows them to interpret in their own way the tasks that have been set. The pattern of movement by an individual pupil resulting from this method is not readily predictable since this will change as the pupil sets out to develop or refine a previously performed action. This explains why 'support' is not generally applicable.

16.2.3 When appropriate, the teacher may give active encouragement and help to an individual pupil, including physically supporting where the movement has become precise and predictable in its every aspect of performance. The teacher and pupil should discuss the techniques of the movement concerned, ensuring that the mechanics are understood. Any interesting solutions to the tasks set should be demonstrated to the entire class and analysed through discussion. This will widen the pupils awareness and understanding of movement.

16.2.4 The self-awareness promoted by individual work should be complemented by co-operative activities which encourage selflessness and consideration for others.

The direct approach

16.2.5 The direct approach covers the formal teaching and coaching of specific actions within the recognised disciplines of competitive gymnastics, such as vault, parallel bars or beam.

16.2.6 This approach should only be used by the teacher or coach with a qualification recognised by the LEA or national governing body and with appropriate teaching experience. Attendance at appropriate in-service training courses will be necessary from time to time to reinforce knowledge and to learn about new developments.

16.2.7 The teacher or coach must fully understand the mechanics of every taught action and the progressions which lead up to it. They must also be aware of the symptoms of physiological and psychological fatigue in a performer and be able to assess the mental and physical readiness of a pupil for each new skill that is taught.

16.2.8 With the predictable pattern of movement, the teacher must be ready to provide support or to stand by a performer, especially in the early stages of the action being learned. Pupils should be taught to support other pupils but only when the teacher is confident of their maturity and ability to do so in a safe manner.

16.2.9 The performing pupil must be made aware when support which has been provided previously is to be withdrawn and must agree to its withdrawal.

16.2.10 More challenging activities require the utmost care. An example is provided by vigorous swinging or circling movements, which can result in premature release from the apparatus, and for which physical support is essential in the learning stages.

16.2.11 Overhead rigs, support belts and other specialised aids should be used only by teachers trained in their use or by competent pupils who have been taught the techniques and who work under the direction of an experienced teacher or coach.

16.3   The Learning of Skills

16.3.1   Good communication is essential between the teacher or coach and the pupil in the learning of skills, together with a clear understanding of their respective responsibilities.

16.3.2   A pupil learning a new skill should have the necessary strength, flexibility and body awareness, and should have passed through the progressive stages leading up to that new skill. For different pupils, the rate at which they achieve success in the progressive stages will vary; it is essential that each stage should be successfully accomplished by an individual pupil before the successive stage is introduced, regardless of the time taken.

16.3.3   Skills learned earlier may have to be re-learned after periods of inactivity such as holidays. Re-learning and consolidation are particularly important at times of significant physiological change which occur during adolescence and with spurts in growth. The reintroduction to gymnastics of a pupil following prolonged absence through illness needs very careful attention.

16.4   Pupil Safety

Discipline

a   Firm discipline and the implementation of established routines contribute to safe practice.

b   Sweets or gum should never be chewed during a physical education lesson.

Warm up

c   A suitably graded warm-up should precede the main part of every lesson.

Clothing and Personal Effects

d   Clothing should allow for unrestricted movement without being loose.

e   Extra clothing (e.g. tracksuits) may be worn for warming-up.

f   All jewellery and other personal effects such as watches should be removed and long hair should be tied back.

g   Handguards may be worn when gripping apparatus, particularly bars.

h   On certain pieces of apparatus, such as the parallel bars or pommelled horse, moderate amounts of soft chalk (magnesium carbonate) should be used to provide a safe grip.

Footwear

i   Gymnastics should be performed with bare feet, or in purpose-designed gymnastics footwear or gym shoes. For work that involves frequent high momentum landings or rope climbing, footwear is kinder to the feet.

j   Footwear should be pliant and close fitting, to enable 'feel' for the apparatus and with enough serrations (or an equivalent feature) on the sole to give good traction. Training shoes with hard plastic soles are inflexible, give poor grip and should not be worn.

'Pirates' and Chasing Games on Apparatus

k   'Pirates' and other competitive chasing games using apparatus as obstacles are dangerous and should **never** be played.

High Flight Rotational Skills

l   Vaults using a box or high table which involve rotation passing through handstand should not be attempted by novices. Pupils should be trained to land under control on both feet in completing all vaults and not to pitch into a forward roll. Physical support must be able to cope with any problems arising from under or over rotation during the learning stages.

(Note: Further advice is contained in chapter 5, including the use of mats.)

TRAMPOLINING

16.5   Introduction

16.5.1   Trampolining is closely allied to gymnastics and much of the advice on safety in the previous section is pertinent. The activity offers an exciting experience to children of all abilities. Whilst challenging the more able, it can under well controlled circumstances, stimulate movement in disabled or mentally handicapped pupils. Whatever the purpose served, great care must be taken to ensure the safety and well being of all participants. Both trampolines and their smaller counterpart, trampettes, can produce serious accidents. Each LEA, EA or self governing school will formulate its own regulations on the use of this rebound equipment.

16.5.2   It is important to remember that any trampolining skill produces risk when the performer fails to generate the right momentum and body positions appropriate to the stunt. 'Awareness' and 'control' are key words.

16.5.3   Teachers must accept that trampolining is constantly modifying its systems in the light of experience. They should therefore be ready to attend in-service training which presents these new developments. Innovation in supporting and the use of safety mattresses are two such areas which contribute to safer working environments. Additionally there are new developments in trampoline design which can more easily facilitate the transportation of the equipment around the gymnasium and into the store room.

16.6   The Teacher

16.6.1   All teachers involved with the teaching of trampolining should be knowledgeable on the basic skills and techniques which are employed and endeavour to pass on to pupils a clear understanding of the mechanics of the moves which are taught. Even a skill as seemingly straightforward as basic vertical jumping feet to feet has a number of fundamental requirements to be learned so that full control and remaining at the centre spot of the bed may be successfully achieved.

16.6.2   It is good practice for the teacher to constantly monitor and check the unfolding and folding of trampolines prior to and after use. The procedures employed should be taught and consistently applied, so that all concerned are fully conversant with the requirements.

16.6.3   For advanced trampolining, teachers and coaches should hold the appropriate award of the British Trampoline Federation.

16.7   Class Organisation

16.7.1   The trampoline in use should always be under the supervision of the teacher. It should be positioned so as to minimise the risk of pupils being distracted as they perform, since concentration is essential.

16.7.2   An experienced teacher should be able to supervise several trampolines at the same time, though it is safer to regard such a multiple arrangement as a clinic where performers do not venture into new skills but practise to consolidate and refine those skills which they can confidently perform. The exception to this would be where a pupil presents a request to the teacher to explore new work but strictly under the direct supervision of the teacher. The requirements are:

a   If the clinic includes raw novices, they should work under the direct supervision of the teacher.

b   Those working on other trampolines must only be revising and consolidating those skills in which they have already demonstrated reliable safe performance to the teacher. Their individual programmes must have the approval of the teacher. These trampolines can only operate where there are sufficient capable spotters in attendance.

c   It is safer if a senior and knowledgeable pupil regulates the flow of teacher prescribed work on any trampoline, apart from the one where the teacher is in direct attendance.

d   Any performer who wishes to attempt any new movement in one of these multi- trampoline sessions must work on the trampoline under the direct supervision of the teacher.

16.8   Pupil Participation

16.8.1   Ensure that all pupils are involved with assembling and folding the trampoline, as described in chapter 5 of this book, and that they understand every aspect of this particular process which is so vital to their safety.

16.8.2   When children are introduced to the trampoline it is advisable, for the first few lessons, to let them wear trainers or gym shoes to give some extra protection against the wheels when erecting or folding the trampoline. This is particularly important when children, for the very first time, lift the wheels clear of the frame. Teachers should be sure that the moment of wheel extraction is well understood by the pupils. If there is any doubt teachers should supervise this activity very closely.

16.8.3   Pupils should mount the trampoline by stepping on to the frame and then the bed, not the springs or cables. Dismounting should be the reverse of this procedure. No-one should jump from the trampoline bed directly on to the floor.

16.8.4   On a single trampoline, there should usually be a minimum of four spotters, who should be in a standing position on the floor at each side and each end of the trampoline frame. They should be instructed on their role, understand the requirements of standing in a ready position, watch the performer and not be distracted, and be physically capable of performing their tasks. Some adjustment to this arrangement is possible where safety mattresses are used to make bridging cover between two trampolines placed together end to end, or where free standing spotting platforms with safety mattresses are attached to the ends of the frame.

16.8.5   The use of a specialist safety throw-in mat, in circumstances where it will assist a performer with the safe learning of a skill, may be under taken by mature and capable spotters who have been taught the necessary techniques and timing.

16.8.6   **Performance**

a   When trampolining long sleeved tops are advisable to prevent friction burns to the forearms when performing activities such as front drops.

b   When bouncing, footwear with soft soles is appropriate provided that it gives sufficient traction. Socks which do not slip are a possible alternative. Bare feet presents a risk of injuries to the toes caused by the gaps in the webbing of the bed and should not be allowed.

c   No performance should begin until spotters are in position and ready.

d   Pupils should jump in a position as near to the centre of the bed as possible, at a height no greater than that at which they can retain complete control of their height and flight.

e   If loss of control is experienced, the pupil jumping should bend the knees and stop at the next contact of the feet with the bed. Jumping should recommence at the centre spot, following an assessment and understanding of why control was lost.

f   Beginners should jump for only short periods of around 30 seconds. The jumping time can be gradually extended but should stop as soon as the pupil begins to tire or to lose concentration.

g   The basic skills should be learned and consolidated separately before sequences and more complex skills are introduced. Individual check-off charts should be used to record progress.

h   Gradual 'step by step' progression over time should be fostered by the teacher, with the emphasis on basic skills, correct techniques and quality. The teacher will need to dissuade any pupil who inclines to over rapid progress and risk taking.

i   Normally only one pupil should be allowed on the trampoline at a time.

j   'Tag-on' games, in which performers in turn add a movement to the sequence routine of the previous performance, are not recommended. They may induce a performer to work beyond his/her ability.

k 'Peer group pressure' whereby spotters vocally encourage a performer to work beyond his/her level of competence must never be permitted.

l At the first signs of fatigue, shown by a deterioration in the quality of performance, loss of concentration or persistent travel, a performer should stop jumping and rest. Teachers must be constantly alert to these symptoms.

m In competitions or displays, only those movements which have been successfully practised and consolidated should be performed. No-one should attempt new records, such as the number of repetitions of a given movement.

n Support for movements that require it must always be available to the performer until both the teacher and the performer are confident that the performer is safe enough to bounce 'solo'.

High Flight Rotational Skills

o These can be dangerous and novices should never be required or allowed to attempt them.

16.9 Supporting Aids

16.9.1 Overhead rigs, safety mattresses, 'throw in' mattresses, support harnesses and manual support are all recognised aids for the coaching of trampolining. A safety mattress may be positioned horizontally at each end of the trampoline and a throw-in mattress can be pushed onto the bed between the performer and the bed during the learning of new movements. Multi-somersaulting and combined rotation and twisting movements should be learned using an overhead support rig.

16.9.2 Bed-level platforms should be used by coaches for direct supervision so that they can intervene with physical support when necessary.

16.10 Trampette Activities

a The use of a standard single trampette is recommended. Double trampettes are more suitable for use in specialist rebound clubs with advanced performers.

b Footwear should be similar to that provided for trampolining (see previous section).

Beginners

c   The trampette should not be used as part of any apparatus combination until adequate training has been given in the basic techniques of jumping and landing from it.

d   Beginners should start with slow, controlled practice runs of just a few paces.

e   The teacher should give close attention to the learning of basic trampette skills with beginners, while maintaining observation and control of the whole class.

Beyond Basic Jumping

f   Each stage in turn should be learned and well consolidated before progressing to the next.

g   In prescribed activities, support should be appropriate to the skill being practised. Support may properly be provided by trained pupils if the class is working well. The supporter should check pupils as they land, and should prevent them from falling backwards or pitching forwards.

High Flight Rotational Skills

h   These can be dangerous and novices should never be required or allowed to attempt them. The same applies to forward rolls on landings; inexperienced pupils should be trained and supported so that they always make a controlled, two footed landing.

Teaching Somersaults

i   Somersaults should not be taught unless the teacher is fully aware of the bio-mechanics, the techniques and the dangers of somersaulting movements.

j   There must be appropriate support at every stage.

k   The teacher must beware of over-rotation which is most often caused by:

♦   pupils maintaining a position such as the tuck or pike for too long during flight;

♦   with forward somersaults, the hips being displaced too far back at the point of take-off, so that the moment of force generated is then too great and subsequent rotation when the body is tucked or piked is too rapid.

l   Beginners should focus initially on perfecting a good take-off technique. Where there is the slightest suspicion of over-rotation, the teacher or supporter(s) must stand by ready to check and steady the landing.

m   Novices must never perform a forward roll immediately following a front somersault as to do this safely requires considerable control and understanding. They should always land in a standing position on two feet with the teacher/coach standing by.

n   The supporter must do everything possible to prevent a performer landing on the head or neck.

o   Learners should not attempt unsupported somersaults until they have demonstrated complete confidence and mastery with direct support and then attendant (shadow) support.

(Note: Please refer also to chapter 5 for information on trampoline equipment).

17: OUTDOOR AND ADVENTUROUS ACTIVITIES

17.1   General Advice

17.1.1   The range of outdoor adventure activities and participation levels of young people is considerable. The inclusion of this area of experience in the national curriculum recognises the potential contribution that it can make to the educational development of young people, with the emphasis on adventure and 'real' experiences in the outdoors. Latent talents and interests are fostered, personal abilities and limitations become evident, with independence and teamwork promoted in the context of a respect and concern for the environment in which the activities take place.

17.1.2   The spirit of adventure and excitement must at all times be complemented by concern for the well-being and safety of participants. Planning and progression are very important elements, as is a recognition of the many variable factors which will impact on a particular venture or activity. It is the adverse combination of these factors which can sometimes result in serious accidents.

17.1.3   Good planning is central to safe practice out of doors. This presumes good leadership. LEA's and governors should have a policy which sets out the competence required of teachers who lead adventurous activities. This should refer to the possession of relevant qualifications, recognised training or proven experience in the field (refer to chapter 2.1 on Qualifications for Teaching Physical Education).

17.1.4   Outdoor and adventurous activities will require competent and experienced teacher-leaders to exercise personal judgment in taking and implementing decisions which are necessary for the safety and well being of the pupils involved.

17.1.5   Helpful guidance is provided in the DfEE publication 'Health and Safety of Pupils on Educational Visits', produced in 1998.

Competent Leadership

17.1.6   Sound judgements are most likely to be made when the person in charge has:

a   An understanding of the 'duty of care' as required of him/her under the law, to apply twenty four hours a day for the duration of the educational visit or venture.

b   Relevant qualifications and skills (including organisational skills).

c First hand knowledge or experience of the intended location.

d Experience of working with pupils in the age range of those involved with the venture.

e Proven qualities of leadership and responsibility which are evident from other aspects of their work.

f The necessary physical and mental fitness to undertake the proposed venture without undue stress.

g A first aid qualification.

Planning, Administration and Organisation

17.1.7 Planning must be thorough, with nothing that is foreseeable left to chance. In particular:

a Sufficient time should be allowed for the implementation of effective and efficient planning. Good practice suggests that a written check list and timescale to cover all aspects of the venture should be established as early as possible. Items for consideration will include a preliminary visit to the site, written advice (including letters and consent forms to parents), meetings, travel, meals, accommodation, activities, equipment and clothing, instruction, responsibilities and supervision (including checks on the qualifications and experience of personnel), finance, insurance, first aid, individual needs (dietary, educational and medical), contingency arrangements and emergency procedures.

b The headteacher, governing body and LEA, as appropriate, should be satisfied that the arrangements are acceptable to the insurers before giving approval to the venture.

c The teacher leader should consider all appropriate written advice from the local authority, the school or any other authoritative source and seek guidance from senior colleagues and professionals with expertise.

d A careful check should be made to ensure that all adults who will have access to pupils during the visit are suitable persons so to do.

e The number of responsible adults required to accompany a party venture will normally be a minimum of two, including the teacher leader. The size and composition of the party, the environment and the nature of the activities are factors in determining the precise number of responsible adults needed.

f Mixed parties on day and residential visits will normally require at least one responsible adult of each sex, including the teacher leader.

g   There will be occasions when working in school grounds and easily managed locations, or with small parties of more mature young people, where only one teacher may need to accompany the pupils.

h   It is accepted practice for Duke of Edinburgh Award Scheme pupils who are properly trained to undertake expeditions with remote supervision.

i   When external agents or tour operators are used, these should be reputable, capable of meeting the school's 'duty of care' requirements and have appropriate financial bonding arrangements with a body recognised by the Department of Trade and Industry.

j   Organised party ventures must conform to relevant European Community directives.

k   Duplicate information should be placed with a named representative of the senior management of a school, who will be the point of contact and communication in cases of emergency.

l   Parents and pupils should be informed of the arrangements and requirements for the visit so that the grouping of participants, the activities, duties and responsibilities are known to all concerned. This should be communicated in writing and additionally through meetings arranged for the purpose.

Participants

17.1.8   The safety and well being of the participants are paramount and care should be taken to ensure that all appropriate measures are taken.

a   Involvement must always be within the threshold levels of individual capability, taking account of all environmental and personal factors.

b   Particular care should be taken to ensure that late changes in party composition are safe and realistic.

c   Group activities must meet the varying abilities of group members and particularly the needs of the least able or least experienced participants. It is essential that those in leadership roles have a good knowledge of the individuals for whom they will be taking responsibility.

d   Young people should be exposed to challenges within their compass.

e	Parents' written consent for their child to participate in the activities should be obtained. They should be advised also on insurance to cover such aspects as health, loss of belongings and travel.

f	Arrangements for care in cases of accident, illness or inability to participate in the planned programme will be necessary.

g	A schedule for the supervision of pupils should be pre-determined.

h	Pupils should demonstrate sufficient skill, experience and maturity under supervision before undertaking more independent activities. Adequate safeguards will be necessary for such ventures. Parental approval is vital.

i	Pupils should be trained in relevant survival techniques.

Activities and Environment

17.1.9	The activities and their settings are fundamental to the success or otherwise of any venture. Those activities which take place away from the main base and particularly in wild or remote areas, will need special consideration.

a	The leader should be experienced in the activities that s/he will be leading and ensure that any other responsible persons involved should be fully aware of their duties and be appropriately experienced for their respective roles.

b	A code of conduct governing pupil behaviour, rules and discipline should be agreed with parents and pupils prior to the venture (refer to Appendix 6).

c	A sufficient number of qualified instructors should be available to allow appropriate instructor to pupil ratios for the safe implementation all of the planned activities. Reference should be made to relevant guidelines from LEA's or national governing bodies. Ratios may need to be improved, perhaps significantly, where pupils with special education needs or behavioural difficulties are participating, depending on such factors as previous experience, the environment, the activities involved and ready access to emergency assistance.

d	Equipment and clothing should be in satisfactory condition and be appropriate to the age and size of participants.

e	An alternative contingency programme should be planned where it is possible that adverse circumstances (such as inclement winter weather) may prevent the safe implementation of the main programme.

f   At no time should young people participate in higher risk activities which are not planned, unsupervised or which the leader has not approved.

Activities with Groups away from the Base

g   In case of an emergency two responsible persons, one being a teacher, should be present with groups engaged in activities away from the base. More than two responsible persons may be needed with larger groups.

h   In the case of an accident or emergency, a planned means of communication of the group with the base or with the fire, police or medical services is useful. A portable telephone or other such means of direct communication by the teacher or instructor may be appropriate, but should not be solely relied upon.

i   Equipment for emergencies should be carried, to include a torch, whistle, survival bag, spare rations (such as chocolate), spare warm clothing and first aid equipment.

j   Clear routes, locations for activities and expected times of arrival should be left with a responsible person at the base with agreed procedures to be taken by that person in the event of the schedule not being met within an appropriate time span.

In Residential Settings

k   It must be accepted by the teacher leader that a duty of care exists for twenty-four hours of each day, extending beyond the main activity schedule to include unprogrammed time and night time.

l   Plans should include arrangements for continuous supervision during the day and evening and for action at night in the event of need.

m   Rooms should allow adequate space and storage for inhabitants without overcrowding.

n   Lighting should be provided in dark areas to facilitate safe passage.

o   Care should be taken to ensure that the residential building has acceptable standards to minimise the possibility of risks from fire and is able to accommodate the effective, safe passage of inhabitants in the unlikely event of an emergency evacuation.

p   Pupils should be made familiar with the interior of the building and the immediate surrounds to which they will have access during their stay at the earliest possible time following arrival.

q Emergency drill procedures should be known and practised.

r Ventures abroad must meet UK emergency procedure requirements.

Use of Outdoor Residential Centres

17.1.10 Many schools make use of outdoor residential centres to provide young people with experiences in the outdoors. Some of these are under the control of local authorities but, increasingly, commercial or private agencies are the providers. Concern has arisen in the past over the management, instruction and safety at some centres.

17.1.11 Schools should satisfy themselves that centres are appropriate and safe before they are committed to using these venues with young people for whom they are responsible. In particular:

a Consideration should be given to using accredited centres, including those which satisfy inspection and licensing under the Activity Centres (Young Persons' Safety) Act, 1995 or which implement the code of practice of the United Kingdom Activity Centre Advisory Committee (ACAC). Helpful guidance is provided in the DfEE publication 'Health and Safety of Pupils on Educational Visits, produced in 1998.

b A visit prior to a first booking is advisable, to view facilities and equipment, to meet with staff, to assess the management of location risks and to talk through and agree the total programme with the centre head.

c Teacher leaders should be assured that the systems for fire and emergency procedures are satisfactory. Emergency evacuation of buildings should be practised by parties upon arrival.

d A resolution of any unsatisfactory issues concerning safety should be implemented before a booking is made. If necessary, advice should be sought from a local authority outdoor education adviser or health and safety officer.

e The arrangements for activities and instruction should be agreed. It is advised that a sufficient number of teachers should be present to enable one teacher to accompany each group under instruction. This will assist teachers to fully exercise their responsibilities in loco parentis.

f In the event of a teacher being concerned that pupils may be at unnecessary risk, the teacher should approach the instructor at a safe interval and appropriate measures should be taken to ensure the continued safety and well being of all the participants.

g   Regular meetings of all staff should be arranged during the visit, to evaluate the course and to discuss and resolve any issues that may arise, especially matters of safety.

Overseas Ventures

17.1.12   Educational visits include ventures abroad, and special care is needed in the organisation of these.   In particular:

a   Reciprocal health insurance arrangements can be arranged for visits to a country in the European Community provided the essential paperwork is carried out well beforehand. The Department of Health and Social Security will provide the necessary forms and information.

b   Collective passports are expedient for group travel. Advice from the Passport Office should be sought well in advance of the visit, as some pupils may not qualify for inclusion under Home Office regulations and special arrangements may be necessary for individual cases.

c   Vaccination is a prerequisite for visiting some countries.

Parental Consent

17.1.13   Reference has previously been made to obtaining parental consent for pupil participation in school ventures. Examples of parent information and consent forms are given at the back of this book in appendices 4, 5 and 6.

17.2   Activities on Land

17.2.1   The range of land based outdoor adventure activities is considerable. Activities covered in this section may take many forms and, with the combinations of activities which can occur, the potential for unsafe practice is considerable.

Camping and Expeditions

17.2.2   Camping takes a variety of forms, from standing camps with some permanent on-site facilities, to the use of lightweight equipment which enables tents to be erected and taken down quickly, as is necessary for backpacking expeditions. Potential hazards concerning sites or activities should be identified and resolved during the planning stage.

Competence to lead

For general advice on leadership in outdoor and adventurous activities, refer to section 17.1.3.

17.2.3   The party leader should be experienced in all aspects of camping and should have made a prior visit to (or have prior knowledge of) the site and location to be used. For camping in mountainous country, leaders should be appropriately trained and experienced. They should either hold a mountain leadership award from the Mountain Leaders Training Board or have an alternative qualification which is recognised by the local education authority. If the group is camping near water and will engage in water based activities, the leader must have knowledge of safe practice in those pursuits.

Staff to pupil ratio

17.2.4   A ratio of one teacher to around ten pupils is recommended, depending on the type of group. A minimum of two responsible persons (including the teacher) should normally be present, in case of illness or accident, with at least one responsible adult of each gender for mixed parties. In circumstances of experienced older pupils with only one teacher, suitable arrangements for dealing with foreseeable emergencies must be in place.

Planning

17.2.5   Adequate planning, training and preparation is essential. In particular, there should be practice in the safe use of cooking stoves, in the pitching and striking of tents and in the packing and carrying of loads before the actual venture takes place.

     a   To prevent or minimise the risk of illness from infected food pupils should be taught how to prepare, store and refrigerate food. Eggs, chicken and similar foods must be cooked thoroughly to minimise the risk of salmonella poisoning.

     b   Advice for safer eating includes preparing and consuming food over relatively short periods of time and using comparatively risk-free foods such as non-cream cakes, salads, fresh fruit and fruit pies.

     c   The use of low flame methylated spirit cooking stoves, in which the integrated unit is so designed that heat is mostly contained within the unit, should be taught in campcraft for lightweight camping.

     d   The leader must ensure that equipment and clothing are suitable for the type of camp being organised.

     e   All equipment should be tested and checked well before the departure date.

On site

17.2.6   The leader should ensure the following:

a   A first camp should be held under controlled conditions and should be located near to permanent shelter.

b   A thorough risk assessment of the site and the immediate locality is carried out, so that all participants are aware of any hazards that may be present and the subsequent constraints to be observed.

c   Tents should be pitched sufficiently far apart to allow free movement and to prevent the spread of fire.

d   Measures for sewage and rubbish disposal should be hygienic and safe.

e   Ball games and running should be banned in the vicinity of tents.

f   No cooking should be allowed inside small tents.

g   Petrol stoves have led to serious problems in the past and are not recommended for youth groups.

h   Gas cylinders and fuel for stoves should be stored outside the tents. Containers should be clearly marked, such as 'methylated spirits', 'paraffin'.

i   Lighting that involves a naked flame should not be allowed inside tents.

j   The leader should know the location and telephone number of the nearest doctor and hospital and have a second contact number should this be needed.

Caving and Potholing

17.2.7   Underground systems, other than show caves and tourist mines, present many of the hazards associated with mountains and water, together with additional dangers from darkness and confined spaces. Rescue can sometimes be difficult, even from places that can normally be reached easily by a fit party. Teacher leaders must always bear this in mind when planning trips. Caving can rarely be absolutely safe but the risks should be reasonable and commensurate with the abilities of the pupils.

Competence to lead

For general advice on leadership in outdoor and adventurous activities, refer to section 17.1.3.

17.2.8 Advice on suitable qualifications for those leading caving may be obtained from the local education authority or National Caving Association. Those engaged in leadership and instruction must be very competent in their knowledge, experience and practice since the potential hazards are considerable. A party entering a cave should be escorted by a minimum of two competent adults, including the teacher leader. Either adult must be capable of returning the party to the surface in the event of an emergency and know the relevant cave rescue procedures.

Staff to pupil ratio

a   The recommended ratio in easy cave systems is two competent adults, one being the teacher leader, to around ten pupils.

b   Group numbers must be reduced if the cave system demands it.

c   A caving party should be a minimum of four people.

Clothing and equipment

17.2.9 Appropriate clothing and equipment are very important.

a   The minimum equipment for each individual is:

♦   warm clothing and a protective overgarment;

♦   a protective helmet with a chin strap and lamp bracket;

♦   boots with strong and well-gripping soles;

♦   an efficient headlamp, preferably electric.

b   If there is any possibility of prolonged exposure to water then a wetsuit, exposure suit, life jacket or other suitable gear must be worn.

c   Each member of the party must carry lighting spares, a whistle and emergency food. Ropes, ladders and other equipment should be taken as required.

d   The leader must carry a first aid kit.

Novice parties

17.2.10   Pupils should not be taken into any cave or pothole system with which the teacher leader is unfamiliar. Those on their first caving trip should be monitored for signs of physical weakness, reckless behaviour, claustrophobia, poor reaction to wet or cold, or any symptoms likely to hinder their safe involvement and progress.

Preparation

17.2.11   Before going underground with a party, the teacher leader should:

a   Have previously visited the cave and be thoroughly familiar with it.

b   Check that the cave owner has given permission to descend.

c   Brief the party on all relevant safety and cave-conservation precautions, giving details of the route to be followed and the features which will be encountered.

d   Check the equipment and clothing of all members of the party, ensuring that their helmets fit correctly and their lights are working.

e   Leave a note with a responsible adult giving the passages to be followed, the expected time of return, the number in the party, the level of experience of the group and the equipment being taken.

f   Leave an identifying object (or person) at the entrance of any cave that is entered.

Underground

17.2.12   While underground, the teacher leader or lead instructor must:

a   Maintain constant contact with the front and rear of the party.

b   Monitor the morale and condition of the party and be prepared to turn back at any stage.

c   Alert the party to any dangers of loose chokes, falling rocks (especially below pitches), static or flowing sumps or false flooring.

d   Take special care to avoid even minor injuries which could require a major rescue.

e   Use a lifeline, handline or some other method to protect at places where a slip could lead to injury.

And on returning above ground:

f   Report back at the earliest time to those concerned.

Vertical pitches

17.2.13   When a group has progressed to the stage of being ready to tackle vertical pitches, the teacher leader or lead instructor should ensure that the following measures are taken:

a   Ladder pitches or roped climbing should first be taught and practised above ground in caving attire.

b   The time required for each ladder pitch should be estimated in advance, and the trip and the group size planned accordingly. Long waits underground should be avoided, particularly if the participants are wet.

c   All ladder pitches must be lifelined using the accepted safe techniques.

d   Lifelines should be held by experienced cavers or by competent pupils under constant supervision.

e   No-one should be allowed on wire ladders in boots with hooked lacing.

f   An experienced caver should descend first and ascend last and a second experienced caver should descend last and ascend first.

Mines

17.2.14   Industrial mines often present totally different dangers and problems from those encountered in natural cave systems and must be treated with the greatest respect. Advice should be sought from the local Inspectorate of Mines and Quarries, which can be found in the local telephone directory under the section Health and Safety Executive. Disused coal mines should never be used for caving.

Radon gas

17.2.15   A concentration of radon gas in some cave systems has produced high levels of radiation which can be damaging to health after repeated exposure. Relevant information may be obtained from the Inspectorate of Mines and Quarries, as above.

Cycle Touring and Mountain Biking

17.2.16   Cycling takes very many forms from basic functional or recreational use through to activities as varied as mountain biking and high powered competitive sprinting and distance events. The British Cycling Federation and English Schools' Cycling Association are bodies which will provide advice on all aspects of cycling.

Cycle Touring

Competence to lead

For general advice on leadership in outdoor and adventurous activities, refer to section 17.1.3.

17.2.17   Advice on qualifications and training for those leading or instructing cycling may be obtained from the local education authority or British Cycling Federation. Leaders should:

a   Ensure the safety of the young people with whom they work, so far as is reasonably possible and within the limits of their control.

b   Take all possible steps to establish a safe environment.

c   Match the activity to the age, experience and ability of the pupils.

d   Prepare the pupils for the activity and raise awareness of their personal responsibilities for safety.

The bicycle

17.2.18   Cycles should be roadworthy with all parts in good condition and operating correctly. Particular attention should be paid to:

a   Tyres being inflated to the correct pressures.

b   Wheels not buckled and hubs running smoothly with no sideways play.

c   Brakes correctly adjusted and capable of stopping the machine plus rider.

d   The frame should not be bent or damaged. The head bearing and bottom bracket bearing should be smooth running without play.

e   The handlebars, brake levers and saddle should be firmly attached so that they are not likely to move whilst the cycle is being ridden.

f   Gears should be correctly adjusted so that the chain engages securely with the appropriate sprocket when using rear and front changers and does not come off.

g   All accessories (pumps, tools mudguards, lights, drinking bottles) should be firmly attached.

h   Any luggage carried should be stowed in purpose-fitted saddle bags or panniers and never carried in the hands or draped over handlebars.

i   A pump, spare inner tube and basic tool kit should be carried.

Position on the bicycle

17.2.19   The size of frame and the position of the rider on the cycle is very important for both efficient and safe riding. The ideal height for the saddle is such that when sitting on the saddle with the heel placed on the pedal at its lowest point, the leg is only very slightly bent. When stopping, the rider should lean the cycle over a little to enable one foot to reach the ground, or slide forward off the saddle so that both feet can be placed on the ground. The handlebars should be set so that with the riders hands within reach of the brake levers the body is set at an angle of approximately 45°. Young riders or novices may initially prefer a more upright stance.

Clothing

17.2.20   Whilst there is specialist cycle wear, almost any leisure wear is acceptable provided it is not likely to become entangled in the chain or wheels. It is important for the rider to remain warm and dry. A considerable chill factor is created by cycling and it is necessary to 'wrap up' to combat this, particularly in inclement weather. Bright or lightly coloured clothing will make it easier for the rider to be seen by other road users.

17.2.21   Helmets should be worn and gloves are recommended. Helmets should conform to the recognised BS EN Standard and the manufacturer's recommendations on use and care should be followed.

Rider Assessment

17.2.22   Young or inexperienced riders should be assessed for riding competence and ability before taking to the road. They should be knowledgeable on signs and traffic lights, keeping to the left, hand signals, positions on the road for negotiating roundabouts and for turning left and right.

17.2.23   Riders must be taught to avoid making any sudden actions such as braking, changing course or slipping from the saddle without warning. The basic skills are best learned and consolidated in a playground or other 'safe' area before being applied on the road.

Planning

17.2.24   Care must be taken to ensure that planned rides are within the capabilities of all the riders, taking account of such variables as traffic conditions, terrain, weather, duration of ride and speed.

Staff to pupil ratios and group riding

17.2.25   The following points should be noted when group riding takes place on the road:

a   The ratio of leaders to pupils should not normally exceed 1:7.

b   A group taken on the road should consist of not more than twelve riders, including two 'leaders'. A larger party should be split into two groups, each with their own leaders.

c   Separate groups should ride at least 10 minutes apart.

d   If the separate groups close to within visible distance of each other, the trailing group should stop at a safe place and wait 10 minutes before proceeding.

e   The group formation on the road should be two ranks when conditions are suitable, with the leaders on the outside of the group, one at the front and one at the rear.

f   The formation will enable the leaders to control the speed of the group, signal effectively, call to each other and speak to riders with instructions or advice.

g   In case of poor visibility, lights should be fitted and the leader's cycle should be clearly identifiable to other riders.

h   Each rider is responsible for looking ahead, and should be taught to warn riders behind of any hazards such as parked cars, potholes or sharp bends. Warnings should be delivered verbally and by hand signals.

i   Those at the rear should warn of overtaking vehicles and those in the outside ranks should give hand signals.

j   When riding in two ranks a distance of one bicycle length should be maintained between pairs and around half a metre between ranks. These distances may be safely reduced with experienced cyclists.

k   When in heavy traffic or on narrow or twisting roads, single file riding is advisable. This may be achieved by the inside rank slowing slightly and the outside rank slipping into the space provided thereby, on instruction from the rear leader.

l   The return to two ranks may be achieved by the reverse of this manoeuvre, again on instruction from the leader at the rear.

Refreshments

17.2.26   In hot weather, with rides that exceed thirty minutes, it is essential for riders to carry a drink. Food (carbohydrate) will also be necessary when rides exceed one hour.

Precautions

17.2.27   Information on the route to be taken and the estimated time of return should be left with a responsible person at base. Riders should have with them some form of identification with their name and address as well as some cash. A first aid kit should be in the possession of a member of the riding party who is competent to use it. The carrying of a mobile telephone is recommended.

Mountain Biking (off-road touring)

Competence to lead

For general advice on leadership in outdoor and adventurous activities, refer to section 17.1.3.

17.2.28   Advice on training and qualifications for mountain biking may be obtained from the local education authority or British Cycling Federation.

17.2.29   Staffing ratios and clothing/equipment should be as for cycle touring, though gloves should be compulsory, footwear should suit the terrain and allowances should be made for potential changes in the weather.

17.2.30   Leaders should have ridden the course recently and assessed its suitability for the group. When leading the group they should take a map, compass and whistle, in addition to the items for cycle touring. A second responsible adult should accompany the party and a mobile phone should be carried, in case of an emergency.

17.2.31   Pupils should be taught and be assessed on off-road riding skills in appropriate locations before they engage in riding a mountain biking course. In conditions that are too challenging, young people should walk with their bikes.

Competence to lead:

For general advice on leadership in outdoor and adventurous activities, refer to section 17.1.3.

17.2.32   Advice on training and qualifications for horse riding may be obtained from the local education authority, British Horse Society and Association of Riding Schools. Riding schools should be recognised by the national governing body, as this will give an indication of quality instruction and the training and suitability of animals for riding purposes.

Clothing:

17.2.33   Suitable clothing should be worn by riders at all times. Basic essentials are:

a   A hard hat which meets the current BS EN Standard.

b   Footwear with low, hard heels. Training shoes or wellingtons which can easily slip from the stirrups are not suitable.

Equipment:

17.2.34   The horse should be fully harnessed with a leather saddle, harness and reins which have been carefully checked before use and are properly adjusted and fitted.

Location

17.2.35   Riders should try as far as possible to avoid traffic and busy roads. Where riding does take place in these circumstances, knowledge and observance of the relevant sections of the Highway Code is necessary.

Pony trekking:

17.2.36   The activity should take place at centres which are licence holders under current legislation. Long hours in the saddle may be entailed and the following recommendations should be noted:

a   Some preliminary riding instruction is advisable.

b   Local advice should be obtained before using routes subject to weather hazards such as fog or slippery conditions following heavy rainfall.

c   Small groups are desirable and should be accompanied by two responsible adults, one or whom should be appropriately qualified and one a teacher.

d Emergency items (first aid, a mobile telephone) should be carried.

Orienteering

Competence to lead

For general leadership in outdoor and adventurous activities, refer to section 17.1.3.

17.2.37 Advice on training and qualifications for leading orienteering may be obtained from the local education authority and British Orienteering Federation. Evidence of experience and competence is adequate for teaching a basic introduction to the activity in school grounds or using observable woodland paths.

17.2.38 **Clothing**

a Footwear should be suitable for the course terrain and the prevailing weather conditions.

b Adequate clothing should be worn to suit the conditions. Complete arm and leg cover is recommended for most wooded events.

c In competition, all participants should carry a whistle.

Course planning and preparation

17.2.39 The organiser should ensure that attention is given to the following points:

a Adequate initial instruction should be given to all participants.

b Prior permission should always be obtained to use a given course, either from the landowner or managing agent. The existence of orienteering maps does not necessarily indicate any right of access. Permission should always be sought.

c Local advice should be noted and implemented.

d Competitors should not be required to cross busy roads or to negotiate major geographical hazards. All hazards should be marked on competition maps and brought to the notice of participants in the prestart area.

e Courses should be appropriate to the age and experience of those taking part. Control points should be located well away from deep water, unsafe buildings or concealed drops in ground level.

f   Only experienced participants should take part in night-time orienteering. They should compete in pairs or in groups and they should keep together.

g   The address and telephone number of the nearest doctor should be displayed at base, together with the location of the nearest telephone.

h   The organiser should have access to first aid equipment.

i   If a participant fails to check in by close-out time, sufficient competent personnel must be prepared to search the area under direction of the organiser.

Problem Solving and Improvised Activities

17.2.40   Problem solving and associated improvised activities can be very valuable in the promotion of applied skills and team building, using 'low technology' equipment. Many activities are relatively low risk but all will need to be carefully planned to ensure that solutions may reasonably be achieved by participation without undue hazards being encountered. In particular:

a   Problems should be clearly and unambiguously presented.

b   Totally 'open-ended' problems with no evident or predictable solutions should not be used.

c   Care for self and others in the group should be the overriding requirement.

d   The challenges set need to be thoroughly assessed for any inherent risks and the effective management of these should be addressed by the teacher with the participants prior to the commencement of the activities.

e   Problems where physical challenge is a feature should be well within the capabilities of all participants and should be closely and responsibly supervised.

f   The teacher must always be prepared to intervene if potentially unsafe measures are adopted by participants.

g   Imposed time pressures should never be such that activities become rushed and lacking in control.

h   Equipment must be adequate, in good condition, suitable and safe for the purposes to which it may be applied, especially the supporting of weight.

17.2.41   Rock climbing and abseiling are highly specialised technical activities which require the utmost attention to safe practice. Those who instruct must be fully aware of the dangers and take all reasonable steps to ensure the safety and well being of those in their charge.

Tuition

For general advice on leadership in outdoor and adventurous activities, refer to section 17.1.3.

17.2.42   Advice on qualifications and training may be obtained from the local education authority, the British Mountaineering Council (BMC) and its administrative body, the UK Mountain Leader Training Board.

Supervision

a   Staffing ratios will depend on the level and purpose of the session, the location and the experience of participants. An introductory session with a teacher leader and instructor should involve about eight pupils.

b   On longer climbs, one instructor should be responsible for no more than three pupils, and each climber should be belayed individually. Climbers must remain roped throughout the climb.

c   When major crags are attempted, there must be at least two adult leaders in the party, including the teacher leader.

Equipment

17.2.43   Equipment is fundamental to safe practice and great care should be taken to implement the following advice:

a   Only approved equipment should be used, all of which must be checked by the leader.

b   Safety helmets to BS EN specification must be included for all climbers, together with gloves for belaying and waist harnesses with a screw-gate karabiner.

c   Footwear should provide good ankle support and a firm grip on the rock.

d   Ropes, karabiners and other specialist items used for climbing and abseiling must meet the relevant BS EN Standards.

e   Ropes should not be allowed to run directly through a loop. A screw-gate karabiner should be positioned between the running rope and the loop.

f   Ropes should be inspected at regular intervals for signs of wear and tear and should be replaced when these are apparent. A record of rope usage must be entered in a log.

On the rock-face:

17.2.44   The leader must ensure the following:

a   The grade of the climb must be within the capability of the least able climber in the group.

b   Climbing or bouldering must not take place without the leader's consent and presence.

c   No-one should lead a climb without the permission of the leader.

d   All knots should be checked by the leader before and during the climb.

e   The standard climbing call system should be observed within the party.

f   Abseiling must always be supervised by the leader.

g   A safety rope must be used for abseiling. This must be belayed separately from the abseil rope.

Artificial climbing walls:

17.2.45   Provision of both indoor and outdoor climbing walls has had a significant influence on climbing, to the extent that new sports have been developed which are dedicated to these facilities. Although generally designed for the purpose with safety a major consideration, great care is still required to ensure acceptable good practice.

a   Artificial climbing (and abseiling) walls should only be used under the supervision of leaders with appropriate qualifications and experience.

b   Ropes and equipment should be of the same standards as that required for rock climbing.

c   Protective mattresses should be of high density foam and contain graphite as a flame inhibitor. They should be covered and held firmly together by a wear sheet to prevent feet entering any gaps. Their use should complement safety measures which make falling improbable.

d   The climbing wall should be approved by the local education authority or the British Mountaineering Council. It should be regularly inspected and maintained.

Skating

Competence to lead:

For general advice on leadership in outdoor and adventurous activities, refer to section 17.1.3.

17.2.46   Whether on ice or roller skates:

a   Suitable clothing should be worn, including protection for the legs.

b   Gloves should worn by beginners for protection on the hands.

c   Boots should provide firm support for the ankles.

d   The skating surface should be regularly maintained and be checked before use. Skating should only take place on a suitably even surface.

e   The activity should be supervised by a teacher and competent leadership should always be present.

f   Rules on procedures for skating should be clearly understood and strictly observed.

g   Advanced skaters and beginners should not generally skate on a rink at the same time.

h   All skating should be in the same (anticlockwise) direction.

Skiing

Competence to lead

For general advice on leadership in outdoor and adventurous activities, refer to section 17.1.3.

17.2.47   Advice on ski course organisation and relevant leader/instructor qualifications may be obtained from the local education authority and the national governing body, Snow Sports GB, or one of the national ski councils.

Clothing and equipment

17.2.48   Ski clothing must provide adequate protection against snow, wind and cold. The following criteria are important:

a   An anorak plus ski trousers/salopettes or one piece ski suit are essential, together with gloves or mits, goggles and a ski hat. Jeans should never be worn. The hat may be a distinctive colour for a party, to enable identification on the slopes.

b   Sun cream should be used to prevent sunburn and lip salve to prevent chapped lips. Both items should be carefully suited to individuals, if necessary with medical advice, as allergic reactions can occur.

c   Ski boots must give firm support to the ankles and the lower legs and be compatible with ski bindings.

d   Skis should generally be no longer than the height of the skier and shorter for novices.

e   Bindings should have the mechanisms properly adjusted for individual skiers for quick release in the event of a fall. These should be checked carefully before skiing lessons commence and adjusted by an appropriately trained technician or other adult with the necessary knowledge.

f   Retaining straps must always be fitted to skis so that, in the event of a released ski, it does not slide out of control down the slope.

g   The length of ski sticks should be roughly equivalent to waist height.

h   On dry ski slopes clothing to protect the arms and legs from friction burns in case of a fall should be worn.

Physical preparation

17.2.49   All skiing trips should be preceded by a programme of regular pre-ski exercises and fitness training sessions. The use of artificial ski slopes will provide valuable experience, with a recommended ratio of one instructor to about twelve pupils.

Skiing and snowboarding on snow in Britain

17.2.50   A day's skiing on local fells should be planned in the same way as a hike in the hills or mounts or mountains. In particular:

a   Participants should be properly clothed for the cold, windy and wet conditions.

b   Sufficient food, hot drinks and spare clothing should be taken along by individuals.

c   The party should be self-supporting. Party leaders should carry emergency equipment (shelter, spare clothing, food and drink, first aid and effective means for communication such as a mobile phone).

d   The group should be adequately supervised by at least two responsible persons.

e   Participants should stay together at all times.

Skiing or snowboarding on snow abroad

17.2.51   The following details should be checked at the planning stage:

a   Adequate insurance cover.

b   Safety of the resort and good slopes with adequate lift systems for beginners through to improvers.

c   Safety of the hotel or other accommodation for fire and emergency procedures.

d   The proximity of the hotel or chalet accommodation to the ski slopes.

e   The availability of adequate drying and storage facilities for clothes, boots and skis or boards.

f   The satisfactory condition of all equipment to be hired and the provision of a technician to check and adjust equipment and to change it if necessary during the ski course.

g   The allocation of ski instructors, appropriately experienced and sufficient in number for the size of the part (one instructor to about twelve pupils).

h   A skiing guarantee, in the event of poor quality snow at the selected resort.

Safety on the slopes

17.2.52   All participants should know and observe the ten points of the Intenationally recognised Ski-Way Code.

a   No pupil should be allowed to ski alone or outside marked skiing areas and trails.

b   Supervised skiing practice and all other snow activities should be carefully monitored.

c   Clear instructions should be given to the pupils on the runs, tows, chairlifts to be used, on check-in and return times, on rendezvous points and on safety procedures.

d   All skiing must be graded according to the abilities of the participants.

e   Tired skiers should stop skiing.

Tuition

17.2.53   Tuition must be by qualified instructors. Daily tuition of four hours (two hours in the morning and two hours in the afternoon) is often provided. If only two hours of daily instruction is given and the pupils are allowed on the slopes at other times, they must be supervised by teachers who have adequate experience and knowledge of the area and who meet the requirements laid down above under competence to lead.

Off the slopes supervision

17.2.54   Appropriate supervision in the hotel and the resort must be maintained at all times, including during any evening entertainment or activity.

Emergency and accident procedures

17.2.55   The party should include a member of staff who knows first aid and can treat minor ailments. In addition:

a   All members of the party should be familiar with accident and emergency procedures for personal accident and fire.

b   Fire drill should be practised on arrival at the resort.

Nordic (Cross Country) Skiing

17.2.56   This activity is very energetic . It is important that:

a   Leaders should obtain the appropriate training and qualification.

b   Routes to be followed should be familiar to the leader and assessed as suitable in the prevailing weather and snow conditions.

c   The group should be appropriately equipped for any foreseeable emergency.

Walking and Climbing at High Level

17.2.57   Walking can take place in a variety of locations, from local walks on pavements and footpaths through to high level mountain and fell walking in remote areas. The advice provided here is largely directed at high level walking since the hazards are likely to be greater in this environment. It must be recognised, however, that risk assessment and management is applicable to all circumstances in which groups engage in walking.

Competence to lead

For general advice on leadership on outdoor and adventurous activities, refer to section 17.1.3.

17.2.58   Advice on training and qualifications in walking and climbing may be obtained from the local education authority and Mountain Leader Training Board (MLTB).

17.2.59   All teachers who lead walking or climbing groups on the fells or mountains should be training in first aid, including the treatment of hypothermia.

Staff to pupil ratios

17.2.60   For fieldwork in less remote areas with easy access to main roads and given reasonable weather conditions, one member of staff to about fifteen pupils is realistic (but with a minimum of two responsible persons, one of whom is a teacher).

In more demanding terrain:

a   The recommended ratio is one member of staff to about ten pupils (with a minimum of two responsible adults, one of whom is a teacher).

b   Groups on unaccompanied (remotely supervised) expeditions, as for the Duke of Edinburgh Award Scheme, should consist of between four and seven pupils.

Clothing and equipment

17.2.61   Waterproof and windproof clothing and a spare sweater are needed at higher levels, even in summer. Boots with a good grip soles are essential. Crampons and an ice-axe are required for snow and ice conditions.

17.2.62   Each member of the group should carry as a minimum:

- a map and compass;
- a whistle;
- a pencil and paper;
- suitable food and drink;
- a torch (in working order, with spare batteries).

17.2.63   Every group should carry the following between the members:

- first aid equipment;

- one lightweight survival bag for every two members of the group;

- a mobile telephone or other effective communication device.

And in winter conditions:

- a sleeping bag for every member;

- for difficult scrambling areas, a climbing rope.

17.2.64   Prior to setting out:

a   The leader should check local weather forecasts and conditions and the location of mountain-rescue posts in the walking area.

b   A route card should be left at the base, indicating the date, where the group is to walk and giving the expected time of return. If plans are changed, the base should be informed.

17.2.65   On the hills:

a   The pace of walking should be reasonable for the slowest member of the group.

b   The group should stay together, with nominated front and back markers.

c   All group members should know the procedure in the event of an accident or emergency.

d   Rest and shelter should be taken in cases of exhaustion and worsening weather.

17.2.66   On the day of return:

a   The leader should report in at base and ensure that the route card is collected.

b   A brief evaluation should be carried out.

17.3   Water Based Activities

17.3.1   The range and involvement of people in water-based activities, both on and in water, continues to grow. Advances in technology have enabled existing activities to be modified and improved and new activities developed so that the scope for choice is considerable.

The awareness of hazards and the management of risks is applicable to all activities and there are fundamental safety principles which should be commonly acknowledged and understood. These include:

♦   conducting the activity in suitable conditions;

♦   using appropriately qualified and experienced leaders;

♦   using appropriate and reliable equipment;

♦   subjecting equipment to regular and rigorous safety checks;

♦   ensuring that participants have the level of water confidence and competence needed for the activity;

♦   knowing and being able to implement appropriate emergency and rescue procedures.

♦   being water confident and a capable swimmer.

17. 3.2   The development of confidence on and in water is essential for safe and enjoyable participation in water-related activities and should be a prime objective of all such activities. In particular:

a   There should be instruction in water safety prior to participation in all water-related activities.

b   The emphasis should at all times be on preventing accidents.

c   Training in safe swimming, in-water survival techniques, self-rescue, rescue of others and resuscitation is recommended and should include cold water immersion as appropriate. It should be noted that younger participants are at greater risk of hypothermia than adults because they have less body fat.

d   The use of personal buoyancy aids or life jackets and any protective clothing that might be appropriate to the activity should be insisted upon.

Inland waters and canals

17.3.3   There is a risk to health from water contaminated by the urine and infected tissues of animals. One example is Weils disease or leptospirosis which is carried by rats and other rodents. Good hygienic practice is essential, with measures which include:

a   Covering any scratches or abrasions with a waterproof plaster prior to entering the water.

b   Avoiding swallowing or inhaling water.

c   Taking a shower after outdoor water sports activities.

17.3.4   Canals can present hazards which should be carefully assessed before use. In particular:

♦   the manoeuvering of craft may be limited by the narrowness of the waterway;

♦   tunnels and swing bridges may present difficulties;

♦   the use of locks requires special boat-handling skills.

♦   the ease of egress from the water at any place.

Leaders of groups should be experienced in using canals and should seek advice and information from the nearest office of the British Waterways Board.

Angling

17.3.5   The activity is popular with many young people and it presents opportunities to develop environmental awareness, raise conservation issues and promote respect for other water users.

Competence to lead

(For general advice on leadership in outdoor and adventurous activities, refer to section 17.1.4)

17.3.6   Leaders should be active and proficient in the activity, be members of a recognised angling club or association, have practical experience of the waters in which angling will take place and be qualified in accordance with the recommendations of the National Anglers' Council.

Bank and shore fishing

17.3.7   The following recommendations should be considered:

a   A staff to pupil ratio of 1 :10, with a minimum of two responsible adults.

b   Participants to be made aware of any potential hazards, such as crumbling banks, variations in the height and speed of tides, slippery weed covered rocks and unexpectedly large waves.

c   The dangers of wading in fast and unfamiliar waters should be emphasised, and instruction given in recovery techniques and the use of a wading stick.

d   Where appropriate, studded felt-soled waders should be worn.

e   Lifejackets should be worn when fishing from rocks. A rescue line or line-throwing buoy should be available.

f   The presence within the party of a person with life saving and first aid competence.

Fishing from boats

17.3.8   Any craft used should be adequate for the activity and large enough for the numbers taking part. If hired, the boat should conform to requirements laid down by the Department of Transport, local authority or other marine safety agency.

Participants should

a   Never fish alone.

b   Be knowledgeable of the local waters, tides and weather conditions.

c   Be proficient in boat handling, rowing and the operation of engines, or engage the services of a professional boatman.

d   Be water confident, yet always wear a personal buoyancy aid while afloat.

And in addition at sea:

e   Wear bright coloured windproof and waterproof clothing and carry spare warm sweaters.

f   Take food, drink and emergency rations.

g   Be satisfied that the boat is equipped with spare and emergency equipment, including two-way radio communication if fishing will be some distance from the shore.

h   Take steps to prevent seasickness if this is anticipated.

Canoeing and Kayaking

17.3.9   Canoeing and kayaking are potentially hazardous and risks must be reasonably assessed and managed without detracting from the challenge and spirit of adventure which is the very essence of the activities. Leaders should take care to ensure that novices experience progressive activities, starting on placid water, for example a swimming pool, which will gradually develop their readiness and capabilities for taking part in situations of increasing challenge with a reasonable expectation of safe performance.

Competence to lead

(For general advice on leadership in outdoor and adventurous activities, refer to section 17.1.4.)

17.3.10   The British Canoe Union has a qualification system of graded awards for instructors relevant to placid and moving (flowing, tidal and white) waters and to the use of different craft (open - and closed - cockpit kayaks and canoes). Leaders should be qualified and experienced at the appropriate levels of instruction for the craft and the water on which they will be taking groups. This should be well within their personal canoeing competence and experience.

All leaders must be capable of performing expired- air resuscitation and must know how to recognise and treat hypothermia.

Staff to pupil ratio

17.3.11   A ratio of one leader to about eight pupils is recommended on still waters and one leader to about six pupils on moving or tidal waters. A minimum of two responsible adults is recommended. On open exposed water, an assistant leader with the ability to perform deep-water rescues would be appropriate.

Clothing and equipment

17.3.12   Clothing should provide warmth and protection from the elements. Waters in and around the United Kingdom are almost always cold and special consideration is needed to ensure adequate warmth during extended periods afloat.

   a   A waterproof anorak is essential as a basic requirement. A wetsuit should be worn in conditions where hypothermia might otherwise occur.

   b   Hard helmets are essential for most types of canoeing.

   c   Wellingtons or heavy clothing should never be worn; lightweight footwear is essential.

   d   Those in canoes or kayaks must always wear a lifejacket or personal buoyancy aid which conforms to the standard CEN393. For certain activities CEN395 (replaces BS3595). The latter is advised for the sea expeditions.

   e   On every canoe or kayak expedition, the leader must carry and have available:

   ♦   a first aid kit;

   ♦   a tow line;

   ♦   distress flares for sea and open water;

- spare paddles and a spray cover (for kayaks);

- a survival bag;

- the means for providing hot drinks;

- a whistle;

- expert advice should be sought concerning the appropriateness of different types of flares.

f   On extended expeditions, each participant should also carry the above items.

g   A mobile telephone should be carried by the leader where there is a reasonable expectation that it will function.

h   New replacement equipment should conform to the new standard CEN395.

The canoe or kayak

17.3.13   All craft should be fitted with buoyancy. If buoyancy bags are used, these should be firmly secured and distributed at the bow and stern, with 13.5 kilograms of buoyancy at either end so that in a capsize they:

- remain in place;

- do not suffer damage or deflation from water pressure;

- cause the craft to float horizontally.

In addition:

a   Painters, if fitted fore and aft, must be secured to keep them well clear of the cockpit. Toggles are generally preferable.

b   Spray decks must be used on graded water and the sea. They should be easily removable in the event of a capsize. Participants must be trained in the removal of spray decks and progressively become accustomed to their use.

c   Items carried should be packed in waterproof bags or containers, stored so that the trim of the craft is maintained, and secured firmly. Equipment in a kayak must not be packed in the cockpit or stored beside the paddler's legs.

d   Footrests should be substantial and should be designed to prevent the canoeist sliding forward on impact. They should be easily adjustable and should not rotate.

e   A canoe or kayak should be brightly coloured so that it may be easily seen and should carry some form of identification.

Repairs to craft

17.3.14   The materials used for the repair of glass reinforced plastic (grp) are hazardous. If inhaled, the chemicals and dust may cause skin irritation or internal damage and there is a fire risk associated with resins. British Standard 4163 (1975) refers to these hazards.

Capsize drill

17.3.15   Capsize drill must form an early part of basic training and must be practised thoroughly. In the event of a capsize occurring:

a   The kayak should be left upside down for use as a buoyancy aid.

b   The canoeist should remain with the craft unless to do so would be dangerous for example if drifting towards a sluice or weir.

c   If close to land, the canoeist should move to one end of the craft and tow it to shore by swimming using a back stroke.

d   In open water, deep water rescue methods should be employed. The group should have learned and mastered these in practice.

Before setting out

17.3.16   The leader should be suitably qualified and experienced in order to:

a   Check the condition and suitability of canoes, kayaks, equipment and clothing (such as windproof anoraks, wetsuits, footwear).

b   Decide whether members of the party have sufficient experience to participate in the prevailing weather and water conditions.

c   Assess local conditions, including currents, tides, and any potentially dangerous features such as weirs by studying guides, maps, charts and tide tables. Great care should be taken when strong tides combine with offshore winds, which will take craft quite quickly out to sea.

d   Obtain local weather forecasts, available in coastal areas from Marine Call (see the appropriate local telephone directory).

e   Arrange a signalling system with the group.

f   Details should be left with a responsible person who will initiate emergency action in the event of the group failing to meet an agreed time of contact with that person.

Also give details to the local coastguard or police of any route to be followed on unsheltered waters for example a coastal trip or of any passage across a large area of exposed inland water. The same authorities must be informed on the party's safe return.

On the water

17.3.17   The leader should ensure the following:

a   Good discipline should be maintained throughout.

b   Large parties should be split into groups of six to eight under competent leaders although the condition of the water may necessitate smaller groups.

c   Normally the slowest paddlers should go at the front of each group and the slowest groups should go first but this procedure merits review on moving water.

d   Groups should keep to a predetermined formation.

e   The leader of each group should be positioned according to the wind and current and to the configuration of the group.

f   A leading canoeist and a last canoeist should be appointed from among responsible members in each group, with the task of ensuring that the group stays together.

g   At the top of short rapids, an inspection should be carried out, from the bank if necessary. The canoeists should then descend the rapids singly and wait at the side in the slack water below until the whole party is safely through. The descent of the group should be monitored and controlled; ideally with lead staff at the walked past rapids where these present too great a challenge for the group.

h   Stops should be made in sheltered places, and extra clothing should be put on when necessary.

i   Mishaps should be dealt with as quickly as possible to prevent the remainder of the party getting cold.

Rafting

17.3.18   Rafting is an increasingly popular activity which may be either a task centred learning exercise or an experience in paddling inflatables on white water rivers.

17.3.19   In either form, leaders should be aware of the particular and local hazards associated with the activity.

Task-centred rafting

a   Leaders should be very experienced in the construction techniques.

b   The criteria used for construction should include advice on safety.

c   The materials used should be suitable for the purpose.

d   Appropriate personal buoyancy and helmets should be worn whilst participants are working on or near the water.

e   Appropriate safety measures should be ready for implementation in the event of a capsize or emergency.

White water rafting

f   Leaders should be highly experienced and be very knowledgeable on the waters to be used and the nature, location and management of all hazards.

g   The British Canoe Union coaching scheme includes many relevant skills and leaders are recommended to seek qualification through the scheme.

h   A standard lesson plan and operating procedure should be used as the basis of the lesson.

Rowing

Competence to lead

(For general advice on leadership in outdoor and adventurous activities, refer to section 17.1.4).

17.3.20   The Amateur Rowing Association is the governing body for the activity. It will provide information and advice on all aspects of rowing, including the awards and qualifications for potential instructors and coaches.

17.3.21   Rowing in all its forms is a strenuous activity and those who engage in it should be thoroughly prepared physically. Attention to the following points will help to ensure that the activity is undertaken safely:

a   The age and physical condition of participants are important factors and young people should not engage in activities and use craft for which they are not properly prepared.

b   Where rowing is part of an outdoor education programme then appropriate personal buoyancy should be worn.

c   The teacher or leader concerned is responsible for ensuring the conditions for rowing are appropriate, the equipment is suitable and a named person is put in charge of the boat.

d   Before being allowed on the water participants should be briefed on:

- local navigation rules and the effects of currents, weirs, sluices and winds;

- the rights and customs of other water users;

- emergency procedures in the event of a capsize or other accidents while rowing.

e   Providers should draw up safety guidelines for the use of their facilities by teachers or leaders.

Dinghy Sailing and Windsurfing

17.3.22   Sailing is a long established traditional activity which has become a core feature of many outdoor and adventurous activity programmes. It can provide satisfaction across a broad range of activities, from the solo handling of small craft through to the teamwork necessary for the effective functioning of a large sailing vessel.

The physical skills necessary for sailing are complemented by those of thoughtful planning, communication and leadership in an activity which is compatible with awareness of, and respect for, the natural environment.

Competence to lead

(For general advice on leadership in outdoor adventurous activities, refer to section 17.1.4.)

17.3.23   The Royal Yachting Association (RYA) and the National Schools Sailing Association (NSSA) will provide relevant advice on qualifications.

Clothing and equipment

17.3.24   Clothing should be warm and should be protected by waterproofs when necessary. At certain times of the year and in cooler weather, wetsuits may be required for windsurfing and for some forms of sailing. The following additional advice should be noted:

a   All participants should be appropriately attired for the activity.

b   When afloat, instructors and crew should wear personal buoyancy which conform to the appropriate European Standard at all times.

c   All crew must be confident in the water when wearing personal buoyancy.

d   All craft should be checked to ensure that they are seaworthy, with adequate secure buoyancy and emergency equipment.

Staff to pupil ratios

17.3.25   The recommended number of crew per boat during instruction is detailed in the RYA booklet 'Guidance for Centre Principals'.

Capsize procedures

17.3.26   Capsize is always a very real possibility when dinghy sailing. It should be experienced as a part of training, along with techniques for righting the dinghy, sailing on and bailing water. In the event of a capsize which cannot be righted, the crew must remain with the boat. With larger dinghies such as 'day' boats that have fixed ballasted keels it might not be practical to capsize such craft but evidence of a thorough risk assessment based on a limited practical scenario should be available.

Before launch

17.3.27   Instructors should take local knowledge into account and should always read or listen to local weather reports (available in coastal areas from Marine Call; refer to the appropriate local telephone directory).

a   Details should be left with a responsible person who will initiate emergency action in the event of the group failing to meet an agreed time of contact with that person. Whenever a group sails in open coastal or tidal waters, the leader should submit complete details of the fleet and the itinerary to the coastguard before sailing.

b   All crews must agree and keep to a sailing area and know the group recall signal.

c   Great care should be taken in conditions of light winds directly off-shore with a strong outgoing tide, when boats may be taken some distance out to sea and returning to land under sail may prove very difficult and laborious. Novices should not be taken out in these circumstances.

On the water

17.3.28   The sailing area should be well defined, known to all participants and strictly observed. A simple code of easily visible and/or audible signals should be understood and used by all crew.

Safety boat

17.3.29   The presence of an appropriately equipped and manned safety boat is essential. Advice on the type of craft suitable is given by the RYA. A minimum qualification for powered craft drivers is RYA Power Boat, Level 2.

First aid

17.3.30   All sailing instructors should be experienced in first aid especially:

   ◆   applying expired air resuscitation;

   ◆   stopping severe bleeding;

   ◆   recognising hypothermia at an early stage, and taking preventative measures;

   ◆   treating shock and concussion;

   ◆   applying inflatable splints in the case of a fracture;

   ◆   dealing with spinal injuries.

   NB RYA Instructor Awards are only valid when supported by a current first aid certificate.

Windsurfing

17.3.31   Many of the principles of sailing apply equally to windsurfing. In addition:

   a   Land simulators, though useful for teaching techniques, require care for safe practice. They should be low and stable and meet RYA standards.

   b   Adverse wind and tide conditions can take windsurfers a long way in a short time, even when capsized. Rescue craft crew need to be vigilant to ensure the safety and well-being of windsurfers for whom they are responsible.

   c   The very early stages with beginners on water will require a high staff to pupil ratio, around 1:6.

Sub Aqua Activities

17.3.32   Underwater exploration often begins with snorkelling but the use of breathing apparatus with appropriate techniques enables greater scope for the enthusiastic diver. As with all water-based activities, there are basic safety requirements to be followed.

Competence to lead

(For general advice on leadership in outdoor and adventurous activities, refer to section 17.1.4)

17.3.33　The British Sub Aqua Club (BSAC) will recommend appropriate qualifications.

Pupil participation

17.3.34　The requirements are:

- all snorkellers must be able to swim at least 50 metres;

- scuba divers should be over fifteen years of age and should have taken the British Sub Aqua Club proficiency test;

- pupils with epilepsy, diabetes and certain other medical conditions must not be allowed to take part;

- all divers should know the techniques of rescue and expired air resuscitation.

17.3.35　Staff to pupil ratios

In pool training:

- Snorkelling:　　　　one instructor for up to ten pupils.

- Aqualung training:　one instructor for up to four pupils.

In open-water:

- Snorkelling:　　　　one instructor for up to four pupils.

- Aqualung diving:　　one instructor for no more than two pupils.

17.3.36　**Clothing and equipment**

a　When diving takes place in UK waters some form of protective clothing, such as a drysuit or a wetsuit, should be worn.

b　All equipment, including masks, snorkels and aqualungs , should conform to the appropriate British Standards/British Standards European Norms.

c　All divers should wear suitable lifejackets, carbon dioxide or air inflated, and each aqualung group should use a surface marker buoy.

Emergencies

17.3.37   Before any training or diving takes place, whether in the pool or in open water, it is essential to make adequate emergency provision including training in the appropriate safety drills.

Open-water dives

17.3.38   For open-water dives to take place a support boat should always be present with at least one stand-by diver. In addition:

a   The leader or instructor should be satisfied that the pupils are physically fit enough and have received appropriate instruction before being allowed to take part in a particular dive. No-one who is suffering from fatigue, a cold or other infection should be permitted to dive.

b   Divers should normally work in pairs, whether for snorkelling or for aqualung diving. Diving without a partner should only be allowed when a lifeline is used and an experienced diver is present.

c   All divers should observe the British Sub Aqua Club Code of Conduct, which is contained in the 'Diving Instructor's Manual'.

d   The skipper of the boat used by the divers should be suitably qualified and experienced. BSAC Diver Coxswain Level III is recommended.

Surfing

17.3.39   Surfing requires the same vigilance as other water-based activities. Participants should be very competent in rough water and be capable of swimming strongly for a considerable period of time in such conditions.

Competence to lead

(For general advice on leadership in outdoor and adventurous activities, refer to section 17.1.4.)

17.3.40   The British Surfing Association's National Coaching Accreditation Scheme provides a course for instructors. It is strongly recommended that leaders should have taken a course leading to a qualification and they must be competent.   The Surf Life Saving Association or The Royal Life Saving Association provide specialist training and qualifications in surf life saving and first aid.

Staff to pupils ratio

17.3.41   A ratio of one instructor to about six pupils is recommended.

Participation

17.3.42   The teaching locations selected and the content of lessons should be appropriate to the levels of ability and experience of participants.

Beginners should:

a   Be paired with shore-based members who are responsible for observing their surfing activity.

b   Wear wetsuits, preferably with cover of their arms and legs.

c   Use boards with adequate floatation for their varying physiques and levels of fitness.

d   Be watched by an active lifeguard at all times when afloat.

e   Be briefed on and keep to the planned incoming and outgoing lane system.

f   Stop surfing as soon as tiredness is experienced.

Swimming in Open Water

17.3.43   Swimming in the sea, lakes or rivers is a potentially hazardous and life-threatening activity which requires very careful assessment and must always be adequately supervised. In particular:

a   Local knowledge and the information provided on markers and signs should always be looked for and respected.

b   Only waters free of pollution and locally recognised as being suitable for swimming should be used. Strong and dangerous tidal undertows are often present in attractive shore locations.

c   Parental approval for swimming should be obtained.

d   Swimming areas should be clearly defined and participants briefed and frequently reminded of these limits.

e   Supervision should be undertaken by persons capable of making a rescue and carrying out resuscitation.

f   Swimming time should be limited in cold water.

g   Weaker swimmers must always keep to areas where they can stand if they need to.

h   Diving should not be permitted.

Water skiing

17.3.44 Water skiing and jumping are very specialised, strenuous activities which usually take place on stretches of water which are reserved for the purpose. They are potentially hazardous and should only take place in highly controlled conditions under suitably qualified leadership. If older pupils of secondary age should, by choice, have the opportunity to ski on water they should be both excellent swimmers and very fit.

Coasteering

17.3.45 A new activity of Coasteering. This is an exciting activity, based on moving along the coast usually in the water for much of the time. It is potentially very hazardous and a high level of organisation should be apparent, this should include:

♦ A thorough written risk assessment.

♦ Standard operating procedures that explain access and escape routes.

♦ Equipment needed including personal buoyancy helmets, wet suits, foot wear.

♦ Group management.

♦ Attention to weather forecasts and change.

♦ Emergency procedures include an effective late back response.

17.4 Activities in the Air

17.4.1 The experience of pupils in air-borne activities is very likely to be limited to conventional flying through package arrangements or other ventures abroad. Such experience is valuable and will raise awareness of the many constraints and procedures which contribute to safety in the air.

17.4.2 Written parental permission for pupils to participate in air-borne activities should be obtained before any activity takes place.

17.4.3 Older pupils in further or higher education may have opportunities to engage in ballooning, paragliding or other such activities which have developed in recent times through technological innovation. All are potentially hazardous and require very specialist expertise and skills to be available. In all tutored situations, care should be taken to ensure that:

a   The activity is conducted under a code of practice or the most recent recommendations of the relevant national governing body or authority.

b   Appropriate tuition is given before participating in the activity.

c   Instruction is provided by capable and qualified practitioners who are very experienced and safe in the activity concerned.

d   Staff to student ratios are conducive to safe practice, possibly as low as 1:1.

e   Novices are fully briefed on the risks, how these will be managed and the procedures to be followed in the event of a foreseeable emergency.

f   Equipment, including any safety devices, is adequate, in satisfactory condition and is always carefully checked and tested immediately before use.

g   Clothing is appropriate and sufficiently protective.

h   Weather conditions and forecasts are favourable.

i   The selected location is recognised as suitable for the activity.

j   In any circumstances of doubt, the activity does not take place or is abandoned.

k   Comprehensive insurance cover has been arranged.

18: SWIMMING, DIVING & LIFE-SAVING

SWIMMING

18.1   Introduction

18.1.1.   Learning to swim provides the essential foundation for many water-based recreational choices and the activity is very appropriately included in the national curriculum. Swimming is health promoting and provides great satisfaction to all its practitioners, who span the age range from young to elderly. The aim must be to teach the basic skills to as many young people as possible. Due to the evident hazard of drowning, the teaching and learning of swimming and water safety requires the utmost care on the part of all concerned.

18.1.2   The Health and Safety at Work Act 1974 places responsibilities on pool owners, managers and users to establish sound procedures to reasonably ensure that swimming related activities are carried out safely

18.2   Normal operating procedures

18.2.1   Normal operating procedures should be written for all pools. These will set out the arrangements for users' safety and should be followed by whoever is responsible for any group using the pool, be it in curriculum time or otherwise. The procedures may vary according to the particular circumstances of the pool and the users.

18.2.2   Normal operating procedures are simply the day to day organisational systems based on risk assessment (see chapter 4). All who assume responsibility for the supervision and safety of any groups using the pool should be made aware of the procedures. Periodic review is important in order to maintain up to date, consistently applied levels of practice.

18.2.3   Operating procedures typically would include information relating to:

- ◆   pool design and depth;

- ◆   potential areas of risk;

- ◆   arrangements for lessons;

- ◆   responsibility for safety;

- ◆   staffing levels and qualifications

- supervision and pupil conduct;

- arrangements for pupils with particular needs e.g. very young children, those with SEN or those with medical conditions;

- pool safety and equipment;

- clothing and equipment;

- maximum numbers;

- first aid provision;

- water quality.

18.3   Pool Design

18.3.1   Leisure pools, many with special water features and irregular shapes, may cause potential supervisory blind spots which need to be checked regularly

18.3.2   Glare across the water surface, from natural or artificial lighting, may restrict sight to the bottom of the pool across large areas. In such circumstances movement by supervisory and teaching staff or some other appropriate action may become necessary in order to maintain maximum visual awareness.

18.3.3   The depth and extent of shallow or deep water areas should be clearly marked and noted by those responsible for safety. Signs should identify these and other potential risks.

18.4   Arrangements for Lessons

18.4.1   Arrangements for the safe supervision of lessons may need to take account of whether the group has sole or shared use of the pool. Shared use with the general public would have further implications for supervision and designated responsibility for safety which would need to be satisfactorily addressed.

18.5   Responsibility for Safety

18.5.1   The duty of care for pupils involved in swimming remains at all times with the teacher. Specialist instructors may be employed by local authorities to assist with swimming lessons and their role will be to complement the skills and experience of the teachers in the safe delivery of the programme. They may also provide essential life saving cover. It is necessary for teachers and instructors to enjoy a good working relationship, with good communication and to understand that the teacher has the responsibility for monitoring the progress of the pupils regardless of who directs the session.

18.5.2 Schools will often use pools on premises other than their own and by law the responsible manager must ensure that the facilities are safe and present no risk to health for visiting groups. This applies equally when schools use swimming pools belonging to other schools, or when the pool is used for the teaching of swimming. It is regarded in law as a place of work.

18.6 Safety Qualifications

18.6.1 Whenever there are pupils in the water, a responsible adult must be present at the poolside who is able to effect a rescue and to carry out cardio-pulmonary resuscitation.

18.6.2 The teaching and life saving awards of the Amateur Swimming Association, the Swimming Teachers Association and the Royal Life Saving Society are desirable qualifications for swimming teachers but it should be remembered that these may not indicate up to date competence in life saving unless retaken from time to time. Local authorities and governing bodies should ensure that swimming teachers and physical education specialists are afforded the opportunity to update themselves in this area.

18.6.3 Teachers are advised that they should regularly practise their previously learned life saving skills and those of a new element in lifeguarding. They should also check that all life saving equipment is adequate, appropriately placed for ready access and in good condition.

18.6.4 Teachers responsible for the delivery of swimming pool programmed aquatic activities including swimming lessons should be aware of the recommendations by the Health and Safety Executive with regard to teachers, coaches and lifeguards holding an appropriate current life-saving award or lifeguard qualification.

18.6.5 Where teachers are responsible for the safety of a programmed session, such as a swimming lesson, it is recommended that they have a current swimming pool life-saving award such as the Rescue Test for Teachers of Swimming.

18.6.6 Those directly responsible for the supervision of a swimming pool are recommended to provide a current nationally recognised pool lifeguard qualification such as the Royal Life Saving Society UK (RLSS UK) National Pool Lifeguard Qualification. This is jointly recognised by the Amateur Swimming Association, the Royal Life Saving Society UK, Institute of Swimming Teachers and Coaches and the Swimming Teachers' Association.

18.6.7   The supervision of activities such as canoeing or scuba diving in pools requires specialist knowledge.

18.7   Supervision

18.7.1   Routines, deep and shallow water and relevant notices should be brought to the attention of pupils when they first visit the pool and be re-emphasised on subsequent visits. Such notices must be clear to users who may have problems with reading. Standard emergency procedures should be practised at regular intervals with the children.

18.7.2   The teacher and/or instructor should be able to see all the pupils throughout the lesson. The bottom of the pool should be clearly visible and any problems of glare or light reflected from the water surface should be satisfactorily overcome.

18.7.3   The teacher or instructor should not enter the water if this leaves no supervising adult on the poolside, except in emergencies or on the very rare occasions when the class is assembled on the poolside while the teacher demonstrates a particular point.

18.7.4   Pupils should be taught to report any mishap to the teacher or instructor; it is helpful if they are paired to check on the well-being of their partners at any time.

18.7.5   Pupils must be registered or counted both before and after the lesson. A number count at times during the lesson may also be appropriate, especially with younger children.

18.7.6   Changing rooms must be adequately supervised.

18.7.7   Pupils in school pools must always have qualified adult supervision.

18.8   Pupil teacher ratio

18.8.1   In any pool the pupil/teacher ratio should be such that it safely meets the varying risks imposed by the pool environment and from the public who may be in the pool at the same time. Whatever the conditions, there must always be supervisory presence able to meet any rescue and resuscitation needs which may arise among the pupils.

18.8.2   In accordance with the general duties and responsibilities placed upon them by the Health and Safety at Work Act 1974 and by the Management of Health and Safety in the Workplace Regulations 1992, owners/operators/occupiers of swimming pools are obliged to take all reasonable practicable measures to ensure teaching and coaching activities are conducted safely. This includes determining the maximum safe ratio of pupils to swimming teachers.

18.8.3　The Health and Safety Executive have clearly identified the risk to the safety of swimmers as being substantially less when undertaking programmed activities compared to swimming in a public session (reference Safety in Swimming Pools; 1988).

A programmed aquatic activity can be defined as having a formal structure, with supervision, control and continuous monitoring from the poolside. This would include school swimming lessons, coaching sessions and other relevant tuition.

18.8.4　As circumstances and the building design of a swimming pool vary greatly, it is not possible to give a definitive set of ratios. The starting point for any such policy must be the completion of a thorough risk assessment as advocated by evolving European legislation . This is known as directed staffing. However, where local requirements are specified these must take precedence.

18.8.5　When carrying out a risk assessment and preparing written procedures, those doing so should consult with swimming teachers, coaches, school teachers and all who take groups to the swimming facility to ensure that the fullest consultation is effected.

18.9　Pupil Conduct

18.9.1　The conduct of pupils when they attend for swimming tuition is of obvious importance. The accepted procedures and underlying reasons should be fully explained to all participants.

♦　All jewellery should be removed or made safe and the chewing of sweets or gum during a lesson should never be allowed.

♦　Pupils should not be permitted to run on the pool surrounds.

♦　Emergency procedures to clear the pool should be practised at regular intervals and should be effected by means of a specified signal, both audible and visual.

♦　Pupils should be encouraged to look for and to report unseemly or unacceptable behaviour, especially when safety is compromised.

♦　Pupils should be encouraged to shower and use the toilet before entering the water.

18.10   Pupils with particular needs

18.10.1   Younger Children.

♦   Infants and young primary children are best taught in shallow beginner pools, with the availability of appropriate aids to floatation and some in-water adult support.

♦   Great care should be taken when teaching very young non-swimmers who are unable to touch the bottom of the shallow end of a pool. They should wear appropriate floatation aids and adult or parent in-water support is essential on a minimum adult to child ratio of one to two and preferably one to one.

18.10.2   Pupils with Special Educational Needs

♦   Where swimming involves young people with special educational needs the class size should be reduced to take account of the age, intelligence and experience of the pupils.

♦   Shallow depth learner pools are much easier to supervise than large public pools, where the presence of the public can present problems.

♦   The help of parents or other responsible adults is very useful.

(Note: More detailed advice on working with pupils with special educational needs is provided in chapter 8.)

18.10.3   Pupils with medical conditions

Pupils with serious medical problems need clearance through the written permission of parents before they can be allowed to participate in school swimming programmes.

Pupils with epilepsy should at all times be observed from the poolside and should work alongside a responsible person in the water when out of their depth. Shimmering water or flickering light may trigger an attack.

18.11   Clothing and equipment

18.11.1   Swimwear should be suitable for the purpose.

18.11.2   Goggles or masks should only be allowed exceptionally, when eyes may be adversely affected by chemicals in the water. When used, these items should be made of unbreakable plastic or rubber materials. Pupils should be taught to remove them by slipping them off the head and not by stretching the retaining band.

18.11.3   If for reasons of culture or religion pupils are allowed into the water in clothing other than usual swimwear, they should be restricted to shallow water until they have shown that they are able to swim competently. Liaison with community leaders can do much to minimise any problems which may arise.

18.12   Pool Safety and Equipment (refer also to chapter 5)

18.12.1   Adequate life-saving, buoyancy aids and first aid equipment , including a blanket, should be immediately to hand.

18.12.2   There should be known access to a telephone giving direct contact from the pool to the emergency services.

18.12.3   Pool depths should be clearly indicated on the walls and teachers should explain their significance, especially to beginners. All signs must conform to the appropriate British Standard/British Standard European Norm.

18.12.4   A pool divider, usually a rope, should normally be positioned for delineating shallow from deep water whenever non-swimmers are present.

18.12.5   A pool should not be used unless and until the water is sufficiently clear to enable the bottom to be visible at all depths.

18.12.6   The doors to a school pool should be locked when the pool is not in use.

18.12.7   Pool operators should know that there are now special recovery stretchers which can more easily meet the need of recovering patients especially where such patients may have suffered head and neck injury.

           Teachers and those on poolside duty should know how to assemble and use such equipment where it is available.

18.13   Water Temperature

18.3.1   The temperature of the water should be about 28°C to enable young people to be comfortable and not become unduly cold during the period of time allocated for swimming.
           The ambient air temperature should be slightly above that of the water to avoid condensation.

18.14 Emergency Action Plan

18.14.1 Risk assessments should be used to identify foreseeable emergencies. Those using a particular pool should be familiar with the recommended action to be taken as set out in a written emergency action plan.

18.14.2 Emergency action plans should establish who assumes leadership in managing emergencies and the action to be taken in relation to such issues as:

- Overcrowding
- Lack of water clarity
- Public disorder
- Fire alarm procedures
- Evacuation procedures
- Bomb threats
- Power failure
- Structural failure
- Toxic gas emission
- Serious injury to a bather
- Dealing with casualties in the water.

DIVING

18.15 General Safety Measures

18.15.1 Diving, by its very nature, can be dangerous and there have been a number of very serious diving accidents recorded in recent years. To avoid such occurrences there are safety measures which need to be observed.

a   Diving sessions should be supervised by a teacher or coach who is thoroughly familiar with modern practice.

b   Pupil numbers should be low enough to allow the teacher to watch all the divers.

c   Pupils should be thoroughly familiar with the water space and environment in which they learn to dive. Diving should never take place in unknown waters.

d   Pupils should be allowed sufficient pool space in which to practise, with no underwater obstructions, to ensure that the risk of collisions during simultaneous dives is avoided.

e   The water must be deep enough to avoid any possible danger of contact with the pool bottom. A shallow entry racing dive should only take place under supervision into water at least 0.9 metres deep.

f   For vertical plain header diving, the water should be minimum of 3 metres in depth and pupils should clearly understand the technique of extending the hands at the wrists immediately after entry to level and raise the body to the surface.

g   Pupils should be regularly advised to exercise great care when diving into water of 1.5 metres depth or less and then only to use a shallow entry dive which they have been taught and are able to consistently perform. Pool signs should clearly indicate those areas which are appropriate for diving.

h   The area for formal diving should be clearly designated and controlled. While diving is in progress no other swimmers should be allowed in or through the area.

i   Appropriate warning signs and notices should be clearly displayed and should be regularly drawn to the attention of pool users.

j   Prolonged underwater swimming following a dive should be discouraged.

k   Raised starting blocks for racing dives should only be used by capable swimmers after receiving instruction on the techniques and with the approval of the teacher. The minimum depth of water is 0.9 metres when racing dives are being used.

18.16   Jumping into Water

18.16.1   Care should be taken with feet first entry jumping which may cause damage to the arches of the feet from striking the pool bottom with force in shallow water. Generally , entry into water less than 1.5 metres in depth may be best effected from a sitting position on the side of the pool.

18.17   Board Diving

a   Only one person should be allowed on any part of the board at any one time.

b   The water should be checked by both the diver and the supervisor to ensure that it is clear of swimmers or any obstruction before a dive.

c   Board divers should demonstrate their competence at low level before progressing to higher levels.

18.18   Plunge (Surface) Dive

18.18.1   All children should be taught to perform and to understand when to use a plunge surface dive from the poolside. It is important that any child taking part in a competitive swimming race commencing with a plunge dive racing entry should be checked for their competency to do so safely, especially where the entry is from a starting block.

LIFESAVING

18.19   The teaching of Lifesaving

18.19.1   When teaching lifesaving, only reaching and throwing rescues should be taught to children below eight years of age. Contact throwing rescues should not be taught to children under fourteen years of age.

18.19.2   Advice on teaching packs and awards for lifesaving at the appropriate key stages in primary and secondary education is available from the Royal Life Saving Society UK.

19: OUTDOOR PLAY

19.1 Introduction

19.1.1 The school playground, particularly in the primary school, provides opportunities for young people to engage in active play in addition to experiencing quiet and environmental areas.

19.1.2 Because of the informality of play and the numbers which are often involved, playground safety and supervision is an important consideration. Pupils may collide with buildings, with other pupils or fall by tripping or misjudging the use of climbing equipment.

19.1.3 The use of balls or bats in crowded areas is hazardous and care needs to be taken to structure activities and designate areas so that risk is minimised.

19.2 The Playground Surface

19.2.1 The surface should be even, maintained in good condition and be free of loose grit. Concrete is not considered a suitable surface for play because it is too hard. Steep slopes or sudden changes in level should be avoided.

19.3 Playground Design

19.3.1 Play areas should be located so that they are well away from windows and walls with sharp corners. The provision of borders (shrub or flower beds) in suitable positions can help to minimise such hazards. Certain parts of the playground may be designated for particular activities, for example ball games or quiet areas.

Spaces for running and vigorous activities should be as open as possible. Play areas should be clearly visible to appointed play supervisors.

19.4 Playground Markings

19.4.1 Playgrounds should promote the dispersal of children at play so that overcrowding is avoided. The provision of a variety of play opportunities and markings well distributed throughout the area will encourage this.

19.5   Playground Climbing Equipment

19.5.1   Before setting up any system of playground equipment usage, the greatest care should be taken to ensure that the following points are considered:

Design and Siting

a   Professionally designed equipment is recommended. Improvised equipment should be approved by the LEA or school governors before being used. Post-installation inspection is essential.

b   Long, low frames are generally better than high ones; currently 2.5 metres is the maximum suitable height.

c   Joints should be smooth and there should be no protruding parts which might trap clothing or cause unintended or unexpected movement.

d   Working surfaces should offer a good grip for the hands and feet to climb on, the only exception being so-called slide and roll surfaces.

e   The diameter of any tube that is to be gripped should be appropriate to the hand sizes of the children who use the frame.

f   Frames designed to offer safe 'escape' systems are better than those with precipitate drops.

g   Frames should be sited away from other structures and positioned where they can be most easily supervised.

h   The surrounding surface should be level, non-slip and uniform.

i   The equipment provided should be suitable for the age-groups to whom it will be available. It should reflect pupils' developmental needs.

j   Playground equipment which meets the appropriate British Standards or British Standards European Norms is generally safer.

Safer Surfaces

19.5.2   There has been considerable effort in recent years to install impact absorbent surfaces beneath and around outdoor climbing frames, especially in public parks, where supervision is usually less thorough than in schools. There is, however, no surface as yet which will prevent head injury or fracture when a child falls from a height greater than one metre. Such injuries are more closely associated with the angle or nature of the impact than by the shock absorbent qualities of the ground surface. A child's weight and skeletal structure are other factors which will influence the extent of any injury.

19.5.3   All new equipment is better if provided with an appropriate surface beneath and around it, forming an apron extending at least 1.75m beyond the outermost points of the base of the frame. For frames which are under 600mm in height, the surface does not require to be impact absorbent. Products and their installation should meet the appropriate British Standards/ British Standards European Norms.

Supervision

19.5.4   Arrangements must be in place for play on climbing equipment to be supervised. In particular:

a   Staff must be familiar with the apparatus and with the abilities of the pupils.

b   Staff and pupils need to be aware of the maximum number of young people that can safely use the frame at any one time.

c   Pupils must wear appropriate footwear that provides good traction between the feet and the frame; smooth soles are dangerous.

d   Small children, particularly those of nursery age, should not use apparatus at the same time as older pupils.

e   Frames should not be used in inclement weather.

f   Where indoor facilities are inadequate, outdoor apparatus may be used for gymnastics lessons in the physical education curriculum under the supervision and control of a teacher.

Ancillary and Voluntary Helpers

19.5.5   If a headteacher decides that outdoor apparatus can be used by pupils at breaks and playtime and employs ancillary staff for supervisory duties at such times, these should be paid employees of the LEA or governing body. If volunteer helpers are used, they should not be placed in sole charge. The headteacher must ensure that all supervisory staff clearly understand their duties and responsibilities.

19.6 Structured Play Activities in Lesson Time

19.6.1   Apparatus is often made available in school for use by nursery and other children at times of supervised structured play.   Items will vary, but may include wheeled vehicles, low wooden climbing structures with platforms and slides, rocking devices and plastic features such as tunnels and cubes. The physical and social skill learning associated with this provision is considerable but care needs to be taken that items meet the highest safety criteria. In particular:

a   apparatus should be assembled and used in accordance with instructions from the manufacturer;

b   equipment should be stable with non-slip bases and be placed on level non-slip surfaces;

c   wooden devices should be smooth and splinter free;

d   landing mats will be helpful where it is anticipated that children might need to absorb their body weight in controlled actions;

e   slides should be gently inclined and end well clear of the ground with a landing mat provided;

f   metal framed items should be smoothly welded in construction rather than bolted. If bolts are used, they should be housed so that they do not project and thereby cause a hazard;

g   items that rock or have moving parts should be selected with special care. They should be designed so that toes or fingers cannot be trapped. The range of movement should be contained within safe limits;

h   ride-on vehicles should be such that speed is constrained and wheels should be wide with soft tyres;

i   plastic shapes into which children may climb should be transparent or with wide openings, enabling external vision of the activity by supervisors.

j   inspection should take place each time the equipment is used and worn or damaged items withdrawn until repaired or replaced. Apparatus with moving parts need careful attention for wear.

19.7 Clothing and Personal Effects

19.7.1   Care should be taken to ensure that clothing and footwear are suitable for the activities.

- Tights, stockings or socks are not suitable.

- Loose garments should be removed or tucked in and cardigans fastened.

- Long hair should be tied back.

- Jewellery, for example watches, bracelets, rings, earrings and badges with pins, should be removed or made safe.

19.8 Activities

19.8.1 In general, children will be aware of their own movement limitations but there will be times when a teacher or supervisor will need to act to ensure safe practice. Children should be encouraged to try different activities but never coerced into activities at or beyond the threshold of their capabilities.

    a   Children should be taught that they must not touch or interfere with other children when they are on apparatus.

    b   It is essential that a structured environment is developed which permits children to explore and be creative within determined limits.

    c   A working atmosphere of involvement and self control by the children should be encouraged.

    d   Teachers, supervisors and nursery nurses should respond to requests made by children for help or advice.

    e   Children should be given freedom of choice to participate or simply to observe.

19.9 Purchase and Maintenance

19.9.1 The purchase of new equipment or the replacement of items which are worn beyond economic repair requires the greatest care. Advice should be sought from the LEA service responsible for supplies and contracts. Before purchasing new equipment the opportunity should be taken to see such items in use by children in other schools and to discuss its appropriateness with teachers.

19.9.2 In addition to the day to day checking by responsible staff, both fixed and portable items of equipment used for indoor or outdoor structured or free play should be subject to an annual inspection and repair programme by an independent specialist in this field of work.

20: OTHER ACTIVITIES

20.1 Introduction

20.1.1 There are numerous examples of new or improvised activities being introduced into the physical education programme. These are important in the interests of development and the promotion of creativity.

Care should be taken to assess any such activity for the hazards that it may present and to ensure the accompanying risks are able to be managed; otherwise the activity should not take place.

20.1.2 Where children are creating their own activity due regard should be given to safety requirements.

The activity should be suited to the abilities of members of the group, taking account of those who are least able. Great care should also be taken in the safe and appropriate use of any equipment, especially if such use is for a purpose other than that for which that apparatus, by design, is primarily intended.

20.2 Bouncy Castles

20.2.1 Bouncy castles are occasionally used by schools for special events, for example to raise funds.

They will nearly always be hired for the occasion and will not form part of the regular experience of teachers and pupils provided by the use of equipment for the physical education programme in a school.

The equipment generally consists of a large inflated structure made of plastic material on which children experience sensations similar to those of other rebound equipment, like trampolines or trampettes, but with a reduced effect in the height of bouncing.

20.2.2 Like all rebound apparatus, bouncy castles should be used with great care and be supervised by experienced adults who are well aware of the risks and understand how these may be reduced to an acceptable level. This is particularly important with children in the very early years where this experience may be totally new and whose awareness of body position and orientation has not yet developed to the extent that they are able to maintain full positional control when bouncing in this manner. The equipment should be securely anchored to ensure stability.

20.2.3   Good practice requires that:

a   The permission of the headteacher, governors and parents should be obtained before children are allowed to participate in the activity.

b   The equipment should be in good repair and subject to a regular inspection and repair programme.

c   High-sided integral padded walls should be provided on three sides to prevent children falling over the edge and onto the ground. The fourth (open) side is for access, egress and observation.

d   A sloping safety apron or thick mattresses should be provided at ground level along the open side and a sufficient number of mature 'spotters' should be situated at arms length intervals to assist children climbing on and off and to prevent children falling over the exposed edge when bouncing.

e   The number of children bouncing at any one time should be kept sufficiently low to reduce the possibility of children colliding with each other.

f   Beginners should bounce only on their feet (not perform seat bounces, for example).

g   Children of similar size should be on the apparatus at any one time.

h   The length of time spent per bouncing session should not be unduly long so that the children do not tire and lose their concentration and bodily control.

i   Children who are known to experience difficulties with their physical control may require 'one to one' assistance holding hands while bouncing. At such times, the number of participants may need to be reduced accordingly.

j   Arrangements may be needed for the cleaning and sterilisation of the bouncing surface from time to time. When this occurs, the material should be thoroughly dry before activity recommences.

k   Onlookers not engaged in the activity should not be permitted to distract those who are bouncing by shouting or calling out.

l   No rotational movements in the air should be allowed.

m   Running from wall to wall should not be permitted.

APPENDIX 1

Physical Education Safe Practice Audit

Preface

This audit has been written in question form to promote discussion of the various topics. The sequence of the order of paragraphs does not denote an order of precedence; all are of equal importance. Section 'A' of the audit is applicable to all schools, whilst Section 'B' relates to special needs schools, special units and schools that have an integration policy.

1 SECTION A

1.1 Safety Policy and Guidelines

1.1.1   Have members of staff discussed the "school's safe practice policy and guidelines" and identified those areas that relate to physical education?

1.1.2   Do the policy and guidelines for physical education feed off and feed into the school's statements?

1.1.3   Is a copy of the Physical Education policy available to all members of staff who teach physical education?

1.1.4   Do you have a system that ensures that the policy and guidelines are discussed in detail, with pupils in practice and with AOTTS assisting with the schools Physical Education programme?

1.1.5   Is the policy and guidelines document reviewed at regular intervals?

2.1 Safety Regulations

2.1.1   Are the following safety regulations available for reference in your school?

     a   National 'Safety in Schools' publications from BAALPE, DfEE, HSE.

     b   LEA safety documents covering all aspects of physical education.

c   School specific safety policies concerning store rooms, showers, entry facilities.

d   Transporting pupils, mini-buses.

2.1.2   Does each member of staff who teaches physical education have access to and regularly read:

a   The school's safe practice policy guidelines in physical education?

b   A copy of each document which is essential to that person according to their job specification?

c   All other relevant safety documents?

2.1.3   What system is used to acquaint pupils with safety regulations and practices?

a   School prospectus/parent information brochure.

b   Discussion of relevant information with pupils.

c   Safe practice written into curriculum units of work, for example lifting and carrying apparatus.

d   Risk assessment and management shared with the pupils.

e   Regulations on permanent display, with clear responsibilities for producing, updating and posting these.

2.1.4   What system has the school introduced to ensure that:

a   Members of staff discuss, and revise as necessary, school safety regulations at regular intervals?

b   Recommendations can be made to the headteacher on all matters appertaining to safety?

2.1.5   What fail-safe scheme is built in to ensure that the essential regulations are discussed?

2.2   Staff

2.2.1   Do any of the staff suffer from an injury or impairment which will prevent them from teaching aspects of the subject?

2.2.2   Do appropriate members of staff have a first aid qualification?

2.2.3   Is any member of staff trained in expired air resuscitation and cardiac compression?

2.2.4   Does any member of staff hold a current life-saving award?

2.2.5   What relevance do the answers to the above questions have to the curriculum co-ordinator/head of department with regard to:

- In service training provision?

- Limitations to programme planning and implementation until qualifications are obtained?

2.2.6   Are new members of staff familiar with school policy when introducing new activities into the programme, for example formal gymnastics, awards schemes, outdoor pursuits?

2.3   Voluntary Helpers

2.3.1   Are these identified as official and approved voluntary helpers?

2.3.2   Has the subject leader supplied the headteacher with details of voluntary helper assistance in physical education, including extra-curricular activities?

2.3.3   Is it understood that a voluntary helper may not be covered by the school's insurance unless these procedures are followed?

2.3.4   Is it recognised that a voluntary helper cannot be left in sole charge of young people and cannot act in loco parentis?

2.3.5   Has the subject leader ensured that helpers who assist with hazardous activities do so under the direct guidance of teachers and follow standard good practice in the activities?

2.4   Partnerships

2.4.1   Has the subject leader obtained the permission of the headteacher and governing body to enter into the field of partnerships (that is involvement of external agents)?

2.4.2   Are insurance arrangements in place and satisfactory?

2.4.3   Have a policy and ground rules been laid down and agreed?

2.4.4   Have the implications of in loco parentis been discussed?

2.4.5   Does work involving partners (for example coaches) conform with the requirements of the national curriculum in physical education?

2.4.6   How will assessment be covered?

2.4.7   Are you familiar with the regulations relating to Substantial Access to children and its implications?

2.4.8   When accepting help from teachers not employed by your LEA does your headteacher review the necessity for a List 99 check?

2.5   Equipment

2.5.1   Is a regular inspection and repair programme arranged and implemented, and carried out by a recognised specialist firm?

2.5.2   Who is responsible for the day to day safety of equipment?

2.5.3   How often does the subject leader inspect fixed and portable apparatus?

2.5.4   What happens to equipment that is condemned as unfit for use on the school's inspection and repair schedule?

2.5.5   Who decides that expendable equipment is beyond safe use and how is it written off?

2.5.6   What long term planning is used to ensure the replacement of condemned equipment?

2.5.7   How is damaged equipment reported to the subject leader?

          (Note: Unofficial repair and/or modification to physical education equipment should not be permitted.)

2.6   Facilities

2.6.1   Are facilities safe from unauthorised use when not supervised, for example are swimming baths locked?

2.6.2   Do any facilities require constant supervision whilst in use, for example showers?

2.6.3   Do any facilities require zoning for safety, for example stock rooms for portable equipment to ensure safe handling?

2.6.4   Do stock rooms require special racking to ensure the safe storage of heavy equipment?

2.6.5   Should any parts of the school grounds be made into restricted areas for reasons of safety?

2.7   Risk Assessment

2.7.1   Has risk assessment of physical education facilities been carried out?

2.7.2   Who is responsible for:

♦   Carrying out the review?

♦   Following up identified risks?

2.7.3   What system is in place for risk assessment in off-site premises or environments?

2.7.4   Is it understood that risk assessment is a legal requirement under the Management of Health and Safety Regulations (since January 1993)?

2.7.5   Are you aware that Fire Risk is now an integral part of physical education risk assessment?

2.8   Accident Procedure

2.8.1   Have members of staff discussed the accident procedure as laid down in the school safety policy?

2.8.2   Has a specific procedure been laid down for accidents in:

♦   school buildings?
♦   the swimming pool?
♦   playing fields?
♦   off-site areas?
♦   transport and travel during curricular and extra-curricular activities?

2.8.3   Do all staff know the procedure to be followed?

2.8.4   Do all members of staff, including auxiliary staff, know who are the qualified first aiders?

2.8.5   Where are your first aid boxes located? Are the contents complete? Are they checked regularly and who is responsible for this?

2.8.6   Do all staff concerned with first aid know the location of the nearest telephone? What steps are taken to ensure the telephone is available during school activities after normal hours when the school office is closed?

2.8.7   What system is applied for the supervision of classes when the member of staff responsible for first aid is withdrawn?

2.8.8   When serious accidents necessitate a visit to hospital, what action would be taken?

2.8.9   What liaison is carried out between the school and parents when an accident to a child occurs? What is the follow up procedure for accidents?

2.8.10   Do all staff concerned with first aid know the school regulations regarding insurance when carrying children in their cars?

2.8.11   Is there a first aid or medical room in the school? Who is responsible for its supervision? Will the child be supervised in the room following an accident? What action will be taken to ensure that no child is left in the room unsupervised, especially after normal school hours?

2.9   Reporting of Accidents

2.9.1   What system is used for the reporting of accidents?

2.9.2   Is there any differentiation between minor and more serious accidents?

           What are the criteria?

2.9.3   Is additional information collated, other than that required on the official form?

2.9.4   What system is used for the storage and retrieval of accident information?

2.9.5.   What system is used to comply with the Reporting of Injuries, Diseases and Dangerous Occurrences Regulations 1995 (RIDDOR)?

2.9.6   Is it recognised that failure to comply with RIDDOR is a criminal offence?

2.10   Health Records

2.10.1   Where are the health records of pupils kept?   Has subject leader direct access to these?

2.10.2   How are members of staff informed of essential health information? Is the system 'fail-safe'?

2.10.3   Does this information include emergency aid procedures for children at medical risk?

2.10.4   Is there liaison between medical officer(s) and the school? What system is in place for reporting any new irregularities or abnormalities which come to light, to the senior medical officer or the school nurse?

2.11   Travelling

2.11.1   Are staff aware of regulations regarding insurance and the use of their own and school vehicles?

2.11.2   What special travel arrangements are necessary for the use of off-site facilities during both curriculum and extra-curricular activities?

2.11.3   Is there a code of behaviour for such travel?

2.11.4   Are children made aware of road safety as it applies to them?

3   SECTION B: SPECIAL EDUCATIONAL NEEDS

3.1   Information and Consultation

3.1.1   Do you examine, in detail, the statement when one is available?

3.1.2   Do you consult with your schools special educational needs co-ordinator SENCO.

3.1.3   Do you consult with parents prior to preparation of a child's programme of work?

3.1.4   What links are formed with the child's medical specialists?

3.1.5   Has the school developed a team approach with other paramedical staff responsible for the well being of the child?

3.1.6   Do the above discussions and research allow you to build up a physical education/medical profile of the child?

3.2 Aids and Appliances

3.2.1   Has the subject leader ensured that all staff who teach physical education are made aware of bags, valves, or other appliances that may affect the child's safe participation in physical education?

3.2.2   Are a child's wheeled appliances such as chairs, trolleys, rollators and walking aids safe for physical education activities? If not, what modifications to the appliances or aids are necessary?

3.2.3   Are aids and appliances that are part of school equipment included in the regular inspection and repair schedule?

3.3 Specific Disabilities

3.3.1   What special instructions have been given to members of staff regarding children who may become unconscious because of:

♦   diabetic coma?
♦   epileptic fits?

3.3.2   What special safety considerations come into effect when deaf children are not wearing their hearing aids?

3.3.3   Are additional safety regulations necessary for hyperactive children or those with dyspraxia when swimming or using apparatus?

3.3.4   Has consideration been given to safe working areas when teaching partially or non-sighted children?

3.3.5   Has careful consideration been given to the type of programme being offered to a child with haemophilia?

3.3.6   Has the problem caused by low blow reflex in spastic children been addressed?

3.4 Hygiene

3.4.1   Is special cleaning necessary to ensure hygienic changing and working areas?

3.4.2   What system is used for the safe disposal of towels, napkins and dressings?

3.4.3   Who is responsibly for the checking of urine bags prior to physical activity?

3.4.4   Who is responsible for expressing urine and faeces prior to physical activity?

3.4.5   Who is responsible for ensuring the availability of urine bags, waterproof pants and towels in physical education?

Pre-School Physical Activity

Apparatus early years is a period of rapid growth and development. Children constantly need new challenges as well as opportunities for consolidation. Play is a tool through which they can develop manipulative skills and growth in discovery and reasoning.

Apparatus

Apparatus used for agility work should conform to British Standards/British Standards European Norms and should only be purchased from a recognised educational supplier (seek advice from LEA). It should be versatile in order to offer a variety of challenges which accommodate the individual differences of children. Apparatus should be durable, stable and free from dangerous projections and it should have a visual appeal to children.

Siting of Apparatus

- Should be well spaced and provide a working area as far as possible from obstructions.

- Should be placed on a surface that ensures good traction.

Indoors

- Beware of proximity to glass and projections.

- Beware of low ceilings and hanging objects.

- Be aware of the problems of glare from sun rays.

Outdoors

- Be aware of any L.E.A regulations or recommendations relating to the use of impact absorbing surfaces under fixed equipment.

- Beware of swinging apparatus intruding into circulation areas.

- Be aware of the possibility of outside usage and vandalism and therefore of the need for daily inspection before use.

Use of Large Apparatus

- Should only be used for supervised play.

- Children should be appropriately clothed and shod.

Indoors

- Mats should be used to indicate dismount points.

- Apparatus used for sliding should terminate on a mat in order to protect the lower spine.

Outdoors

- Should only be used in clement weather conditions.

- Particular care should be taken of sliding activities especially if head first or backward sliding is allowed.

- Fixed sliding apparatus should terminate in a platform approximately 300mm from the ground

Children's Clothing

- Clothing and footwear should be compatible with the environment, indoors and outdoors and with the activity:

  Indoors: children should wear non-slip footwear or be in bare feet.

  Outdoors: normal footwear can be worn except when using climbing apparatus.

- Clothing should not be loose in order that it does not snag on apparatus.

- Long hair should be tied back.

- All jewellery and watches should be removed.

The Teacher

- Should wear footwear and clothing that allows for easy, quick and safe movement.

- Should check the apparatus prior to each activity session for stability, loose fastenings, splinters.

- Should involve the children as meaningfully as possible in checking the equipment.

- Should stand in a position where they can view all the activities.

- Should have the children under constant observation.

Activity

Children should be:

- Encouraged, but not coeced, to try activities.

- Taught not to interfere or touch each other.

- Informed at regular intervals of the 'limits' of the activity they are attempting.

- Encouraged to work in a quiet atmosphere.

- Given the freedom of choice to participate or observe.

- Where educationally appropriate, taught that some apparatus can and may move when being used.

Play Equipment

- Should only be purchased from a recognised educational supplier.

- Use of this type of equipment requires the same vigilance as that given to the use of large equipment.

- There is a need to regulate the use of mobile toys. Careful thought should be given to the need for specific areas of play to ensure this type of toy does not create high risk situations.

Inspection and Repair

- All apparatus and equipment should be included in the school annual inspection and repair schedule.

- Where the class or group is not attached to an existing primary school special arrangements must be made for an annual inspection.

- It is essential that the recommendations in the inspection report are acted upon immediately.

- Where educationally appropriate children should be taught to identify any wear and tear of equipment and report it.

Qualification and Supervision

♦ Play on portable or fixed equipment should be supervised by a qualified infant or nursery teacher.

♦ AOTT's should never be left in sole charge of such activity.

In-Service Training

♦ Teacher and AOTT's are strongly recommended to take advantage of the LEA's primary schools Physical Education in-service training programme.

APPENDIX 3

Notification of Proposed Educational Visit or Journey

This form should be completed by the party leader and submitted to the headteacher for information and the approval of the headteacher and governors.

School ———————————————————— Party leader ————————————

Educational visit / journey reference number ————————————————

Accompanying teachers (first named to be deputy leader) ————————————

Other accompanying adults ——————————————————————

Outline details of visit, journey, costs, itinerary ————————————————

Date (s) ————————————————————— To —————————————

Pupil age range ———————— Probable number of boys ——————— girls ————

Travel arrangements ————————————————————————

All proposed activities ————————————————————————

Has the party leader previous experience of leading groups which involve these

activities? ————————————————— yes / no ————————————

Relevent qualifications / experience of leader ——————————————————

Relevant qualifications / experience of teacher and other adults listed above

Staff / adults with emergency aid qualifications
If school minibus to be used, name driver (s) ———————————————————

Will special insurance cover be arranged?   yes / no

If yes, name of company and brief details of cover ————————————————

Will the visit be arranged through a commercial company? yes / no

If yes, name of company ————————————————————————

ABTA covered?   yes / no

Signed ————————————————— (Party leader) ——————————

Date ———————————————————

Passed to headteacher on (date) ————————————————————

Visit approved: yes / no   Signed ——————————— (Headteacher) ————

Date ——————————— Notes ————————————————————

APPENDIX 4

Information on Proposed Educational Visit or Journey

Dear Parent,

The Governors and I have given approval to the following educational visit, on which it is hoped that you wish your child to participate.

The following information is provided to help you with this decision:

Details of visit / journey_____

Date (s) _____   To _____

Activities to be included during the visit _____

_____

_____

_____

Party leader_____   Deputy leader _____

Other teachers _____

Other adults _____

Age range of group_____   Probable number: boys_____ girls _____

Accommodation arrangements _____

_____

_____

Travel arrangements_____

_____

_____

Insurance arrangements_____

_____

(Note: Where private insurance will be taken out by the school on behalf of the pupils, details can be obtained from the party leader.)

Any special requirements (clothing etc.) _____

_____

_____

continued...

For the visit or journey to be a valid and safe educational experience, sensible active involvement is required from all participating pupils. To ensure that the maximum value is gained the School has particular requirements regarding behaviour and application. These are contained in a 'code of conduct', a copy of which will be sent to you in order that both you and your child are aware of the expectations.

If you require further details, please do not hesitate to contact _____ the party leader.

OR

A parents evening will be organised by _____ , the party leader, at which further details of the visit will be available and there will be an opportunity for you to raise questions.

If after consideration of all the details you wish your child to be included on the visit, would you please inform me accordingly by returning the slip at the end of this letter.
I will then arrange to forward the necessary forms for you to complete.

Yours sincerely,

_____ (Headteacher)

•••

_____ School   School visit or journey

I would like my child _____ in form _____

to be included in the school visit / journey

to   _____

on   _____

Please send me the following forms for completion and signature:

1. Agreement and medical details.

2. Code of conduct.

Signed   _____

Relationship to child   _____

Date   _____

APPENDIX 5

Parental/Guardian Consent and Medical Information Form for Educational Visits, Overnight Stays and Outdoor and Adventurous Activities

This form to be completed in full by the parent/guardian and returned to the school

School _____

1   Details of visit

Visit to _____

From _____ (date/time) To _____ (date/time)

I agree to my son / daughter / ward

Full name _____ Form/class _____

taking part in the above stated visit and having read the information sheet, agree to her/his participation in any or all of the activities described. I acknowledge the need for good conduct and responsible behaviour on her/his part.

2   Emergency details

a)   I agree to my child being given any medical, surgical or dental treatment, including general anaesthetic and blood transfusion, as considered necessary by the medical authorities present.

b)   I may be contacted by telephoning the following number (s):

Home (full number) _____

Work (full number) _____

My home address is _____

c)   Please state an alternative contact point:

Telephone number _____

Name and address of contact _____

continued...

d)   Child health service details:

Medical card number ──────────────────────────────

Family doctor (name, address and telephone number ──────────────

3   Medical information

(Cross out the YES or NO which does not apply)

Does you child suffer from any of the following conditions?

Asthma	yes/no	Bronchitis	yes/no
Chest problems	yes/no	Diabetes	yes/no
Epliepsy	yes/no	Fainting Attacks	yes/no
Heart Trouble	yes/no	Migraine	yes/no
Raised Blood Pressure	yes/no	Tuberculosis	yes/no

If YES to any of the above, please provide details:

──

──

──

Does your child suffer from any other condition requiring medical treatment, including medication?   yes/no

If YES, please provide full details:

──

──

──

Is your child allergic or sensitive to any medication, insect bites or food?
                                              yes/no

If YES, please provide full details:

──

──

continued...

Has your child been immunised against the following diseases?

Poliomyelitis   yes/no
Tetanus (lock jaw)   yes/no

If YES to tetanus, please give date if known _____

Is your child taking any form of medication on a regular basis?

Yes/no

If YES, please give full details, indicating the type of medication and dosage.

_____

_____

Please ensure that your child has adequate supplies of medication and dosage.

To the best of your knowledge, has your child been in contact with any contagious or infectious diseases, or suffered any recent condition that may become infectious or contagious?

yes/no

If YES, please give full details:

_____

_____

_____

4   Insurance cover

I understand that the visit is insured in respect of legal liabilities (third party liability) but that my child has no personal accident cover unless I have been specifically advised of this in writing by the organiser of the visit.

I also understand that any extension of insurance cover is my responsibility unless advised differently by the School.

continued...

5   Declaration

♦   I have read the attached information provided about the proposed educational visit and the insurance arrangements.

♦   I consent to my child _____ taking part in the visit, and, having read the information sheet, declare my child to be in good health and physically able to participate in all the activities mentioned.

♦   I have noted where and when the pupils are to be returned and I understand that I am responsible for my child getting home safely from that place.

♦   I am aware of the levels of insurance cover.

♦   I have completed the required medical form and return it with this consent form.

♦   I will ensure that any change in the circumstances which will affect my child's participation in the visit will be notified to the School prior to the visit.

Signature of parent/guardian _____

Name in block letters _____

Address _____

_____

APPENDIX 6

Code of Conduct for Pupils on Educational Visits

1   It is good and safe practice for schools to agree a 'code of conduct' with parents and children before young people participate in educational ventures. Acceptance of a code will provide party leaders with the necessary authority to carry out their responsibilities.

2   The agreed code of conduct should be formalised and sent to parents along with the agreement and medical forms, for the joint signature of the child and the parent(s).

   The items suggested below will help to enable a sound policy to be developed.

   Each pupil should:

   ♦   Observe normal school rules.

   ♦   Co-operate fully with leaders at all times.

   ♦   Fulfil any tasks or duties set prior to and during the visit.

   ♦   Participate fully in all activities and sessions during the visit.

   ♦   Be punctual at all times.

   ♦   Not leave group sessions or accommodation without permission.

   ♦   Always return to the meeting point or accommodation at agreed times.

   ♦   If granted indirectly supervised time, be in groups of not less than three young people.

   ♦   Avoid behaviour which might inconvenience others.

   ♦   Be considerate to others at all times.

   ♦   Respect all requests and requirements made by staff and accompanying adults.

   ♦   Behave at all times in a manner which reflects credit on self, to the party and to the school.

   ♦   Abide by laws, rules and regulations of the countries and places visited.

   ♦   Comply with customs and duty-free regulations.

♦ Not purchase or consume alcohol, tobacco products or purchase dangerous articles such as explosives and knives.

♦ If in doubt on any matter, consult with staff.

♦ Accept that a full written report of any misconduct will be forwarded to the headteacher and to the parent(s).

APPENDIX 7

Useful Addresses

England and the United Kingdom

- British Association of Advisers and Lecturers in Physical Education, Mill House, The Street, Great Snoring, Fakenham, Norfolk, NR21 0AH

- Central Council for Physical Recreation, Francis Street, London SW1P 1DE

- Department for Education and Employment, Sanctuary Buildings, Great Smith Street, London SW1P 3BT

- The Duke of Edinburgh's Award Scheme, Gulliver House, Madeira Walk, Windsor, Berks. SL4 1EU

- The Health and Safety Executive (Information Services), Broad Lane, Sheffield S3 7HQ

- The National Coaching Foundation, 114 Cardigan Road, Headingly, Leeds LS6 3BJ

- The Physical Education Association of the United Kingdom, Ling House, Building 25, London Road, Reading, Berks. RG1 5AQ

- The Royal Society for the Prevention of Accidents, Cannon House, The Priory, Queensway, Birmingham B4 6PS

- Sport England, 16 Upper Woburn Place, London WC1H 0QP

- Exercise (England), Solcast House, 13-24 Brunswick Place, London N1 3QY

Northern Ireland

- Department of Education for Northern Ireland, Rathgael House, Balloo Road, Bangor, County Down BT19 7PR

- The Sports Council for Northern Ireland, House of Sport, Upper Malone Road, Belfast BT9 5LA

- The Health & Safety Agency, 83 Ladas Drive, Belfast BT6 9FJ

Scotland

- The Scottish Education Department, New St Andrew's House, St James Centre, Edinburgh EH1 3SY

- The Scottish Sports Council, Caledonia House, South Gyle, Edinburgh EH12 9DQ

Eire

- Department of Sport, Tourism & Recreation, Frederick Buildings, South Frederick Street, Dublin 2, Eire.

- Department of Education, Hawkins House, Dublin 2, Eire

- Cospoir, The National Sports Council, Hawkins House, Dublin 2, Eire

- Gaelic Athletic Association, Croke Park, Jones Road, Dublin 3, Eire

Wales

- The Education Department Welsh Office, Government Buildings, Ty Glas Road, Llanishen, Cardiff CF4 5WE

- The Sports Council for Wales, National Sports Centre for Wales, Sophia Gardens, Cardiff CF1 9SW

baalpe
BRITISH ASSOCIATION OF
ADVISERS & LECTURERS
IN PHYSICAL EDUCATION

what is it? An Association for advisers, lecturers, inspectors, consultants, advisory teachers, teachers with management responsibilities and other professionals with qualifications in physical education, sport and dance.

what does it do? It exists to promote and maintain high standards and safe practice in all aspects and at all levels of physical education.

It extends professional support to all members through a range of courses and seminars and by providing insurance cover and advice appropriate to their needs.

It publishes a bulletin of physical education which members receive three times in each year, newsletters for members and a range of publications which are for sale generally.

It has an area network and members have termly area meeting and access to meetings arranged by other areas if they so wish.

insurance Members working for a local authority or education institution have insurance cover for all eventualities. Extra cover for those working as independent consultants, expert witnesses or planning consultants can also be arranged.

services to non members Non members may subscribe to the bulletin of physical education, attend conference, seminars and summer school and may purchase any of the range of leaflets and publications produced by the association.

the bulletin This is published three times a year and features articles on current issues, guidelines and information about recent and relevant research, courses, publications, resources and equipment.

It also offers a forum for sharing views and opinions and for professional debate.

conferences A national conference for physical education, sport and dance is held in July each year with keynote speakers, workshops, discussion groups and an exhibition.

summer school A full range of residential and day courses, both theory and practical, are offered.

seminars A number are arranged through the year and topics include inspection, assessment and safe practice.

fee Membership categories -
full: £75
overseas: £90
associate: £40
past service: £25
commercial: £50

information about membership -
please contact the treasurer:
Tony Pannell, Mill House,
The Street, Great Snoring,
Fakenham, Norfolk NR21 0AH (tel
01328 820227
fax 01328 820868)

bulletin subscriptions and orders -
contact the publisher:
Studies in Education,
Driffield Road, Nafferton, East
Yorkshire, YO25 0LY
(tel pm only & fax: 01377 256861)

publications information and orders
- presently contact Saltwells EDC:
Dudley LEA Publications
(BAALPE), Saltwells EDC,
Bowling Green Road, Netherton,
Dudley DY2 9LY (tel: 01384
813706 fax: 01384 813801)

publications   A range of
books, leaflets and videos is
available, which covers:
Safe practice in physical
education;
Secondary school gymnastics
(book & video);
Teaching and learning
strategies in physical
education;
Physical education for children
with special educational needs
in mainstream education;
Achieving excellence -
Subject leader in physical
education.

New publications are being
prepared.

Key Word Index

A

accidents   4, 19, 23, 25, 49, 68, 107, 108, 114, 122, 128, 134, 135, 140, 141, 161,
             167, 187, 202, 209, 236, 244, 260, 275, 276, 292
activity centres   26, 57, 214
adults other than teachers   4, 23, 32, 33, 34, 117
angling   237
apparatus   5, 40, 41, 42, 51, 53, 59, 60, 61, 62, 65, 66, 67, 68, 70, 101, 102, 121, 122,
             123, 124, 128, 132, 133, 134, 135, 140, 141, 143, 144, 199, 200, 201, 202, 207,
             246, 265, 266, 267, 269, 270, 273, 275, 279, 280, 281, 282
archery   192, 193, 194
arthritis   84
association football   176
asthma   56, 79, 84, 85, 108, 287
athletics   5, 30, 65, 78, 83, 91, 131, 143, 147, 148, 153, 155, 157, 161

B

badminton   185, 189
baseball   189, 191
basketball   129, 175, 176, 178, 179
behavioural difficulties   85
bouncy castles   269
boxing   91, 167, 168
brittle bones   86
BSI   4, 59

C

camping   215, 216
canoeing   238, 239, 256
cardiac conditions   87
caving and potholing   217
CEN   4, 239, 240
cerebral palsy   87
Children Act 1989   26
circuit training   85, 161, 162
climbing frames   59, 264
climbing walls   229
clothing   23, 70, 75, 76, 78, 93, 102, 113, 121, 159, 162, 165, 166, 168, 171, 173, 175,
             176, 179, 180, 181, 183, 185, 188, 192, 201, 210, 212, 213, 216, 218,
             219, 222, 224, 225, 226, 230, 231, 232, 234, 236, 238, 239, 241, 242, 244,
             247, 251, 254, 258, 259, 264, 266, 281, 285
clumsiness   84, 88
code of conduct   212, 286, 291
coeliac   89
common law   19, 20
community use   73, 141
competence to lead   216, 218, 221, 224, 225, 226, 230, 234, 237, 239, 243, 244, 247, 248
contact   26, 27, 30, 42, 43, 44, 50, 58, 60, 61, 62, 67, 68, 73, 86, 91, 92,
             94, 99, 109, 112, 113, 124, 127, 143, 152, 156, 167, 168, 172, 176, 177, 178,
             179, 180, 181, 182, 183, 188, 205, 211, 217, 219, 241, 245, 259, 261, 262,
             286, 287, 289, 295
continuity   36, 38
cooling down   163
cricket   78, 151, 167, 177, 189, 191

M

N

O

P